ENCYCLOPEDIA OF THE
Animal World

Vol 6   Cow sharks — Dodo

Bay Books Sydney

COWFISH *Lactophrys quadricornis,* one of the trunkfishes found in the warmer parts on both sides of the Atlantic. The body is encased in a stout armour of plates and is triangular in cross-section, with light blue spots and lines on a yellow background. A related species from the Indo-Pacific area, *Lactorra cornutus,* has a pair of long forward-projecting horns above the eyes. FAMILY: Ostraciontidae, ORDER: Tetraodontiformes, CLASS: Pisces.

COWRIES, marine gastropod molluscs with beautiful shells but lacking an operculum. The larger species, *Cypraea,* are found in the tropics but small cowries, *Trivia,* also occur intertidally in temperate latitudes.

The shells of cowries are unusual as they do not have a brown periostracum over the outside as do most other molluscs. This means that the shell has a high polish on its outer surface, which accounts for another of their popular names, Porcelain shells. The shells are well marked, often in spots of different colours, giving a dappled effect. The precise biological significance of these striking colour schemes is difficult to ascertain as the shell is not normally visible when the mollusc is active, being then totally enclosed by a pair of opaque mantle lobes. Thus the colours cannot be some form of protective camouflage. The mantle lobes themselves are brightly coloured, often with tubercles, and may well be providing protective colouration.

The adult shell is not typical of this group of molluscs, as it does not have a spire and the mouth is a long narrow slit with its sides rolling inwards like a scroll. Often there are distinct differences between the sexes (sexual dimorphism) as, for example, in *Cypraea gracilis* where the males are brown and the females are red.

The animals crawl by means of very complicated waves passing over the muscular

Cowries, with one seen in section to show the spiral.

Tiger cowrie *Cypraea tigris* in life, showing the shell partially obscured by the mantle lobes.

foot. Most cowries are rather slow, the fastest species, such as *Cypraea exanthemum,* crawling at no more than 6 in (15 cm) per min.

Cowries are unisexual and internal fertilization occurs after mating. In the European cowrie *Trivia monacha,* superfluous, or senile, spermatozoa are digested by special cells in the female reproductive system. This arrangement presumably enables fresh sperm to swim up the female tract and so fertilize the eggs efficiently. In the very closely related Arctic cowrie *T. arctica* such a system is not present.

Cowries feed on sponges, Sea anemones, coral polyps, and Sea squirts, animals more or less fixed to one spot, and this explains why, for carnivores, they are relatively slow moving animals. When feeding on Sea squirts their jaws bite off pieces of the 'test' and then they burrow into the soft parts of the animal, the radula conveying the debris back into the gut. The small cowries, *Trivia,* found in European waters, lay their egg capsules inside these feeding pits, the exposed parts of the capsule being moulded by the ventral pedal gland of the cowrie.

Cowries have a well developed senseorgan, the osphradium, in the mantle cavity which may be sensitive to minute traces of dissolved materials in the sea water and it is thought that cowries may be able to locate

their prey by using this chemoreceptor. They have a short gut producing the enzymes necessary to digest their protein-rich diet. FAMILY: Cypraeidae, ORDER: Mesogastropoda, CLASS: Gastropoda, PHYLUM: Mollusca.   P.F.N.

COWRIE MONEY. From early times the common cowrie of the Indian Ocean *Cypraea moneta* has been used as a form of money. From its home around the shores of the Indian Ocean, the Money cowrie has been carried to many parts of the world and its appearance in archaeological sites has shed light on the trade routes of early civilizations. Money cowries have turned up in Scandinavia and were even used by the North American Indians. In the 19th century they were such an important form of currency in Africa that a large trade grew up, to import them to England from the Indian Ocean then re-export to Africa.

COW SHARKS, a family of primitive sharks that can be immediately recognized by the presence of six or seven gill slits (there being five gill slits in all other sharks except the Frilled shark and the Saw shark *Pliotrema,* in which there are six, but in the former the first pair are continuous under the

The coyote or Prairie wolf has suffered less than the Timber wolf largely because it is smaller.

head). The Cow sharks are also known as the Comb-toothed sharks in reference to the graduated series of cusps on the teeth (descending on both sides of the centre of the tooth in the upper jaw but from one end of the tooth only in the lower jaw). The Cow sharks are large fishes, some species exceeding 10 ft (3·3 m) in length and occasionally one is reported over twice that length. There is a single dorsal fin and the teeth of the lower jaw tend to form a kind of pavement, with several rows in use at any one time. There are probably only three species in this family, one with six gill slits and two with seven.

The Six-gilled shark *Hexanchus griseus* is a large and bulky fish with a long tail and is found in all the temperate seas, usually in fairly deep water. Large individuals of 15 ft (4·5 m) are often caught and a specimen of 26 ft (7·8 m) was reported from Cornwall, England in the last century. These fishes are caught commercially on long lines off Cuban coasts, sometimes at depths of over 5,000 ft (1,500 m) but they are also known in shallow waters.

The Seven-gilled sharks are represented by the Broad-headed form, *Notorhynchus maculatum*, of the Indo-Pacific region, found chiefly in fairly deep, temperate waters; and the Narrow-headed form, *Heptranchias*

perlo, found in the Atlantic, Mediterranean and off Japan and Australia. The first species is the larger of the two, reaching a length of 10 ft (3·3 m) compared with about 7 ft (2·1 m) in the latter.

Members of this family are all ovoviviparous, the young hatching within the uterus of the female and later being born. At birth, the young are fairly small and may be quite numerous, 108 embryos being recorded from one female Six-gilled shark (only nine embryos have been found in a Narrow-headed seven-gill shark, however). FAMILY: Hexanchidae, ORDER: Pleurotremata, CLASS: Chondrichthyes.

COYOTE *Canis latrans*, or Prairie wolf, a North American wild dog closely related to the wolf *Canis lupus*, but smaller in size. Weighing between 25–30 lb (11·5–13·5 kg), the coyote has grizzled black and yellow fur with black markings on the tail and shoulders. Although originally an inhabitant of the Western Plains of the United States, this species, unlike most carnivores, has expanded its range in recent years and is now found as far east as the New England states. The coyote's success is largely due to its cunning and opportunism. Whereas the wolf, a co-operative pack hunter, cannot survive in the absence of large hoofed mammals, the

coyote takes advantage of numerous food sources, including young ungulates, small rodents and rabbits, carrion, insects, fruits, and even rubbish from garbage dumps. Its ability to hunt in packs composed of family groups, in pairs, or alone and to alter its habits as external conditions change is reminiscent of the jackals which occupy a similar ecological niche in Africa and southern Asia. Both the coyotes and jackals are constantly hunted by man who believes that they prey upon domestic livestock, but their cleverness in evading traps and snares has so far prevented their extermination. In the United States recent attempts to reduce the coyote population with poisoned carcasses have not only killed members of this species but have taken their toll of other wildlife as well.

Like wolves, coyotes maintain and defend territories and if numerous food sources are available a pair may spend years covering a small area 10 miles (16 km) in circumference. Scent marks are left at various places in the home range, a behaviour which indicates to more mobile coyotes that the area is occupied. Within each pair's territory there are likely to be favoured rest sites, one or more dens, and places where surplus food is cached.

Coyotes may pair for life; certainly the male aids in rearing the young which are born in March or April after a 63 day gestation. While the cubs are helpless and need constant tending, the male does most of the hunting. Later, both parents hunt and, during weaning, they regurgitate partly digested meat to the litter to ease the transition from a milk to meat diet. The family often remains together during the lean winter months, constantly on the move in search of carrion or larger mammals weakened by cold and hunger.

The gestures and facial expressions used by the coyote during social interactions are similar to those of the wolf and domestic dog *Canis familiaris*, but its howl is unique, consisting not only of a pure wolf-like howl, but also of yaps and barks. Coyotes often howl in chorus, and because of their peculiar vocalizations, one can easily mistake a group of three 'singing' animals for a pack of six or seven. When aggressive, they use a deep-throated growl very different from the soft whine that bitches use to call the young. FAMILY: Canidae, ORDER: Carnivora, CLASS: Mammalia.   D.G.K.

COYPU *Myocastor coypus*, a South American rodent superficially resembling a large musk-rat or small beaver. It is the sole member of the genus *Myocastor* which in turn is the only member of its family, the Capromyidae, on the South American continent. A few related species, generally known as hutias, are found on several islands of the West Indies.

Coypus have a head and body length of almost 2 ft (60 cm) when fully grown and weigh up to about 15 lb (7 kg). They are aquatic animals but the tail, which is about two-thirds the length of the head and body, is quite round in section, not flattened as in most aquatic animals. The fur is yellowish brown above and grey below. The underfur, especially on the underside of the body, is dense and soft, and coypu pelts, known in the trade as 'nutria', are prepared by cutting along the upper surface of the body to leave the underside intact and by removing the longer bristly guard hairs. An unusual adaptation to an aquatic life is the very high position of the teats on the female's flanks, allowing the young to suckle while the mother is swimming.

Coypus are found throughout the southern half of South America wherever there is water. However, they have been kept all over the world on fur farms from which they have frequently escaped (and, in the case of the USSR, been deliberately released) and have become established in the wild. Such colonies can be found in eastern England, many parts of Europe and the USSR and in much of North America. In some areas, e.g. in East Anglia in England, they are considered a pest because of damage to crops such as sugar beet, but in Russia wild coypu are considered a valuable asset. They are artificially fed in winter and systematically trapped for their fur.

Although primarily herbivorous, coypus are known to vary their diet with shellfish. In Britain and North America, where they have been more intensively studied than in their native South America, coypus feed on sedges, reeds and other aquatic herbs, selecting especially the succulent bases of the shoots just above root-level. Breeding, at

Coypu, a rodent which can be both a pest or profit-making, according to circumstances.

least in the northern hemisphere, appears to continue all year, and the young, usually about five in a litter, are very well developed at birth and are very soon accomplished swimmers. Depending on the habitat the nest may be in a burrow in a river bank or in a heap of vegetation built on the surface of a marsh. FAMILY: Capromyidae, ORDER: Rodentia, CLASS: Mammalia.   G.B.C.

CRAB PLOVER *Dromas ardeola,* a large wading bird and sole member of the family Dromadidae. It is not a true plover (family Charadriidae). In size, it is similar to the godwits *Limosa* spp, about 15 in (38 cm) long, while the plumage resembles that of the avocets and stilts (Recurvirostridae). Apart from black mantle feathers and primaries, the whole plumage is white. It has a fairly long, straight and stout bill, no doubt an adaptation for dealing with its chief prey, Shore crabs. The sexes are alike.

The Crab plover is a coastal species, restricted as a breeding bird to the northern and western coasts of the Indian Ocean, from the Persian Gulf to East Africa, though non-breeding individuals are regular as far south as Madagascar. Among waders, its breeding biology is unique on several counts. It lays a single largish white egg. Most wader species lay two or more eggs, which are coloured to provide camouflage. As the Crab plover's nest is placed at the end of a long burrow there is no need in its case for camouflage. The species nests colonially, excavating burrows in sand for a distance of several feet. The chick is nidicolous, being fed by the parents in the nest; other wader

chicks are nidifugous, leaving the nest soon after hatching, and in only a few species are the young fed by the parents. As far as is known, the young Crab plovers are fed on the same crustaceans and molluscs as those which form the chief food of the adults. FAMILY: Dromadidae, ORDER: Charadriiformes, CLASS: Aves.   P.R.E.

CRABS, name given to a wide range of decapod crustaceans having a reduced abdomen that is carried tucked forward underneath a broad carapace, which is often wider than long, and the insertions of the legs are widely separated on the underside. When

A male Land crab of the West Indies, the Duppy crab *Cardisoma guanhumi.*

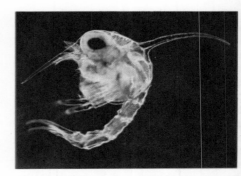

First zoea larva of European Shore crab *Carcinus maenas.*

Opposite: a Ghost crab *Ocypoda cordimana,* of Rottnest Island, Australia, beside the mouth of its burrow in which it spends most of the day.

walking or running many crabs move sideways or obliquely, but the most skilled runners can move forwards, backwards or sideways with great facility. A typical crab has a pair of well developed pincers and four pairs of walking legs, making five pairs, or 10 legs in all (Gk: *deka,* ten, *podos,* foot). One or two of the hind pairs of legs are reduced or even absent in certain families. Some of the fast running crabs appear to use only two pairs of legs when travelling at high speed.

A crab's gills are housed in chambers on each side of the thorax. These open near the bases of the legs, and also have a forwardly directed opening near the bases of the antennae. Water is moved in and out of the gill chamber by a flap, the scaphognathite, which is attached to the outer edge of one of the mouthparts (second maxilla), and projects back into the gill chamber. Normally the

A Stone crab *Lithodes maia,* in the Bergen Aquarium, so named for its resemblance, when the legs are tucked into the body, to a stone.

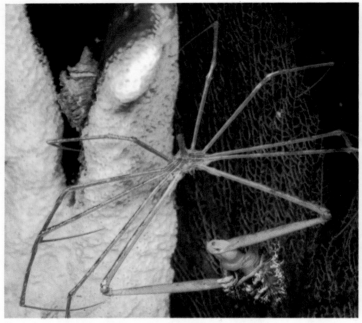

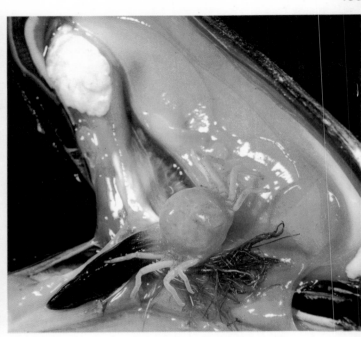

Spider crab *Stenorhynchus seticornis*, of the tropical Atlantic.

Pea crab *Pinnotheres pisum* in Common mussel *Mytilus edulis*.

water is drawn in at the bases of the limbs and passed out over the bases of the antennae. But the current can also be reversed, and frequently is in forms such as the *Masked crab. Another remarkable adaptation is seen in some of the crabs that spend much of their time out of water. *Aratus pisoni* climbs in mangrove trees and passes water from the gill chambers out of the front openings. When the crab is in air the water flows as a thin film down the front of the underside to the bases of the limbs where it regains entry to the gill chamber. This seems to be an admirable adaptation for recirculating and aerating water from the gill chamber. *Sesarma cinereum* goes a step further and circulates water over its back as well as down its underside. The water is guided over the crabs back through a series of small channels and groups of hairs.

The eyes of crabs are borne on stalks which vary greatly in length in different species. An extreme example is found in the genus *Podophthalmus* where the eyestalks resemble matchsticks, and there is a joint just before the eye.

Internally the anatomy of a crab is basically like that of a *crayfish (see also Crustacea), but with various proportions altered to fit the crab form. The nervous system shows the greatest modification in the true crabs where the ventral chain is condensed into a single nerve mass in the middle of the thorax.

Crabs are often scavengers, eating whatever they can find, but they are also active predators, and their pincers are capable of killing small fish and breaking open the shells of various molluscs. In addition to these generalized methods of feeding there are

specialized techniques in certain families. The Porcelain crabs for instance have one of the mouthparts equipped with long feathery setae that are swept through the water to catch small particles which are then transferred to the other mouthparts and eaten.

Male crabs often have larger pincers than females and the male abdomen is usually much narrower. When eggs are laid they become attached to the female's abdominal appendages and form an egg mass between the abdomen and the underside of the thorax. The abdomen, which normally fits neatly into a broad groove is thus displaced and bulges downwards when the female is carrying eggs.

Crab eggs are often brightly coloured with carotenoid pigments, and may be red, yellow, blue, brown or green. They vary in size and number in different species of crab, but a fairly large marine crab may lay up to a million eggs at a time. Typically, from the egg hatches a zoea larva, which moults several times before changing into a more crab-like

A crab of the family Xanthidae, common in tropical seas. One species is called the Barometer crab because its spots expand as the barometer rises.

form (see crustacean larvae). Many of the semi-terrestrial and freshwater forms develop directly from the egg into miniature crabs.

Crabs vary greatly in size and shape. The smallest species measure only $\frac{1}{4}$ in (6 mm) across the carapace, but the largest have a carapace over 1ft (30 cm) in width, and the legs of the giant Japanese Spider crab may span nearly 9 ft (3 m). This diversity in size and shape has enabled crabs to colonize a wide range of habitats. Most species are marine, living among rocks, or burrowing in sand and mud down to considerable depths in the sea. Others have invaded fresh water, particularly in the tropics, and yet others have become semi-terrestrial, often ranging far away from water, although they generally prefer moist places.

The 4,000 or so true crabs are arranged in 26 families, including the following.

Family Dromiidae	-- Sponge crabs. These are primitive crabs with the last pair of legs modified to hold pieces of sponge which may eventually grow to cover the whole back of the crab
Family Calappidae	- Shame-faced crabs, with large flat pincers that fit neatly together in front of the carapace and hide the front of the crab.
Family Raninidae	- Frog crabs
Family Corystidae	- Masked crabs
Family Portunidae	- about 300 species, including swimming crabs and the Shore crab *Carcinus*

Family Cancridae	– heavily armoured crabs with oval carapaces, including the European Edible crab *Cancer pagurus*
Family Xanthidae	– heavily armoured, short-legged crabs, resembling the Cancridae, but differing in the way the antennules fold. Over 900 species, mainly in tropical regions, include the Giant crab *Pseudocarcinus*
Family Pinnotheridae	– Pea crabs
Family Grapsidae	– over 300 species, including Kelp crabs and the Chinese Woolly-handed or Mitten crab *Eriocheir sinensis*. Many tropical species live in mangrove swamps.
Family Ocypodidae	– includes Ghost crabs, Fiddler crabs and Soldier crabs
Family Majidae	– Spider crabs

Crab spider concealed in blossom, waiting for prey. It moves sideways, like a crab.

The following families belong to the suborder Anomura, but include forms commonly called crabs.

Family Porcellanidae	– Porcelain crabs
Family Paguridae	– Hermit crabs
Family Coenobitidae	– Tropical hermit crabs and Robber crab *Birgus*
Family Lithodidae	– Stone crabs and King crab
Family Hippidae	– Mole crabs, burrowers in sand, often abundant on tropical shores

SUBORDER: Brachyura, ORDER: Decapoda, CLASS: Crustacea, PHYLUM: Arthropoda. J.G.

CRAB SPIDERS, so-named because of their superficial resemblance to crabs. Their bodies are often flattened, their legs are extended laterally and they can walk sideways. They build no snares, are short-sighted and rely on strategy and ambush to capture their prey.

In temperate regions the Thomisidae are the dominant Crab spiders but in warmer climates they are joined by the Heteropodidae and Selenopidae which may reach body-lengths up to 2 in (5 cm). *Heteropoda venatoria* has become established in most tropical countries but the many specimens which reach Europe with bananas cannot survive. The Thomisidae rarely exceed $\frac{1}{3}$ in (8 mm). *Xysticus* is a world-wide genus whose bars and spots blend with its earthy habitat. The short-sighted male must not risk losing a female he has found so he seizes her by a leg and binds her to the ground with silk once he has found her.

Examples of ambush and camouflage are often remarkable. The Asian *Misumenops nepenthicola* cheats Pitcher plants *Nepenthes* of some insect prey by sitting inside the pitchers. A black South American *Bucranium* feeds on black ants and carries the sucked skeleton of one aloft like an umbrella. Asian *Phrynarachne decipiens* mimics bird droppings visited by flies with a small platform of silk on a leaf in the centre of which its white and black body is stationed. *Misumena vatia,* common in Europe and North America, can change from white to yellow or vice versa to blend with the petals of flowers in which it sits. Experiments have shown that the presence of a dark spider in the same flower will deter insects from alighting on it. ORDER: Araneae, CLASS: Arachnida, PHYLUM: Arthropoda. W.S.B.

CRAKE, term used for certain birds of the family Rallidae, a group of shy, typically marsh-dwelling birds, though some are found in drier situations. The word 'crake' is equivalent, or alternative, to 'rail', as in the land-rail *Crex crex,* also known as the corncrake. In other cases, as in the genus *Porzana,* some species will be known by one name and other species by the other. Which name is used seems to be a matter of local tradition as there is no ornithological distinction between crakes and rails. The term crake however is more common in England than elsewhere (see rails). FAMILY: Rallidae, ORDER: Gruiformes, CLASS: Aves.

CRANEFLIES, unspecialized flies with slender bodies, narrow wings and extremely long legs which easily break off. Thus Daddy

Black crake *Limnocorax flavirostra*, of the marshes of Africa.

Cranefly or Daddy long legs, female, *Tipula* sp.

long legs has become a common name. They tend to settle in cool damp places, under leaves and between grass stems. They are slow flying and vulnerable to predators. Many of them bob up and down when they are perched, by bending and straightening their legs. Others hang upside-down holding on by the forelegs and rhythmically waving the hindlegs. Some of these movements are probably involved in sexual attraction and are seen mainly in larger species. Some of the smaller gnat-like species form mating swarms of males, seen just before sunset or sunrise monotonously dancing up and down. At intervals a female enters the swarm and is captured by a male. They then both drop to the ground.

Craneflies feed little as adults and then take only nectar. It is the growing larvae which consume the most food. They are tough-skinned, known as leatherjackets, and have biting mouthparts. They live just under the surface of the soil, attacking roots and stems of a wide range of plants including crops of various kinds. In warm weather they will feed at night above ground and cut through the stems at ground level. The larvae of *Tipula paludosa* are common farm pests and irregular bare patches in a field often betray their presence. This species lays eggs in the soil and the fully grown larvae pupate there in early summer. Adults emerge in two to three weeks. Other species have larvae which are semi-aquatic, some live among moss and others in rotten logs. All of them are moisture loving and dry weather kills them in large numbers. See leatherjackets. FAMILY: Tipulidae, ORDER: Diptera, CLASS: Insecta, PHYLUM: Arthropoda.   R.F.C.

CRANES, large, long-legged, spectacular birds with a superficial resemblance to herons and storks, but hardly ever perching in trees. With the rails (Rallidae) and some other families, they constitute the order Grui-formes. They have existed since the upper Eocene, over 40 million years ago, but currently there are only 14 species arranged in

five genera. And some of these are in danger of extinction.

Cranes stand from 30–60 in (76–150 cm) tall, of which the long legs and neck make up a considerable proportion. The plumage varies from white to slate grey or brown, and the inner secondary feathers of the wing are curled or elongated to form a mass of plumes that droop over the hind end of the body when the wings are folded. The head is ornamented with plumes or has areas of red featherless skin and the tail is rather short.

The bill is strong and straight; the legs and feet are also strong, with the toes connected at the base by a membrane. The hind toe is elevated, apparently playing little part in normal locomotion. The voice is loud and resonant—typically trumpeting but in others more whistling—aided by the unusual formation of the trachea which, in the males of most species, is coiled upon itself. These tracheal coils occupy part of the sternum and in some species even penetrate the breast muscles.

Cranes are world-wide, being absent only from South America, Madagascar, the Malayan Archipelago, New Zealand and Polynesia. Typically they are found in open country: marshes, plains, prairies, lakes and seashores. In the breeding season they are particularly shy and nest in wild remote

Migration routes of the European crane *Grus grus* during the autumn passage to its wintering areas.

nesting areas

wintering areas

migration routes

areas. Most species are migratory.

Outside the breeding season most cranes are strongly gregarious, migrating and wintering in large flocks. They fly strongly on long, wide wings, usually in an echelon or V-formation, and when travelling long distances fly at considerable altitudes. They fly with neck and legs extended and commonly call in flight, presumably as an aid in keeping the flock together.

The food of cranes is very variable. They will take most kinds of small animal and perhaps even more vegetable material, particularly fruits and roots. They forage in cultivated fields whenever possible and the understandable antagonism of farmers in an increasingly competitive and demanding market has been one of the reasons for the decline in numbers of cranes. In certain countries where cranes are partial pests there are governmental schemes for protecting crops and indemnifying farmers. In Canada for example, insurance against damage to crops by wildlife, including cranes, was instituted in Saskatchewan in 1953 and in Alberta in 1962. Also, exploders are used to scare cranes off the standing crops on which they feed and alternative 'lure crops' are provided.

One of the most outstanding characteristics of cranes is their habit of dancing. This may occur at any time of year, in winter as well as the breeding season, and may involve single birds or groups of either or both of the sexes. It is probably seen, however, in its most highly developed form in the dancing displays of a mated pair. Typically, the birds walk around each other with rapid steps and partly spread wings, bowing, or bobbing their heads, and alternately jumping into the air in a manner which is graceful in spite of their bulk. From time to time they stop suddenly, erect. They also throw a stick or other pieces of vegetation into the air, either catching it or stabbing at it as it falls. Prodigious jumps may be performed during the dance.

Cranes nest on the ground or in shallow water, and the nest varies from a shallow scrape in the soil to a bulky collection of vegetable material. Sometimes even within a single species the nest may vary considerably in form. Occasionally one, normally two and rarely three eggs are laid. They are incubated by both sexes, which also both take part in the care of the precocial young.

Crowned cranes and crocodile in Nairobi National Park. A strikingly beautiful bird renowned for its dances (opposite top).

Siberian white cranes, a species now much reduced in numbers (opposite centre).

Crowned cranes, widely distributed in Africa and notably abundant in Uganda, of which country it is the national emblem (opposite below).

Most living species of cranes are in the genus *Grus*. The present centre of the group is eastern Asia but there are 7 species spread across Eurasia. The Common crane *Grus grus* breeds from northern and eastern Europe across most of Asia. It was a regular breeder in Britain until around 1600, but it dislikes interference and human cultivation and has gradually been pushed eastwards. It stands about 44 in (112 cm) tall and is slate grey with a white streak from the eye down the neck. There is a red patch on the back of the crown.

The Common crane breeds in wet or damp open countryside such as swamps and marshes with or without scattered trees or scrub. In winter it prefers more open country, including dry grassland and steppe. In certain areas of the Siberian tundra it is replaced by the Siberian White crane *G. leucogeranus,* though this species is now much depleted.

In North America the type of habitat occupied by the Common crane in Eurasia is the territory of the Sandhill crane *G. canadensis*. This species is similar in many ways to the Common crane, being about the same size, basically grey with darker wing tips, and with red on the head. However, it is the forehead which is red and not the crown. Some birds have the feathers of head, neck or body stained red-brown from iron in the water. In both the Sandhill crane and the Common crane the red colouration on the head is the result of red-pigmented warty skin clearly showing through the few short, hair-like feathers. The young of both species are brown, with fully-feathered heads.

The breeding range of the Sandhill crane is considerable, extending from the Canadian, United States and Russian arctic southwards. The American population apparently consists of several groups, some resident and some migratory. There is a resident population in the southeastern United States, of which the birds in Florida in 1942 totalled some 2,650 individuals. There is another resident population, of apparently similar size, in the Caribbean. A small population breeding in Michigan, estimated in 1944 as 27 pairs, migrates to the southeastern United States. The majority of the American Sandhill cranes breed in the northern United States and Canada and migrate in winter to the southwestern United States and Mexico. In November 1963 there were over 200,000 individuals of this population in western Texas and eastern New Mexico. Clearly, the total population of Sandhill cranes in North America could be well over 200,000 birds, and fears that this may be one of the species of cranes nearing extinction seem to be unfounded. Protection schemes are probably effective enough, and early enough, in this case for the species to survive in safe numbers. The Russian population of this species

Young Australian or Brolga crane, also known as the 'Native companion', because of its readiness to stay near human beings.

Demoiselle crane of Europe, Asia and Africa.

may well be a considerable one, although exact figures are not at present available, and the world population of the Sandhill crane might be a million birds.

Studies carried out by officers of the Canadian Wildlife Service have provided information on the general ecology and bionomics of this species. The populations which winter in southwestern United States and Mexico begin their northward migration in late March, passing through the Canadian prairies in April. Only a few cranes stay in the prairies during the summer, the typical breeding habitat being the tundra. But during the southward migration in autumn, the time of the grain harvest on the Canadian prairies, flocks of thousands of birds gather in the fields to forage. They may stay from late August to early October, and in this time can do a considerable amount of damage, at least when foraging in unharvested grain fields.

Sandhill cranes, like other species of Gruidae, have long made use of cultivated land for feeding. Audubon reported Sandhill cranes feeding in cultivated fields in Mississippi as early as 1821, and they have been reported as damaging grain in the Prairie Provinces of Canada from the early 1920's. Although the birds take a very wide variety of food—various fruits and seeds and invertebrate animals in particular—they forage in grain fields by preference, and when there is a standing crop cause damage by trampling as well as by consumption.

During the night the cranes rest in temporary roosting areas some little distance from where they feed. They leave the roosts around dawn and fly to the feeding areas, which are seldom far from water. They typically return to the roosts around midday, and make a further feeding trip in the afternoon, returning to the roosts again at sunset.

It has been estimated that 100 acres (40 ha) can produce enough grain for 18,000 cranes, but this does not allow for wastage. In practice there are never more than 4,000 birds feeding in 100 acres, although 30,000 cranes may occupy one roost. The situation is clearly not a simple one, but damage is kept to a minimum by a combination of exploders and other bird scarers, 'lure' crops of grain and controlled hunting—a system which has been found to be effective for the control of ducks in parts of Canada and the United States.

The other American species of crane, the Whooping crane *G. americana*, is far from being a nuisance because of the depredations of large flocks. On the contrary, this species, endemic to North America, has become famous among conservationists and ornithologists through the efforts made to save the few remaining birds from extinction. This species was one of the 13 species or races of birds named as being on the danger list by the International Technical Conference on

The climate is subarctic but during the cranes' breeding season the mean monthly temperature is over 50° F (10° C). Precipitation is relatively low but local fluctuations may result in very wet or very dry conditions. In the former case there is a lower breeding success due to flooding and delayed nesting. A drier season does not affect the birds so adversely as the potholes are of variable depth and so some always retain their water.

The cranes arriving in the breeding area in spring are already mated, but although they leave the wintering area in Texas in family parties, the young do not arrive in the north with the adults. Somewhere along the migration route the family group becomes dispersed and this would seem to be a major factor in both the causation and the prevention of the population decline. The young do not seem to be experienced enough to undertake their first northward journey alone and this is the section of the population which suffers most. The Sass River population, which is probably the most important Whooping crane group, produced 32 young between 1954 and 1965 from the same five or six breeding pairs of adults. These young did not return to the Sass River area and did not contribute to production from other areas, as shown by the number of birds returning to the Texas refuge for the winter.

Another major factor in the population dynamics of the Whooping crane is the fact that although two eggs are laid, and usually hatched, only one young, even under the most favourable conditions, is reared. In fact only one young survives the hatching period, the second one to hatch, or about to hatch, apparently being destroyed by the adults. The technique has been developed, therefore, of taking one egg from each full clutch found and incubating it artificially. Cranes can be reared and bred successfully in captivity (of the 68 birds known at the beginning of 1969, 18 were captive) and there is hope that protection in the wild and breeding in captivity may eventually result in the wild population being successfully re-established.

Certain Asian species of *Grus* are also reduced to dangerously low numbers. The Siberian White crane has already been mentioned. From the number of birds seen in the traditional winter quarters of the species, it would seem that the population is much reduced. This species winters in two major areas: the birds from western Siberia fly to India and the shores of the Caspian Sea, and the eastern birds to China. The Indian population has recently numbered as few as 60 birds.

The Manchurian crane *G. japonensis* breeds in a few areas of Manchuria and in Hokkaido, Japan. This is another largely white species with black wings and red crown, but it also has a large grey streak

Sarus crane, the familiar crane of India and south-east Asia.

the Protection of Nature organized by UNESCO at Lake Success in 1949.

The Whooping crane stands 4 ft (1·2 m) high and has a wing span of 8 ft (2·4 m). It is white with black wing tips and has a large featherless area of red on the forehead and crown, on the front of the face and in a large moustachial streak. It would seem that this bird was not abundant even in the days of the first colonization of America by Europeans, though flocks of thousands were reported into the 19th century. By 1920, however, the population was down to 50 individuals, and the lowest level was reached in 1941 when there were only 23 individuals left, two of them in captivity.

After the Second World War an intensive programme of publicity, conservation and research was begun by government and private agencies in Canada and the United States. The small Texas wintering area of the species became the now famous Arkansas National Wildlife Refuge, and a substantial propaganda campaign was aimed largely at reducing the numbers of Whooping cranes

shot by accident or in ignorance by hunters during the migration period for Sandhill and Whooping cranes. Then in 1954 a major breeding area for the species was discovered in an existing national park in Canada. This made possible protection and research in both wintering and breeding areas of this migratory species, and the subsequent improvement in the numbers of Whooping cranes must in large part be the result of this major long-term conservation effort.

In January 1969 the total number of Whooping cranes had risen to 68. This increase is largely due to conservation operations instigated as a result of research into the breeding ecology of the population in the Sass River area of the Wood Buffalo National Park in the Canadian North West Territories. The habitat in the nesting area is marsh with numerous shallow potholes and a sparse covering of trees and shrubs. The cranes feed in the potholes which are shallow enough for them to wade in, and in this shallower water grow such plants as the bulrush, with which they make their nests.

running down each side of the neck. It seems that most of the birds winter in Japan, where they are strictly protected, but the breeding population in Hokkaido in 1962 was no more than 200.

The Hooded crane *G. monacha,* is another species which previously was a common winter visitor in Japan. The bare head-patch in this species is red and black. The breeding area again covers parts of Japan and Manchuria, but the winter flock consists of only a few hundred birds.

The White-necked crane *G. vipio* is grey with white throat and hind neck and white secondary wing feathers. It has a red face and forehead. It breeds in eastern Siberia and winters in Japan and also, like several other cranes, in parts of China and Korea. In Japan and Korea at least the various species of cranes have been protected for well over 50 years, but the depredations of the occupation forces after the Second World War and the havoc caused to cranes' wintering

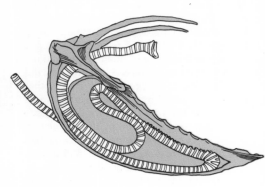

The long windpipe of a crane is folded on itself and lodged in a cavity of the breastbone.

grounds in the Korean war have had a very serious effect upon a number of species.

The Sarus crane *G. antigone,* is a very impressive bird, even for a crane, standing some 5 ft (1½ m) tall. It is blue-grey with a bare red head and upper neck and breeds in northern India and adjacent regions. The little-known Black-necked crane *G. nigricollis* lives in central Siberia. The remaining species of the genus is the Australian crane *G. rubicunda,* also called the 'native companion'. It is a silver-grey bird with a green crown and red on the face and back of the head and neck, and is found in southern New Guinea as well as Australia.

In eastern Europe and through much of central Asia to the south of the forest belt inhabited by the Common crane is found a member of one of the other crane genera, the Demoiselle crane *Anthropoides virgo.* This bird is only about 3 ft (1 m) tall and has soft grey plumage with black flight feathers, face and front of neck, and white plumes curving back and down from behind the eye. It is very handsome and is frequently kept in captivity. It winters in most of northeastern

Africa and the greater part of southern Asia.

On the South African plateau the Blue, or Stanley, crane, *Tetrapteryx paradisea,* is in some degree the ecological equivalent of the Demoiselle to the north. It is only found in South Africa but is still quite common there. It is basically similar to the Demoiselle but has black secondary wing feathers extending far beyond the tail.

Another South African species is the Wattled crane *Bugeranus carunculatus,* which is found in East Africa also. This is a large dark bird, grey above, black beneath and with the upper breast, neck and much of the head white. The face bears red warts, or carunculations, and below it hang two white-feathered wattles, or lappets. This seems to be another species which is on the decline.

Finally, one of the most striking of all the cranes: the Crowned crane *Balearica pavonina,* which is a widely-distributed species, found over much of Africa from Abyssinia and the Sudan southwards. It is 38 in (96 cm) tall and there are several races, one of which, from South Africa, is regarded by some authorities as being a separate species. The Ugandan race is particularly common and forms the Ugandan national emblem. The species is seen on the postage stamps of several African countries.

The Crowned crane is basically a dark-plumaged bird, with rufous on the hind part and white on the wings, but its most striking feature is its head with the crown which gives it its name. This crown is composed of a tuft of stiff straw-coloured feathers standing up in a fan from the back of the head. The head is otherwise covered with short black plumes and the bare cheeks are white. The bill is proportionally shorter than in other cranes.

The striking appearance of the Crowned crane is enhanced by the dances which it performs, the crown being displayed to full effect in the bobbing and bowing. This is one of a number of species of birds which have provided models for the dances of local tribes in West Africa.

In many parts of the world cranes have long been regarded as symbols of longevity. In Japanese folklore they are supposed to live for hundreds of years. They do not of course live for even one hundred years, yet, in common with many other large birds with a low breeding rate, they do live for a long time. The oldest known crane was a Siberian White crane which died in captivity at the age of 59. Cranes probably breed for much of their lifetime, and if conservation programmes can be made effective in protecting the populations of cranes on the danger list, their future could well be assured. It would clearly be a great loss to science and to all those with an interest in nature if any more species of cranes became extinct. FAMILY: Gruidae, ORDER: Gruiformes, CLASS: Aves. P.M.D.

CRAYFISHES, freshwater decapod crustaceans, having five pairs of walking legs, with the first pair enlarged and modified to form characteristic stout pincers. The second and third pairs also bear small pincers. The body is elongated and the tail is large, bearing a fan formed by an enlarged and flattened pair of abdominal appendages. A characteristic escape movement of a crayfish is to shoot backwards using a violent flexing of the fan.

The Common European crayfish *Astacus astacus* lives in streams and ponds, where it takes a varied diet, including snails, insects and plants. When dealing with large pieces of food the first three pairs of walking legs may all be involved in tearing pieces off and thrusting them into the mouthparts. These cut up the food even more, but the final grinding is done in the first part of the gut, where there is a gastric mill. This has hardened walls and powerful muscles which run from the mill to the exoskeleton. Movement of these muscles causes the hardened patches in the walls to move together and break up the food.

The crayfish respires by means of gills, which are housed in a branchial cavity on either side of the thorax. They are arranged in series at the bases of the thoracic limbs. Water is pumped in and out of the branchial chamber by a flap at the base of one of the thoracic limbs which serve as mouthparts (2nd maxilla). Water flows into the chamber near the bases of the hindlegs and out as a jet past the bases of the antennae. This is convenient from an excretory point of view, because the main excretory organ, or green gland, of the crayfish opens to the exterior at the base of each antenna.

In November the female of the Common European crayfish lays a batch of relatively large eggs. These are attached to the underside of the abdomen and carried for six months until they hatch. The young emerging from the eggs have the same general structure as the adult, but the form is more rounded and the limbs are not fully developed. This direct development contrasts with most marine decapods, lobsters and crabs, which have larval forms differing greatly from the adult. The European crayfish takes two or three years to reach maturity and may live for a total of 20 years.

Crayfish are most commonly found in streams with a high calcium content as they have heavy chalky exoskeletons. Regions of granite or other rocks, that yield little or no calcium to the surface waters, are lacking in crayfish. Most crayfish are not very tolerant of high temperatures and seek the shade at midday.

In winter crayfishes tend to burrow into the banks of their streams and the greater the likelihood of the water freezing the deeper they burrow. Some of the larger species do considerable damage to the banks of rivers, and some have extended their burrowing habits to other times of the year, becoming semi-terrestrial. There is one record of crayfishes invading a snake den in North America and devouring the torpid snakes during their winter hibernation when they were too sluggish to retaliate.

In North America over 200 species of a single subfamily, the Cambarinae, are found east of the Rocky Mountains. Paradoxically to the west of these mountains the crayfishes belong to the same subfamily as the European crayfish (Astacinae), and only five species are found along the Pacific Slope from British Columbia to California.

The crayfishes of the southern hemisphere are usually placed in a separate family (Parastacidae) from those in the northern hemisphere. These southern forms are found in Australia, New Guinea, New Zealand, South America and Madagascar, but not on the mainland of Africa. In Australia there are over 50 species in the genus *Euastacus* and of these, those that live in the northern tropical regions of Australia are confined to cool mountainous areas. In New Guinea, in Lake Piniai in the mountains of the western region, there are at least six species of *Cherax*. The same genus also occurs on the mainland of Australia and in the Aru Islands. The largest of all the crayfishes, *Astacopsis franklini,* occurs in Tasmania and reaches a weight of 9–11 lb (4–5 kg).

Crayfishes occur mainly in the temperate regions of the world and where they occur in the tropics they are restricted to cool mountainous areas. In the tropical regions where there are no crayfishes the fresh waters have been invaded by other decapods, particularly shrimps of the families Atyidae and Palaemonidae, which reach a large size, comparable to that of a crayfish.

Crayfishes are esteemed by man as food wherever they are found. A wide range of traps and collecting techniques have been developed. Australian aborigines wade shoulder deep in water, with a basket clenched in their teeth, locating the crayfishes, or yabbies, with their toes. When a crayfish is found it is caught by hand and transferred to the basket. They are also cultured artificially. In Europe it has been found that the most suitable form for cultivation is the American species, *Orconectes limosus*. This has been introduced into several European countries as it is more easily reared than the native species. Its life-cycle contributes to this greater ease of cultivation. The eggs are laid in April or May and take only five to eight weeks to hatch.

It should be noted that the name crayfish, or crawfish, is also sometimes applied to some marine forms, also known as Spiny lobsters or langouste. These belong to a separate group (Palinura). FAMILIES: Astacidae, Parastacidae, ORDER: Decapoda, CLASS: Crustacea, PHYLUM: Arthropoda.
Ja.G.

Common European freshwater crayfish with 3-spined stickleback *Gasterosteus aculeatus* in its claw.
Baby crayfishes clinging to the underside of the mother with their hooked pincers.

CREEPERS, term used in the name of a number of species of birds in certain families of the order Passeriformes. It usually forms part of a compound word, as in tree-creeper (Certhiidae), honeycreeper (Coeribinae) and woodcreeper (Dendrocolaptidae). In America the word creeper is usually synonymous with the Brown creeper *Certhia familiaris,* the species which is also found in Europe and there called the Tree creeper, or treecreeper. ORDER: Passeriformes, CLASS: Aves.

CREODONTA, a group of fossil mammals which were carnivorous. They are known from latest Cretaceous to Oligocene times in Europe, Asia and North America, but survived later, into the Miocene, in Africa; they failed to enter South America.

As with all groups of early fossil mammals, it can be difficult to distinguish creodonts from their contemporaries, so there have been repeated changes in classification. The giant *Andrewsarchus,* for example, with a skull 3 ft (1 m) long (a lion or large bear skull is about 1 ft (30 cm) long), has been often quoted as the largest creodont and therefore the largest carnivorous mammal. It is now regarded as a *condylarth. At the moment it is undecided whether creodonts should be placed in the Carnivora or the Insectivora.

CRESTED SWIFTS, or tree-swifts, relatives of the true swifts (Apodidae) which they resemble. They differ in the males being brightly coloured, and in their habit of perching, and building their nests, on tree branches.

The three species of *Hemiprocne* are restricted to tropical Asia where they live in open woodland, secondary forest and gardens. As with the true swifts, all their food is gathered on the wing and includes wasps and bees.

The nest is a tiny cup of saliva, bark and feathers glued to the top of a slender branch. The single egg is glued into the nest which only just accommodates it. The mottled-brown nestling sits still on the branch, protected by its general resemblance to a knot or piece of lichen. FAMILY: Hemiprocnidae, ORDER: Apodiformes, CLASS: Aves.

CRICK, Francis H. C., b. 1916, British molecular biologist. He took his first degree in physics and later joined a team using physical methods to study the structures of biological molecules. His collaborative studies in the early 1950s with J. D. Watson, incorporating evidence obtained using X-ray crystallography by M. H. F. Wilkins in London, led to them putting forward the idea that the molecule of the genetic material deoxyribonucleic acid (DNA) is a double helix. This is one of the most significant scientific discoveries of the 20th century, and was

Female Wood cricket *Nemobius sylvestris.*

recognized by the award of a Nobel Prize to Crick, Watson and Wilkins in 1962.

CRICKETS, jumping insects of small to moderate size closely related to the bush-crickets and belonging to the family Gryllidae. There are about 1,000 species and although the group is mainly tropical there are many temperate species.

The antennae are thread-like and composed of more than 30 segments. Behind the head is a saddle-shaped structure, the pronotum, protecting the front part of the thorax. There are usually two pairs of fully developed wings, but in some species these are reduced in size or completely absent. The hindwings are membranous and fold up like a fan when at rest, forming two 'spikes' that protrude from beneath the shorter and tougher forewings. The females have a rod- or needle-like egg-laying instrument (ovipositor) at the tip of the abdomen and both sexes have a pair of long and conspicuous cerci.

The eggs are usually laid in the ground, but in the tree-crickets of the subfamily Oecanthinae, which are exceptional in living in trees and shrubs, they are laid on bark, in the pith

The head of a Giant cricket.

of twigs or in the stems of various plants. The young are similar to the adults in appearance, but lack wings. They reach maturity after moulting from eight to 11 or more times, an unusually large number for insects of this size. The young stages often pass through a resting phase during the winter or, in the tropics, the dry season, and so may take as long as a year to become adult.

Most male crickets can 'sing' by rubbing the hind edge of the left forewing against a row of teeth on the right forewing. The sounds produced are often quite musical and in some parts of the world crickets are sold in cages, to be kept as singing pets. The females are unable to sing but both sexes have a hearing organ in each foreleg.

A few species of crickets have become associated with man and have been spread by him to many parts of the world. The best known example is the European house-cricket *Acheta domesticus* which now occurs in indoor situations throughout the world and is sometimes sufficiently numerous to be a pest.

Crickets are usually nocturnal, often living in burrows during the day and feeding on a wide variety of both plant and animal matter.

The closely related mole-crickets (Gryllotalpidae) live almost entirely in burrows, which they dig with their much modified, mole-like forelegs. Both sexes, when alarmed, can eject an evil-smelling liquid from the tip of the abdomen. Unlike those of the true crickets, the females can produce sounds, differing from the males' song but produced in a similar way. In warm countries mole-crickets are sometimes sufficiently abundant to cause damage to crops. FAMILY: Gryllidae, ORDER: Orthoptera, CLASS: Insecta, PHYLUM: Arthropoda. D.R.R.

CRICKET FIGHTS. As well as keeping crickets for their song, the Chinese were accustomed to keep them for fighting. Male crickets were pitted against each other in special bowls, with all the ceremony of a prize fight. The past honours of the contestants were recited before they were goaded into action with a fine hair. The fight was usually to the death and money changed hands on the result. From an exclusive pastime of the rich, cricket fighting became a widespread sport of the peasants and may by now have died out.

CRINOIDS, scientists' slang name for Sea lilies and Feather stars.

The Striped drum *Equetus pulcher*, one of the croakers, a fish living in the seas around Florida and the Lesser Antilles which makes sounds, presumably to communicate with its fellows.

CROAKERS, also known as drums, a family of perch-like fishes capable of producing a great range of sounds. There are nearly 200 species of croakers, a few from freshwaters but most are marine. There is a single dorsal fin, the anterior portion spiny and the remainder composed of soft rays. The body is fairly elongated, the scales are easily shed, and the liver is extremely rich in vitamin A. The noises produced by these fishes result from the vibration of muscles that run from the abdomen into the swimbladder. The muscles vibrate rapidly (about 24 times a second) and the swimbladder acts as a resonator (if collapsed by pricking with a pin no sound is produced). In most fishes the swimbladder is a smooth bag-like structure,

but in the croakers it branches into arborescent or tree-like processes around its periphery. Possibly these branches determine the kind of sound produced. The function of the drumming noises is not yet fully understood. In some species the noises are most intense during the breeding season and at feeding periods. A species of *Nibea* from Japan forms large shoals of up to a million individuals which appear to be able to synchronize their drumming. Many of the species have large otoliths or ear stones and in the past these were considered useful in curing colic. A few members of the genus *Menticirrhus,* which includes the Atlantic minkfishes, lack a swimbladder and can only produce rather weak noises by grinding their teeth.

The croakers are fairly large fishes, usually with well-flavoured flesh, and some species are important as sport fishes. The American freshwater drum *Aplodinotus grunniens,* found particularly in the freshwaters of the southern states, also occurs in the Great Lakes where it is known as the sheepshead. A large specimen may weigh 60 lb (28 kg) but archaeologists have found the bones of drums in Indian camp sites which show that fishes of 200 lb (90 kg) were once caught. The average size of fishes caught nowadays is only 5 lb (2·5 kg).

Of the three European species, the meagre, the Brown meagre and the corb, the first is the largest, reaching 6 ft (1·8 m) in length and providing considerable sport.

The croakers are usually rather dull coloured, but the Striped drum *Equetus pulcher* from tropical regions has longitudinal bands of black and white on the flanks and the dorsal fin is enlarged resembling a black flag. The largest of the croakers is the totuva *Cynoscion macdonaldi* from the Gulf of California which reaches weights of 220 lb (100 kg). In South Africa, the croaker *Atractoscion aequidens* is considered a great delicacy and is known as salmon or geelbek. It is not common and when caught it is usually cured, but a certain sharp practice exists amongst the local fishermen who cure the much more common but inferiorly flavoured croaker *Johnius hololepidotus.* As the cured fishes greatly resemble each other in appearance except for the shape of the tail, the latter is cut off by the fishermen to complete the deception. The drums are important commercial fishes in many areas and in India they are used to provide a source of low quality isinglass from their swimbladders, as well as for food. FAMILY: Sciaenidae, ORDER: Perciformes, CLASS: Pisces.

CROCODILE BIRD, several species of wading birds that commonly associate with basking crocodiles, some even sleeping on them. In Africa, three waders have been recorded regularly feeding close to crocodiles, or actually feeding on their ectoparasites; these are the Egyptian plover *Pluvianus aegyptius* (see courser), the Spurwinged plover *Vanellus spinosus* and the Common sandpiper *Actitis hypoleucos.* The name 'crocodile-bird' was used by Herodotus and Pliny for an African bird (or birds) which took food from the gums of basking crocodiles, or even entered their mouths; but such behaviour has been documented very rarely in recent years, and almost certainly is not a regular behaviour pattern of any wader. ORDER: Charadriiformes, CLASS: Aves.

CROCODILES, 13 species belonging to the order *Crocodylia, the others being known as alligators, caimans and gavials. They differ from alligators and caimans in that the large fourth tooth in the lower jaw which fits into a notch in the upper jaw remains visible even when the mouth is closed. Moreover, the teeth of the upper and lower jaw are more or less in line, those of the lower jaw engaging between the teeth of the upper jaw. The two ribs on the first cervical vertebra diverge considerably. Bony scutes are usually restricted on the underside to the front of the thorax.

The best known species of true crocodiles is the Nile crocodile *Crocodylus niloticus* which occurs all over Africa south of the Sahara, as well as Madagascar and the Seychelles Islands. Only a few decades ago it died out in southwest Asia (the River Zerka in Israel). At one time this species reached lengths of up to 33 ft (10 m) but nowadays it is hard to find specimens more than 20 ft (6 m) long. In western and central Africa, as well as in Ujiji on Lake Tanganyika, lives the 13 ft (4 m) Long-snouted crocodile *Crocodylus cataphractus,* the snout of which is up to $3\frac{1}{2}$ times as long as it is wide at the base. In contrast, the Broad-nosed crocodile *Osteolaemus tetraspis,* of western and central Africa, has an extremely short snout and is rarely more than 6 ft (1·8 m) long. It has brown eyes and is said to spend more time in

The snouts of crocodilians are distinctive: 1. gavial, 2. crocodile, 3. alligator.

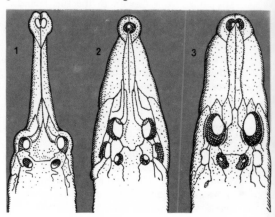

Australian crocodile.

the jungle than in water. It feeds mainly on freshwater crabs and soft turtles using its comparatively blunt teeth.

In Asia lives the 13 ft (4 m) long mugger or Swamp crocodile *Crocodylus palustris,* mainly in India and Ceylon, perhaps also in Burma. It differs from the very similar Nile crocodile by its somewhat shorter snout and the less regular arrangement of the scutes on the back, the central longitudinal rows being somewhat broader than those at the sides. The Siam crocodile *C. siamensis,* which has somewhat the same length, is restricted to Thailand and Indo-China and the islands of Java and Borneo. It is characterized by a triangular raised portion in front of the eyes, with the apex of the triangle facing forward, and a longitudinally directed bony ridge between the eyes. Despite its name, the somewhat longer Sunda gavial *Tomistoma schlegeli* does not belong to the gavials (Gavialidae) but to the true crocodiles. Although its snout is extremely long, and up to five times as long as its width at the base, this does not stem from the main part of the skull in the manner of a beak but gradually merges with the skull. This species is found on the Malayan peninsula as well as on the islands of Sumatra and Borneo.

The Estuarine crocodile *Crocodylus porosus* is spread over a vast territory stretching from Ceylon to the Fiji Islands, including northern Australia. It lacks the large post occipital scutes, the scutes on the back overlie only small oval ossifications and on the snout there is a pair of scute-like bony ridges extending from the front corners of the eyes up to the nose. The Estuarine crocodile reaches 33 ft (10 m) in length and lives at the mouths of rivers and in salt water. It can be seen swimming many miles from the coast in the open seas.

Similar bone ridges on the snout, even though shorter and less pronounced, are found in the New Guinea crocodile *C. novaeguineae* and the Philippine crocodile *C. mindorensis,* which also occurs in the Sulu

Archipelago. Both forms, which differ from the Estuarine crocodile by the well built post occipital scutes and the completely ossified scutes on the back, are perhaps only geographical races of a single species; their length is up to roughly 10 ft (3 m).

Apart from the Estuarine crocodile, in northern Australia we find the Australian crocodile *C. johnsoni* which is only 8 ft (2·5 m) long and is recognized by its long narrow snout.

True crocodiles are also at home in the New World. The most northern species is the light olive coloured American or Sharp-nosed crocodile *C. acutus* in the south of the Florida peninsula, on the islands of Cuba, Jamaica and Hispaniola, as well as from Mexico southwards over the whole of Central America to Venezuela, Colombia, Ecuador and Northern Peru. It is characterized by its narrow and long snout having a bulbous dome in front of the eyes. The scutes on the back are somewhat irregular and form only four to six interconnected longitudinal rows. Whilst this species reaches almost 12 ft (3·5 m), the Bulbous crocodile *C. moreletii,* found in the east of British Honduras and in Guatemala, is only a little more than 8 ft (2·5 m) long and is almost black when aged. Here, too, the snout carries a lump in front of the eyes but has a much broader and shorter effect than in the previous species. Restricted to Cuba there is the barely 7 ft (2 m) long Cuba crocodile *C. rhombifer* which has a triangular raised portion in front of the eyes similar to that in the Siam crocodile. The older individuals are almost black and exhibit light yellow spots on the back legs. The only wholly South American species is found in

the region of the Orinoco river, namely the Orinoco crocodile *C. intermedius* which reaches the stately length of up to 15 ft (4·5 m). It differs clearly from all other American species of crocodile by its extremely narrow and very elongated snout. FAMILY: Crocodylidae, ORDER: Crocodylia, CLASS: Reptilia.   H.W.

CROCODILES DISTINGUISHED. Even when alligators and crocodiles are seen together in a zoo it is not easy to tell which is which unless one knows their particular characters. Alligators have a blunter snout and, when the mouth is shut, the upper teeth overlap the lower teeth. In crocodiles the two rows of teeth are in line but the enlarged fourth lower tooth fits into a notch in the upper jaw and is visible whereas it is covered in alligators. It could be said that the crocodiles leer while the alligators have a toothy grin.

CROCODYLIA, order of reptiles adapted for freshwater, marine and terrestrial life. First appearing in the Triassic, the order represents today the only surviving group of the *Archosauria. In all members the nostrils and eyes are set high on the head allowing almost complete submergence of the body without impairment of breathing or sight. The long jaws are armed with simple conical and socketed teeth. Externally the body is protected by horny scales which are underlain, at least on the back region, by bony scutes. The toes of both the short fore-and long hind-limbs are webbed and the tail is powerfully

Crocodiles hatching in Murchison Falls Park, Uganda. Mother opens nest for babies to crawl out.

Crocodiles basking. It was long believed a crocodile opens its mouth by raising the upper jaw.

developed for propulsion in water. The eggs are laid on land. Several extinct groups, notably the geosaurs (see Marine reptiles), were marine. Today, the order comprises the alligators, caimans, crocodiles, and gavials.

The flat head terminates in a generally long snout which carries numerous teeth often of various sizes. The cranium has clearly formed upper and lower temporal openings (temporal foramina) and there is no opening for a pineal eye (pineal foramen). New teeth grow throughout life and drive the old ones out of their cavities. The tongue is fast to the base of the mouth cavity and cannot be projected out of the snout. The internal nostrils open at the extreme hinder end of the palate well into the throat. In front of these is a flap of skin closing them from the mouth cavity. So crocodiles can breathe even if the snout is opened under water because their external nostrils are located on a hump and project above the surface of the water when the animal is immersed. The eyes also are high up on the head and the ear, in contrast to all other reptiles, is protected by a flap of skin keeping out water.

The back carries large, roughly square, horny scutes arranged in more or less regular longitudinal and transverse rows, with generally a large scute along their centre. Beneath these there are strong dermal plates, smaller than the horny scales only in the Estuarine crocodiles. Large isolated scutes are also disposed along the sides and on the outsides of the legs.

The legs are strongly developed but only serve for walking on land. While swimming, the crocodile draws the legs back against the body and moves through the water only by side to side movements of its tail. The front legs carry five toes and the rear legs only four toes, all of which may be more or less strongly connected by webs. Only the three inner toes carry horny claws. Some transformations in the inner structure of the front legs show that crocodiles, like practically all Archosauria, can be traced back to originally two-legged (bipedal) ancestors.

The body terminates in a long laterally flattened muscular tail. At its upper surface, on lamelliform scales, there is a high and initially double crest which merges into a single crest at about the middle of the tail.

The entire underside of all crocodiles is covered with smaller rectangular horny scales arranged in regular transverse and longitudinal rows. Internally to these, and especially in the alligators, and particularly the caimans, there are large bony plates. In true crocodiles these are only occasionally on the chest. Directly behind the rear legs there is the longitudinally directed anal cleft from which, in the case of the male, there projects the single erectile penis.

The skeleton is strongly ossified. Behind the solid skull there are nine cervical vertebrae, of which the first two also carry short ribs, 14–15 thoracic and lumbar vertebrae, two pelvic and 30–40 caudal vertebrae with frontal cavity (procoelous). The shoulder

girdle is very simply constructed and consists of only five bones (two scapulae, two coracoids, one inter-clavicle). The pelvis is perpendicular to the vertebral column and is composed of three paired bones (two pubes, two ischia and two ilia).

In the oral cavity there are salivary glands only in the vicinity of the pharynx. For this reason crocodiles feed almost exclusively in the water. The stomach lies transversely to the longitudinal axis of the body and usually contains stones which probably serve not so much for grinding the food but as ballast in swimming and diving. The posterior intestine, ureters and genital ducts open into a common cloaca. A diaphragm, not homologous with the diaphragm of mammals, separates the thoracic and stomach cavities. It is likely that this assists crocodiles to make bellowing noises during which their sides vibrate so intensely that the water spurts upwards. Probably this bellowing serves to mark acoustically the boundaries between the individual territories.

Although the heart is completely separated into two auricles and two ventricles, arterial and venous blood mix at an opening at the beginning of the two aortae. This connection is probably necessary to balance out the very different gas pressures in the two parts of the blood vessel system during diving.

Glands open between the upper scales on the back and their secretion keeps the scales supple. A large musk gland opens on both sides beneath the head adjacent to the two halves of the lower jaw; other musk glands are sited in the cloaca.

The nervous system and sense organs are highly developed. Of all the reptiles, the cerebral cortex is most strongly folded in crocodiles; these animals are therefore capable of noteworthy performances in which we may justifiably see the beginnings of a rudimentary intelligence. Smell, hearing and sight are also efficient. A reflecting layer (tapetum lucidum) at the back of the eye serves to make the most use of the available light at night, crocodiles being particularly active at twilight. The pupil also dilates at this time and contracts to a fine vertical slit in bright light.

When young, crocodiles feed on worms, beetles, crabs and Amphibia, later on fish and waterfowl and when old even on medium-sized mammals. Some species drag their prey into cavities along the banks and leave them to decay a little before eating the carcases.

The sexes of crocodiles can hardly be differentiated externally except in the Mississippi alligator and the Ganges gavial. After mating, which takes place in the water, the female lays up to over 100 chalky-shelled eggs in nests, the construction of which varies in different species. There are all kinds from simple pits in the sand to heaps of mud and decaying vegetable matter. After 8–12 weeks the young hatch out with a length of 8–12 in (20–30 cm), depending on the species. Shortly before hatching some young crocodiles emit quacking sounds while still in the egg. This is to call the mother who stays in the vicinity and helps to release the crawling young from the nest and lead them to the water. During the first few weeks the young remain hidden in the water and are even said to climb onto bushes so as not to be devoured by the older crocodiles. At 8–10 years crocodiles become sexually mature. Depending on the species, they reach maximum lengths between 6 ft (1·8 m) and 33 ft (10 m) and they are believed to live considerably more than 100 years.

The order Crocodylia is divided into three families: the alligators (Alligatoridae), including the true alligators and the caimans, the true crocodiles (Crocodylidae) and the gavials (Gavialidae) represented by only one species. Altogether eight genera with 21 species are recognized. CLASS: Reptilia. H.W.

CROSSBILLS, finches with peculiar crossed mandibles for extracting seeds from the conifer cones which provide almost their entire food. They also have large feet for gripping the cones and are adept at climbing among the branches, using feet and bill to pull themselves along in parrot-fashion. They are found in northern regions throughout the world. The three species differ in body size, size of bill and preferred food. The largest, the Parrot crossbill *Loxia pytyopsittacus* has a heavy bill and feeds from the hard cones of pine; the medium-sized Common crossbill *L. curvirostrus* has a medium bill and feeds from the softer cones of spruce; while the smallest Two-barred crossbill *L. leucoptera* has a slender bill and feeds from the delicate cones of larch. This is true as a general tendency, but each sometimes takes cones of other types. In all three species, the males are coloured brick-red, with brownish wings and tail, and the females and young are greenish; but the two-barred, as its name implies, also has white bars across its wings.

Most of the conifers on which crossbills feed produce their seeds in mid-summer. The seeds remain in the cones overwinter and fall the following spring when the cones open. Crossbills can obtain seeds from cones at any stage of ripeness but, owing to their special bill-structure, cannot pick fallen seeds from the ground below. So in the few weeks between the falling of one crop and the formation of the next, they have to turn to alternate foods: to insects or to seeds of deciduous trees and herbaceous plants.

Crossbills nest high on the branches of conifers, laying three to four bluish-white spotted eggs. So that the young can be raised while seeds are still plentiful, all three species nest early in the year before the seeds have fallen. The main breeding season of the

Common crossbill lasts from January to March. In the winter of 1940/41, some nests were found near Moscow when temperatures were down to 0°F (−18°C); but inside the nests, while the female brooded, they reached 100°F (38°C). It is perhaps because the young are often raised in cold snowy weather that they develop more slowly than other finches and stay in the nest for up to 30 days.

The migrations of crossbills are also unusual, being adapted to their special food-supply. Cone-crops vary enormously in size, both from place to place in the same year and from year to year in the same place, a good crop usually being followed by a poor one. The birds therefore move around every summer, settling wherever cones are plentiful. Here they will remain for a year, but will move on at the end of the year in search of new areas rich in seed. Thus the crossbills differ from other migratory birds in making only a single movement each year. In addition, these movements sometimes develop into 'irruptions', in which the birds leave their home range in enormous numbers and appear in regions quite unsuited to their needs. This is supposedly caused by widespread crop-failure or 'overpopulation'. Ir-

rupting Common crossbills have reached Britain from northern Europe and Russia at least 17 times in the last 70 years. It was as a result of an invasion in 1909 that the colony breeding in the pine plantations of East Anglia was established, though some breeding has occurred in other areas after every irruption. The other two species behave similarly, but invasions of the Two-barred crossbill, which lives mainly in northern Russia and Siberia, rarely reach Britain. FAMILY: Fringillidae, ORDER: Passeriformes, CLASS: Aves.   I.N.

CROSSOPTERYGII, a group of fishes very important in evolutionary history because it is generally agreed that numbered amongst them are the ancestors of all amphibians, reptiles, birds and mammals, including ourselves. Strictly the Crossopterygii comprise two sub-groups, the Rhipidistia and Actinistia or coelacanths. One species of the latter is alive today but all the Rhipidistia are extinct. The rhipidistians were freshwater forms ranging in geological time from the Lower Devonian to the Lower Permian (390 million—260 million years ago). Like the living lungfishes (Dipnoi) they had lungs and their fins show a structure antecedent to that

The Common crossbill can pick seeds out of cones but cannot pick them up from the ground.

Carrion crows build their nests in trees inland but build on a rocky ledge on the coast.

of the tetrapod limb. However, the closeness of their relationship to the Dipnoi is in dispute. SUBCLASS: Crossopterygii, CLASS: Pisces.

CROWS, perching birds, usually sombre-coloured of the family Corvidae which contains 100 or so species. The term is also used in a more restricted sense for members of the typical genus *Corvus*, though some of these species have their own names, e.g. 'raven', 'rook' and 'jackdaw'. Crows outside *Corvus* include magpies, jays, nutcrackers, choughs and piapac. In some parts of the world the names 'crow', 'jay', 'magpie' and 'chough' have been given to birds outside the Corvidae.

The crow family is probably the most advanced in the order of perching birds (Passeriformes) and also in the Aves. It includes the largest members of the order and the most psychologically advanced ones. Furthermore, certain species have a fairly complex social organization, or perform activities which in mammals would probably be labelled 'play'. The family is a cosmopolitan one, only being entirely absent from New Zealand and certain Pacific islands, and is clearly highly successful. This success, however, has not come about through extremes of specialization and adaptation to restricted ecological niches, but rather through a generalized structure and adaptability of behaviour which enables corvids to benefit from a wide range of environmental circumstances.

Corvids range in length from 7–28 in (17–71 cm). The typical crows are usually entirely black, or black with white, grey or brown. At close quarters the black plumage can usually be seen to have a blue, green or purple metallic sheen. The jays and magpies are more variable in colouration, often showing much blue or green, and they are frequently crested or have long tails. Bright wing or tail bars are seen in some. The bills of most members of the family are stout and moderately long, very strong in some such as the ravens, which can open carcasses and skulls with relative ease. The nostrils are protected by forwardly-directed bristles which presumably help to exclude foreign material during feeding. Both pairs of limbs are strong; thus the corvids are highly efficient in locomotion both on the ground and in the air. Some species, such as the raven *Corvus corax* and the chough *Pyrrhocorax pyrrhocorax,* show a highly developed mastery of the air exceeded by few other animals. The sexes of corvids are similar in appearance.

The family is most common in the northern temperate zone. The range of the genus *Corvus* is that of the family, except that the only corvids in South America are jays. The various species of the family are found in a wide variety of habitats ranging from high mountains and sub-arctic regions to tropical jungle and human conurbations. Most species are omnivorous, taking a wide variety of food, often opportunistically. Many act as scavengers and will feed on dead or dying animals as well as on garbage, and have thereby aroused the enmity of farmers and gamekeepers. Most species will take the eggs or young of other animals, as well as weak adults or anything small enough which they catch unawares. They may thus be regarded as partial predators. A number of species feed on the shoreline.

The breeding of corvids is, in many species, colonial, though other species, e.g. the Carrion crow *Corvus corone,* are gregarious only outside the breeding season. The pair-bond is close, several species pairing for life and both sexes taking part in rearing the young. The nest is typically rather large, made of stout twigs and placed in a tree or bush or on cliffs or buildings. In a few species, such as the magpie *Pica pica,* the nest is domed, and in the jackdaw *Corvus*

Hooded crow at nest and in flight. Although differing in colour, it and the Carrion crow are probably one species.

monedula it is less bulky and placed in a hole in a tree, building, or cliff face or in the ground. Eggs vary from two to ten in number and are usually cryptically coloured varying from cream to blue with dark markings. Incubation takes two to three weeks and the nestling period is five to six weeks, according to the size of the bird and other factors.

One of the most complex examples of the intelligence of crows is provided by the many learning experiments carried out on the raven by Otto Koehler. He found it possible to train a bird to open the lids of a series of boxes until it had found a predetermined number of food pieces, randomly distributed. It would go no further after it had found the appropriate number. One jackdaw even learned to open black boxes until it had had two pieces of food, green boxes for three, red boxes for four and white boxes for five. This involves the ability to remember the number of things presented in a sequence. Experiments with a raven demonstrated a different ability—the ability to compare the numbers of things in groups presented simultaneously. Thus a raven learned to open a box patterned with the same number of spots as on a key card when that box was presented among several other boxes with different numbers of spots. The magpie has been found to have similar counting abilities. It is true that these experiments involved only a few individual birds and were carried out under laboratory conditions, yet they do give an indication of the kind of ability which corvids can call upon in certain circumstances.

The raven is a Holarctic bird, with different dialects in different parts of its range, as is the case with other widely-distributed birds. It also extends into Central America. It is solitary for much of the year and is now restricted to the wilder and more remote areas. The rook *C. frugilegus,* on the other

hand, is Palearctic only in its distribution, and is common wherever there are large trees in which to build its groups of nests or 'rookeries' and suitable land on which to forage. It is both gregarious and colonial and is 18 in (46 cm) long. The jackdaw, another colonial species, has a similar distribution but is only 13 in (33 cm) long. The two species are frequently found together, particularly when feeding. The Carrion crow and Hooded crow, both probably *C. corone,* are found through most of the Palearctic region. They are $18\frac{1}{2}$ in (47 cm) long, the Hooded crow being distinguished by a grey back and belly. In North America these two species are replaced by the Common crow *C. brachyrhynchos,* a very similar species and also, to a certain extent, by the slightly smaller Fish crow *C. ossifragus,* which feeds particularly along rivers and tide-lines.

Another typical species of *Corvus* is the Pied crow *C. albus,* which is common through much of tropical and southern Africa and is the only corvid of any kind found in Madagascar. Several other large species of *Corvus* are found in Africa which provides plenty of scope for corvine-type activities. *Corvus* species are also common in Asia and Australasia, frequently in association with man.

The members of the crow family other than *Corvus* have their own entries else-

where. But, mention must be made of the more divergent forms of the Corvidae. In the plateaus of central Asia live the ground jays of the genera *Podoces* and *Pseudopodoces,* small, long-legged running birds with sandy bodies and dark wings and tail. And in Africa live two species of which the classification is uncertain. The piapiac *Ptilostomus afer* is like a small dark-coloured magpie and is quite common in parts of west and central Africa. It is frequently found in association with man or other animals and, like many other corvids, perches on the backs of wild or domesticated mammals. Stresemann's bush crow *Zavattariornis stresemanni,* grey above, white below, with blue-black wings and tail, is an inhabitant of the thorn bush country of southern Ethiopia and is about the size of a jackdaw. Relatively little is known about it.

The family of crows, by their widespread occurrence, their frequent association with man and their highly-developed mental abilities—including the faculty of vocal mimicry shown by a number of species—has become one of the best known groups of birds. Widespread in human legend and folklore, one corvid or another is familiar to almost everyone. FAMILY: Corvidae, ORDER: Passeriformes, CLASS: Aves.   P.M.D.

CRUCIFIX FISH, a fanciful name given to certain marine catfishes of the genus *Arius* in parts of South America and the West Indies because of the resemblance of the underparts of the cleaned skull to a figure with outstretched arms. The body is formed from the parasphenoid bone, the two lateral pro-

Upper and lower views of the skull of the Crucifix fish (a species of marine catfish *Arius*), showing the resemblance to a monk with outstretched arms (left) and to a crucifix (right).

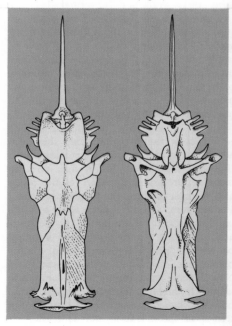

cesses resembling arms, while the Weberian ossicles form a halo. The upper side of the skull can be seen as a monk or Roman soldier, the dorsal spine being the spear and the ear-stones or otoliths rattling like the proverbial dice with which the soldiers cast lots for Christ's garments. When appropriately painted, the skull gives a satisfying blend of the fortuitous and the contrived. FAMILY: Ariidae, ORDER: Cypriniformes, CLASS: Pisces.

CRUSTACEA, the class of animal in which are found crabs, shrimps, woodlice, barnacles and Water fleas, together with a great number of forms that have no common names. There is such a great range of form within the class that it is not possible to give a concise definition that will include all the aberrant forms, but most Crustacea can be described as aquatic arthropods, breathing by gills or by their general body surface and having two pairs of antennae or feelers on the head. Obvious exceptions to this definition are the Land crabs and woodlice, which have given up the aquatic habit, and the parasitic forms,

Axius stirhynchus carrying eggs. Female.

some of which lose all their appendages and can only be recognized as crustaceans by their larvae.

The best way to understand the structure of the Crustacea is to examine one of the larger forms, such as a prawn or a crayfish. After becoming familiar with the detailed structure of such a form comparisons with other smaller, and often more highly modified forms, can usefully be made. Taking the crayfish as an example has a classical precedent. Thomas Henry Huxley wrote a book on the crayfish in 1880, which has become one of the classics of zoology and is still useful today.

The body of the crayfish is segmented, but the segments are only distinct in the abdomen, those of the thorax being covered by a large flap extending from the back of the head. This flap, or carapace, is found in many other Crustacea, but is often absent. Each segment bears a pair of appendages and although the thoracic segments are obscured by the carapace the appendages are quite obvious. In the head region, too, the append-

Tail-fan and statocysts of *Neomysis integer*, an Opossum shrimp.

Sea slater, a relative of the woodlouse.

ages give a guide to the basic segmental plan. Starting at the front the following sequence is found: antennules, antennae, mandibles, first maxillae, second maxillae, first, second and third maxillipeds, chelipeds (pincers), four pairs of walking legs, five pairs of swimmerets and finally at the tip of the abdomen the uropods which form a tail fan. The mandibles and the two pairs of maxillae constitute the

basic mouthparts, to which have been added the three pairs of maxillipeds from the thoracic region. This means that in the crayfish there are six pairs of appendages concerned with manipulation of food near the mouth. To these one can also add pincers which can seize and tear up food.

The digestive system of the crayfish is one of the most complex found in all Crustacea. There is an internal grinding and filtering mechanism. The walls of the stomach are thickened in patches and in these thickenings are developed calcareous plates or ossicles. Muscles run from the thickenings to the exoskeleton and by their contractions the ossicles are caused to move in relation to each other and grind up the food in the gut. Large particles are prevented from moving further down the gut by an elaborate filter. Digestion is aided by a set of digestive glands called the hepatopancreas, which perform the functions of the liver and the pancreas. Numerous enzymes are produced and many different substances are digested and stored in the hepatopancreas. In many of the smaller Crustacea the gut is a simple tube with no obvious hepatopancreas, so that all the digestive processes must be carried out by cells in the gut wall.

The gills of the crayfish are attached to the bases of the thoracic limbs and the sides of the thorax near the limb bases. They are enclosed in a chamber formed on each side by the overhanging carapace. Water is pumped in and out of the gill-chamber by means of a flap on the base of the maxilla, the scaphognathite. Other Crustacea have different arrangements of their gills. Sometimes, as in the Isopoda, the

Longitudinal section through a typical crustacean, to show anatomy. 1. eye, 2. supraoesophageal ganglion, 3. gizzard, 4. midgut, 5. heart, 6. pallium, 7. antenna, 8. antennule, 9. antennal gland, 10. mandible, 11. first maxilla, 12. second maxilla, 13. maxillary gland, 14. gill, 15. reproductive organs, 16. intestine. Inset top right: cross section through the body of a polychaete worm, for comparison with (inset bottom right) the appendages of a typical crustacean. 17. gill, 18. dorsal cirrus, 19. dorsal parapodium, 20. supporting bristles, 21. ventral parapodium, 22. ventral cirrus, 23. gill, 24. basipodite, 25. exopodite, 26. endopodite.

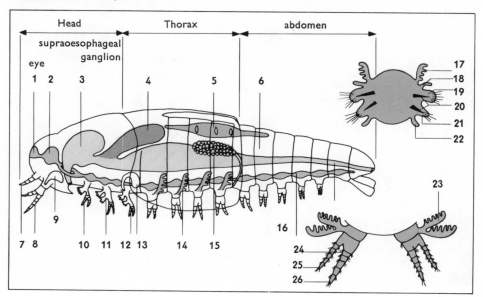

Gooseneck barnacles *Pocillipes polymerus* on a Californian seashore.

The crayfish of the rivers of Europe, the first crustacean to be studied in detail.

abdominal limbs are flattened and serve as gills. In many of the smaller forms there are no gills and the general body surface is sufficiently permeable to allow respiratory exchange to take place.

The blood of the crayfish circulates through the gills and then passes upwards into the pericardial cavity which surrounds the heart, which in the crayfish is short and almost square when viewed from above. In many primitive Crustacea the heart is long and tubular, but whatever the shape the basic mechanism is the same. When the heart dilates blood enters through small valves or ostia. These allow the blood to flow into the heart, but do not allow any outflow. When the heart contracts the blood is forced out through the arteries which lead to various parts of the body. In some of the smaller Crustacea there is a simple heart with a single pair of ostia and a single very short artery. Other small Crustacea lack a heart, their blood being moved around the body by the movements of the limbs.

In the crayfish the main organ of excretion is the antennal gland. This has an internal end sac, a duct or canal and a bladder. The antennal gland also functions in other decapods and in amphipods, but in many other Crustacea a similar gland opens on the maxilla. A few Crustacea, such as *Nebalia* and *Hutchinsoniella* have both glands well developed. In some groups the antennal gland functions in the young, but degenerates when the maxillary gland takes over in the adult. In addition to these glands there may also be excretion via the gut. If coloured substances are injected into the blood they are quickly moved to the lumen of the gut.

The crustacean nervous system is built on the typical arthropod plan. There is a pair of complex cerebral ganglia forming a brain above the gut in the head. The brain is connected to a chain of ganglia running underneath the gut. The number of ganglia in the chain varies with the length of the body and in some forms, such as the crabs, the chain is condensed into a single mass with nerves radiating from it.

The most conspicuous sense organs are generally the eyes, although these are often absent from cave-dwelling and deep-sea forms. Simple eyes are often found in larval forms but most adults have compound eyes, that are sometimes stalked. In some of the crabs the stalk may be very elongated and jointed.

Whether crustaceans hear in the same way that we do is somewhat problematical. Certainly some of them have receptors called statocysts which contain small particles rest

The crawfish *Panulirus ornatus*, family Palinuridae, commonly called Ornate crawfish or Ornate spiny lobster, of the seas of northern Australia and Papua-New Guinea.

ing on delicate setae (bristles), functioning in one way similar to our ears in that they help the crustacean to maintain its balance. It also seems likely that a few forms at least can perceive vibrations. The statocysts may not be the only means of perceiving vibrations as some of the very fine setae that project from various appendages may also be sensitive to vibrations. Most setae seem to be sensitive to the mechanical stimulus of touch, but some have very thin walls and may be concerned with the senses we call smell and taste, but which can be grouped together as chemo-sense. Receptors for the chemical senses are most abundant on the antennae and mouth-parts.

The classification of Crustacea reflects their diversity and is best summarized in a table.

Subclass	Cephalocarida – *Hutchinsoniella*, *Lightiella*, *Sandersiella*
Subclass	Branchiopoda
Order	Lipostraca – fossil only, *Lepidocaris*
Order	Anostraca – Fairy shrimps
Order	Notostraca – Tadpole shrimps
Order	Conchostraca – Clam shrimps
Order	Cladocera – Water fleas
Subclass	Ostracoda
Subclass	Cirripedia – barnacles
Subclass	Mystacocarida – *Derocheilocaris*
Subclass	Copepoda – *Cyclops, Calanus*
Subclass	Branchiura
Order	Branchiura
Subclass	Malacostraca
Division	Hoplocarida
Order	Stomatopoda – Mantis shrimps
Division	Phyllocarida

Order	Leptostraca – *Nebalia*
Division	Syncarida
Order	Anaspidacea – *Anaspides*
Order	Stygocaridacea – *Stygocaris*
Order	Bathynellacea – *Bathynella, Parabathynella*
Division	Peracarida
Order	Spelaeogriphacea
Order	Thermosbaenacea – *Thermosbaena, Monodella*
Order	Mysidacea – Opossum shrimps
Order	Cumacea – *Diastylis*
Order	Amphipoda – sandhoppers, Whale lice
Order	Isopoda – woodlice, gribble
Order	Tanaidacea – *Apseudes*
Division	Eucarida
Order	Euphausiacea – krill
Order	Decapoda
Suborder	Natantia – shrimps, prawns, cleaner shrimps, Pistol shrimps
Suborder	Reptantia
Tribe	Astacura – crayfish, lobsters, Norway lobsters
Tribe	Palinura – Spiny lobsters
Tribe	Anomura – Hermit crabs, King crabs *Paralithodes*, Robber crabs, Porcelain crabs
Tribe	Brachyura – Spider crabs, Shore crabs, Fiddler crabs, River crabs, Ghost crabs

A notable feature of this classification is that the subdivisions become finer towards the end. This is because the Decapoda are a large and successful group, with many conspicuous and familiar examples, while some of the other groups, such as the Stygocaridacea, are small and known only to

specialists. It will be convenient to deal wi the 'specialist groups' here, and to deal wi the more familar forms under their ow separate headings.

The subclass Cephalocarida was fir described in 1955, since then four distin species in three different genera have bee described. They are all small, not more than few millimetres in length, but are of outstan ing interest because their trunk limbs are of primitive type which could have given rise all the varieties of limbs found in mor advanced Crustacea. Basically the cephal caridan limb is a three branched affair, wit an inner jointed branch and two flap-lik outer branches. The inner jointed limb coul give rise to the typical shrimp type walkin leg. The two outer flaps could give rise t swimming limbs of the type found in th Branchiopoda such as Fairy shrimps an Tadpole shrimps.

The head of a cephalocaridan is rounded i front and bears a short carapace which cover only the first body segment. The body is ver elongated and consists of 20 segments, seve or eight of which bear the characteristi limbs. The little that is known of the biolog of cephalocarids indicates that they have very low reproductive rate. *Hutchinsoniell* appears to produce only six eggs in a year an has to pass through 18 stages before i becomes mature.

The first member of the subclass Mysta cocarida was described in 1943 from th coast of Massachusetts. Others have sinc been found on the coasts of South Americ Africa and Europe. They are very smal worm-like crustaceans, under $\frac{1}{2}$ mm in length

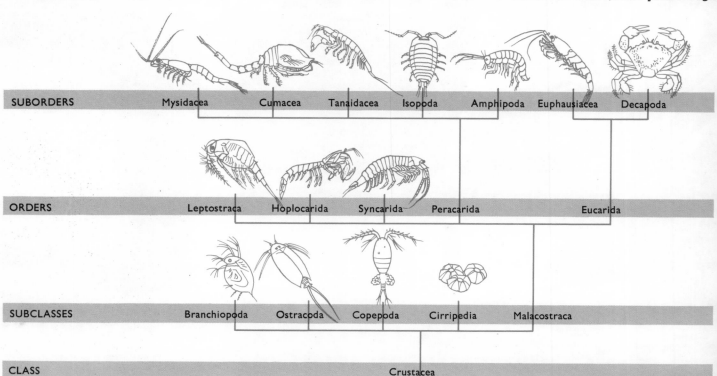

SUBORDERS — Mysidacea — Cumacea — Tanaidacea — Isopoda — Amphipoda — Euphausiacea — Decapoda

ORDERS — Leptostraca — Hoplocarida — Syncarida — Peracarida — Eucarida

SUBCLASSES — Branchiopoda — Ostracoda — Copepoda — Cirripedia — Malacostraca

CLASS — Crustacea

A Shore crab *Carcinus maenas* exposed on the sand near the castings of a lugworm *Arenicola*.

with branched antennae that they use to push their way through the spaces between sand grains. The other head appendages are well developed, but the trunk limbs are small. All the known species lack eyes and belong to the genus *Derocheilocaris*. They feed on small particles which they filter from the water lying in the spaces between sand grains. The young emerge from the eggs with only three pairs of appendages and pass through ten stages before becoming adult.

The habit of living between sand grains has also been adopted by members of the orders Bathynellacea and Stygocaridacea. The first specimens of the latter group were described from South America in 1963, but the first bathynellid was described from a well in Prague in 1882, and was not found again until 30 years later. Now there are over 50 described species of this group from places as far apart as Japan, South America and Africa. Both groups live predominantly in fresh water, but a few bathynellids have been found in brackish water. The body of *Bathynella* is long and cylindrical; the largest species reaches a length of $\frac{1}{5}$ in (5 mm), but most are much smaller. The thoracic limbs have two branches, but the abdominal limbs are reduced to vestiges or are absent. The stygocarids are similar in many respects to the bathynellids, but differ in possessing statocysts, or gravity receptors, in their antennules. This feature is lacking in the bathynellids, but is present in the anaspids, which are generally larger forms, reaching a length of 2 in (5 cm). All three groups are placed together in the division Syncarida, and have in common the absense of a carapace and a brood pouch. The anaspids are the only

ones with eyes and even one of the anaspids lacks eyes. All the present day Anaspidacea live in Tasmania or South Australia, although closely related fossils are known from other parts of the world. As far as is known the development of the Syncarida is direct, so that there are no larval forms and the young resemble the parents except in some aspects of limb development.

The division Phyllocarida includes a single order, the Leptostraca, containing only nine species. Their general form is dominated by the large bivalved carapace and a relatively narrow abdomen. The largest species reaches a length of $1\frac{1}{2}$ in (4 cm), but most are only about $\frac{2}{5}$ in (1 cm) long when adult.

Nebalia bipes has been studied in the greatest detail. The abdomen has seven distinct segments, whereas all other orders of the Malacostraca appear to have only six, although seven may be apparent in the embryos. At the tip of the abdomen of *Nebalia* there is a pair of caudal rami. These are quite different from the uropods found in most other Malacostraca and resemble the rami found in the Copepoda and in the Fairy shrimps. The only other malacostracans with caudal rami are some of the Syncarida. The eyes of *Nebalia* are stalked and bright red. *Nebalia* is a filter feeder, using the eight pairs of thoracic limbs, which are all similar in structure and beat in a metachronal rhythm. The filters are borne on the inner edges of the limbs, and food is trapped in the midline between the two rows of limbs. As well as bearing filters the limbs also bear series of brush-like setae which push the trapped food forwards to the mouth. The females of *Nebalia* carry their eggs between their thoracic legs and the young emerge as miniatures of their parents.

Nebalia bipes lives in mud on the lower part of the sea shore, but some of its relatives, for example *Nebaliopsis typica,* have become planktonic, and have a gut modified for feeding on tiny planktonic eggs. There is an enormous sac opening into the gut, so that *Nebaliopsis* can make the most of any chance encounter with a floating mass of eggs.

The next division, the Peracarida, consists of a highly diverse and successful group of middle-sized Crustacea, their major common feature being a brood pouch. In most peracaridans the brood pouch is formed by a series of plates extending from the bases of the thoracic limbs. The three best known groups, the Opossum shrimps, the Amphipoda and the Isopoda, are dealt with under their own headings. The remaining groups are not so well known, although the Cumacea and Tanaidacea are widespread and common in the seas of the world.

There are about 500 known species of the

The blood vascular system in a generalized crustacean. The heart (H) lies dorsally in the thorax. A main artery (CA) carries oxygenated blood to the head region, another, the sternal artery (SA) carries blood to the thorax and a third (PA) runs to the abdomen. These connect with a ventral vein (VV) from which capillaries take the impure blood to the gills (G) where carbon dioxide is lost to the surrounding water and oxygen is taken in, the oxygenated blood being returned to the heart for circulation through the body.

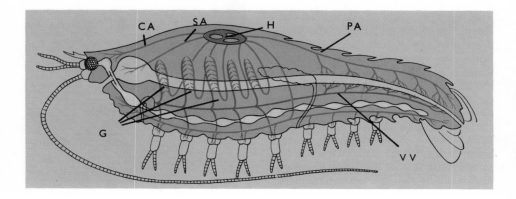

order Cumacea. The head of a cumacean is relatively large and the abdomen is long and narrow so that the general appearance is that of a small tadpole. The largest species reaches a length of $1\frac{1}{3}$ in ($3\frac{1}{2}$ cm), but most species are much smaller. There is a short carapace which fuses with two or three of the thoracic segments and overhangs to enclose a single gill on each side. The carapace also extends forwards in front of the head. A cumacean normally lies buried in sand with only the forward extension of the carapace projecting above the surface. This enables water to be pumped in over the gills and then out again as a forward flowing current under the inward

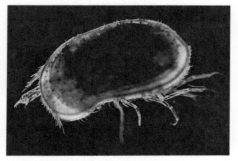

An ostracod *Cythere albomaculata.*

current. The inward current also brings in small food particles which are trapped on a filter and then pushed into the mouth.

The cumaceans are found in all the seas of the world and some are known from brackish water, but none is known from fresh water.

The members of the order Tanaidacea have a small carapace which is fused to the tops of the first two thoracic segments and overhangs to cover a single gill on each side. In general form they resemble isopods and were at one time included as a suborder of the Isopoda, under the name Chelifera. This name refers to the fact that most tanaids have the first pair of legs modified to form a stout pair of chelae or pincers. These are generally more powerfully developed in the males than in the females. The majority of tanaidaceans live in the sea, but a few species have been recorded in brackish and fresh water. The largest species is a deep-sea form, *Herpotanais kirkegaardi,* which reaches a length of 1 in ($2\frac{1}{2}$ cm). Most of the species burrow in mud, or construct tunnels among algae and hydroids. Others live in crevices on rocky shores. The main food appears to be organic debris, and some species seem to be able to filter small particles from the water when large particles are not available.

The two remaining orders of the Peracarida are both small and both contain cave-dwelling forms. The Spelaeogriphacea contains a single species, *Spelaeogriphus lepidops,* which was described from a cave in South Africa in 1957. The carapace is even smaller than that of the tanaidaceans and fuses with only a single segment of the thorax.

The body is elongated and bears seven pairs of walking legs on the thorax. The abdomen has four pairs of swimmerets and a rudimentary fifth pair. In addition there is a well developed tail fan. The biology is unknown, but *Spelaeogriphus* has been observed to swim as well as walk.

The Thermosbaenacea differ from all other Malacostraca in having a dorsal brood pouch formed by the carapace. Males have a small carapace, covering two or three segments of the thorax, but in females the carapace expands to hold an average of ten relatively large eggs. The largest member of the order is about $\frac{1}{6}$ in (4 mm) in length. There are at present only two known genera: *Thermosbaena,* with five pairs of walking legs and *Monodella* with seven pairs. All the forms seem to feed by scraping or biting organic debris. Apart from the peculiar brood pouch the chief interest of the Thermosbaenacea lies in their distribution. *Thermosbaena* was discovered in 1923 in a hot spring at El Hamm, Tunisia, where the water temperature reaches 118° F (48°C). The other genus, *Monodella,* is known from several underground localities around the Mediterranean. The first species of *Monodella* was described in 1949 from Italy, others have since been described from Yugoslavia and Israel, but it now seems that the group is even more widespread than was originally thought, because a species of *Monodella* has been

Chamaeleon prawn *Hippolyte huntii,* capable of changing colour according to its background.

Brine shrimp *Artemia* copulating.

found in a cave in Texas. PHYLUM: Arthropoda.   Ja.G.

CRUSTACEAN LARVAE.

Some Crustacea undergo direct development, emerging from the egg in a form resembling the parent, but the majority of crustaceans hatch in a form that differs greatly from the parent. There is considerable diversity among crustacean larvae, but there is one form that is found in such a wide range of different groups that it must be regarded as the basic primitive crustacean larva. This is the nauplius larva.

In its basic form the nauplius has a simple unsegmented body, a single eye and three pairs of appendages. These appendages are the antennules, antennae and mandibles. The antennules are generally simple in structure with a few sensory setae (bristles) and they are often held out in front of the head. The antennae are often relatively large and complicated, with two branches and numerous long setae. These setae may be feather-like in form, increasing the surface area. The branched antennae are used in swimming, so that the increase in the surface area of the setae makes a larger, more effective, paddle. Sometimes the bases of the antennae are enlarged, with projections towards the mouth, and they may assist in feeding. The mandibles are usually a little smaller than the antennae. They may aid to some extent in swimming, but generally their bases are modified to aid in pushing food into the mouth which lies on the underside of the unsegmented body.

When the nauplius develops signs of segmentation it is known as a metanauplius and some crustaceans hatch at this stage. A nauplius or metanauplius is known from all the following crustacean groups: Anostraca (Fairy shrimps), Notostraca (Tadpole shrimps), Conchostraca (Clam shrimps), Cladocera (Water fleas – only *Leptodora* has a nauplius, all others develop directly), Copepoda, Cirripedia (barnacles), Euphausiacea (krill) and some prawns (especially in the family Penaeidae).

In some groups, such as the Fairy shrimps and Tadpole shrimps, the change from nauplius to adult is very gradual. The trunk becomes more elongated, segments develop and additional limbs appear. When sufficient trunk limbs are present they take over the swimming role from the antennae. Once all the trunk limbs have developed the Fairy shrimp is virtually an adult and needs only to become sexually mature to complete the life-cycle.

In other groups there are more sudden changes at certain stages in the life-history. In the copepods, such as *Calanus* and *Cyclops,* the nauplius moults five times, still keeping its characteristic form. At the next moult it suddenly changes into a copepodid, which resembles the adult in general form, but has fewer limbs. The copepodid moults five times

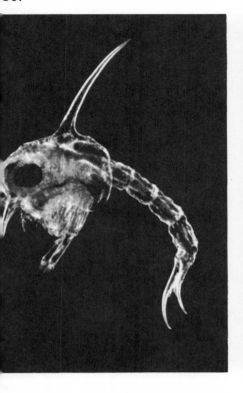

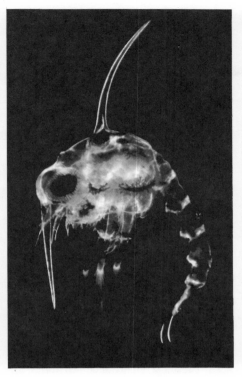

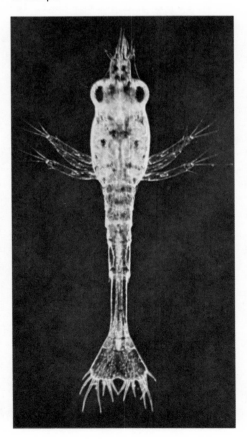

and at each moult it adds to the completeness of its limbs. Once the adult stage has been reached the copepod does not moult again. In some parasitic copepods the larval development may be abbreviated. The eggs of the family Choniostomatidae, which are parasites on other Crustacea, give rise to copepodid larvae with only two pairs of legs. These larvae seek out a host and then moult, losing their swimming legs and developing rounded bodies. They thus reach essentially the same form as the adult. In a few chonoistomatids there is a quiescent stage between the copepodid larva and the adult. This is called a pupa, but it should not be regarded as equivalent to the pupa of an insect.

In the barnacles an additional stage is added into the life-history. The nauplius larva is followed by a cypris larva. The cypris has a bivalved shell like an ostracod, but it differs from an ostracod in having more pairs of swimming legs and relatively large antennules. It is the cypris stage which seeks out the final spot where the barnacle will spend the rest of its life. The antennules of the cypris have cement glands and the secretions from these glands are used to attach the larva to its chosen spot. Once it is attached to a solid surface the cypris changes into the adult form. In the Acorn barnacles this process involves the loss of the cypris shell and the formation of the characteristic turret of plates. The swimming legs enlarge and become the cirri which are used by the adult to catch food.

In the Euphausiacea, or krill, there is a long sequence of larvae, beginning with the nauplius. This is followed by a metanauplius,

and then by a stage which develops a carapace and an elongated trunk. This is the calyptopsis larva, and it also differs from the earlier stages in having paired eyes, although they are not yet movable. It also has some limbs on its thorax, but none on the abdomen. When the abdominal limbs have developed and the eyes have become stalked and mobile, the larva is known as a furcilia. The furcilia passes through a series of moults and gradually changes to the adult form.

The penaeid prawns also hatch as a nauplius or metanauplius and then pass through three stages: the protozoea, zoea and post-larval stage, before becoming adult. Each of these stages may include several moults. The distinguishing characteristics of each stage are related to the development of the limbs and the way in which the larva swims. The nauplius and metanauplius swim by means of their antennae and they lack thoracic limbs. The protozoea also swims with its antennae, but it has paired eyes and thoracic limbs. The zoea stops using the antennae, using instead the thoracic limbs, and finally the post-larval stages swim by beating their abdominal limbs, which is the adult mode of swimming.

The lobster (*Homarus*) hatches from the egg with all its thoracic limbs, but with no abdominal limbs. It is thus at the same stage as the zoea of the penaeid prawns. At the next moult some of the abdominal limbs appear and the young lobster enters the post-larval stages, which resemble the adult. The freshwater relatives of the lobster, namely the crayfishes, hatch at a later stage of development. Although their proportions differ from those of the adult they are already in the post-larval stage and lack only a few of the abdominal limbs.

The Spiny lobsters, such as *Palinurus*, have a remarkable larva called a phyllosoma. This has a flat transparent body and long spreading thoracic limbs. The eyes are borne on long stalks and the abdomen is minute. This larva drifts in the plankton of the sea and moults ten or 11 times, increasing in size, but not altering its general form very greatly. Then it changes rapidly at the next moult into a small lobster-like creature with very long antennae that are often flattened at the tip. This form is called a puerulus and during the course of several moults it changes to the adult form.

Most crabs hatch from the egg as a zoea, with stalked eyes, well developed thoracic limbs, but few or no abdominal limbs. After several moults, the actual number varying in different species of crab, the zoea changes into a megalopa. This is essentially a minute crab with large eyes (giving it its name) and a thin abdomen which extends backwards like a tail instead of being tucked forwards as in the adult. At the next moult the abdomen is tucked forwards and the young crab enters its post-larval stages, resembling the adult in most respects except size and sexual maturity. As the young crab grows there is often disproportionate growh of some parts of the body in relation to other parts. Often the pincers become relatively larger as the crab grows, or there may be a change in the ratio of the length to the width of the carapace.

The Hermit crabs have a life-history similar to that of the true crabs, but the stage following the zoea is known as a glaucothoe. This generally has appendages on both sides of the abdomen and the last pair, the uropods, are often asymmetrical, with the left one larger than the right. When the glaucothoe changes to the adult form the abdominal appendages on the right side (except the uropods) are lost. The abdomen becomes swollen and curved and is hidden inside the empty shell of a marine snail which the hermit carries about for protection.

So far we have been discussing the larval development of free-living Crustacea, although the abbreviated development of some parasitic copepods has also been mentioned. In the parasitic isopods there is an extension of development beyond the normal isopod condition, so that forms resembling free-living isopods are immature and are called larvae, and the adult parasites are grossly distorted forms that would not be recognizable as isopods if it were not for their early stages.

Isopods of the family Gnathiidae are parasitic on fishes. The first stage emerging from the egg is a fairly typical little isopod and is known as a zuphea. This larva can swim and it seeks out a fish and then gorges on its blood. When fully gorged the third fourth and fifth segments of the thorax are distended to twice the diameter of the rest of the body and the larva is then called a praniza. The praniza leaves the fish and hides in a crevice, sometimes for over a month while it digests its meal of fish blood. Then the praniza moults to reveal the next zuphea stage which sets off to find a new fish and in turn becomes a praniza. During the life of a gnathiid there seem to be three zuphea stages and three praniza stages before the adult. After the final meal the last praniza stages gather in groups in crevices and change to the adult form which does not feed.

The isopods of the suborder Epicaridea are parasites on other Crustacea. Their earliest larval stage is quite a normal isopod, called an epicaridium. The epicaridium can swim actively and seeks out a planktonic copepod, such as *Calanus*. The epicaridium then moults and changes into a microniscus, which does not swim, but feeds on the blood of the copepod for a week. The microniscus then moults and changes into a cryptoniscus, which leaves the copepod and seeks out a final host. The most highly modified forms are those which use crabs as their final hosts. The cryptoniscus enters the gill-chamber of the crab, penetrates the gill wall and enters the body cavity. It then moults, loses all its limbs, and becomes maggot-like in shape. The adult female develops from this stage by increasing in size and produces a large ovary which distorts the body into grotesque bulges. The males remain in the cryptoniscus stage and live in the brood pouch of the female.
PHYLUM: Arthropoda. Ja.G.

CRYPTIC COLOURATION, the means by which animals conceal themselves from their enemies using the normal colouration or shape of their bodies, or by bringing about colour changes to suit particular backgrounds.

A common method of concealment is for the outlines of an animal to be blurred. This may be brought about in a number of ways. First let us consider countershading. A cylindrical object lit from above will have a shadow cast along its lower sides producing a dark patch. This applies equally to the body of an animal, but if the lower side is lighter in colour than the back, the effect of the shadow is offset and the contour of the animal is less obvious. The fur on the belly of a hare is much lighter than that on the back, a contrast which is startling when the animal lies on its side, but when a hare crouches to the ground it becomes difficult to detect. Many fishes have dark backs and silvery undersides. In this case the camouflage serves a double purpose for viewed from below against the silvery appearing surface of the water, the fishes are inconspicuous because the colour of their undersides comes so near to that of the background. Countershading is reversed in some animals. The Nile catfish, for example, has a light back and a dark underside—but it habitually swims upside down! Much the same applies to the larva of the Eyed hawk-moth, for its colouration is reversed but so is its normal posture on a twig.

Countershading reduces the effect of the shadow but it is also possible for the shadow to be eliminated by the animal taking on a depressed form so that the sides of its body meet the ground in, as it were, a flange. A young Stone curlew will crouch down on the ground when it is alarmed and press its head and neck onto the ground while the feathers spread out sideways. As it is also cryptically coloured, is is very difficult to pick out. A number of lizards of rather flattened form crouch down and expand their bodies sideways. One gecko, *Uroplates fimbriatus,* has fringes along the edge of its jaw and a broad flange on each side of its tail, all of which help to reduce the amount of shadow when it is resting.

Another important group of camouflage patterns are those which are exemplified by disruptive colouration. An animal which blends with its background and has some way of reducing its shadow will effectively be invisible but it is rare for the background which an animal inhabits to be uniform, so that a colour which blends in one place may make the animal conspicuous in another. But it is the 'continuity of surface bounded by a specific contour or outline' which makes an animal recognizable as such and distinguishes it from the background. So concealment can be brought about if this contour is made difficult to recognize. Disruptive colouration of stripes and patches take the eye of the observer away from the shape which bears them. The effect is greatly enhanced if one of the colours is the same as the background for then those parts of the animal 'disappear' and the coherence of the whole shape is quite lost. The brown and grey-brown colours of a number of adult moths succeed in this admirably when for instance they settle on lichen covered bark. Very obvious contrasting elements in a pattern may be particularly effective in destroying what would otherwise be an obvious feature. A very obvious feature in fishes, birds or mammals are their shining eyes. But their prominence is often reduced by the eye being incorporated into a black

The European nightjar *Caprimulgus europaeus*, like all other nightjars, roosts and nests on the ground, which it matches superbly; the brill *Scophthalmus rhombeus* lives on sandy bottoms and is sand-coloured; the Crab spider can change slowly from white to yellow, and vice versa, to match flower petals; the Gaboon viper *Bitis gabonica* is almost invisible among leaf litter, and the brownish coat of the Sportive lemur *Lepilemur mustelinus* has a neutral quality among tree-trunks.

stripe along the side of the head and even down the length of the body. Other black stripes may help to disrupt the animal's outline; the fish, *Eques lanceolatus,* is a good example of this. Where the pattern is high-lighted with light colours beside dark lines a three-dimensional effect is produced; in this way a snake like a copperhead becomes difficult to see against fallen leaves for the smooth surface of the animal appears to consist of planes at all angles like the curled and scattered leaves on the forest floor.

Many ground-nesting birds like lapwing or curlews, lay eggs which are typically shades of buff or olive-green broken by irregular patches of brown, making them difficult to pick out against the broken background of their surroundings. Some species of ground-nesting birds, such as the Australian Ground pigeons, however lay conspicuous white eggs but these are then concealed by the crypti-cally coloured body of the parent who stays on the nest when danger threatens instead of abandoning it as a curlew will do.

In some animals lines of contrasting colour come together when the animal rests, so that the coincident lines produce a disrupting pattern which by being continuous, across body and leg for example, disguises the animal's shape. Some of the tree-dwelling amphibians provide splendid examples of this. The treefrog *Megalixalus fornasinii* has longitudinal bands of colour which, when it rests with its legs tucked against its body, fuse into two broad light bands which make it difficult to distinguish.

The stripes of a zebra are doubly conceal-ing for they disrupt the outline when the animal stands in the open, but in the tall grasses the vertical lines reflect the verticals of the grass stalks and hide the animal by fusing it with the background. Such direct mimicry of the background as concealment coloura-tion is often observed. Some flatfishes are able to adapt their body colouration to fit in with the background upon which they are lying. The changes are brought about by alterations in the proportions of various chromatophores or pigment cells in the skin. Similar changes in chromatophores take place in prawns and other Crustacea. They are mediated through the eyes which in turn affect the nervous and hormonal control of the chromatophores (in fishes mainly nervous, in Crustacea, hor-monal).

Imitation of natural objects will render animals inconspicuous provided they are in a place where those objects are abundant. Stick insects not only are long and thin, but also stand on a twig with their bodies held out on an angle very similar to that of a twiglet branching from the main twig. One such, *Parasosibia pana,* rests with its head down-wards, grasping the twig with its second pair of legs, the rest of its body is held away from the twig at an angle, the hindlegs being held

closely against the body. Looper cater-pillars take up similar positions. Other insects mimic leaves, the resemblance being so detailed that the animal bears markings like the veins of a leaf and even, in some, like birds' droppings or like the moulds which grow on the leaf.

It is difficult to conceive that these patterns could have arisen without serving a purpose, and experiments prove their effectiveness. It is a simple experiment to place adult water-bugs in tanks with sandy bottoms where the colours of some of the insects make them less conspicuous than the others against the sand. A minnow or two put in a tank will eat some of the bugs and it is clear that those taken by the minnow are in the main those less well concealed. In industrial Britain the black form of the Peppered moth is replacing the light form, but where industrial air pollution is lower, the white one can be found in greater proportions. The light ones are particularly well disguised when they settle on lichens on a tree trunk but the effect of air pollution is to destroy the lichens. The bare bark which is left rapidly becomes blackened by the soot-laden air and against this bark the dark one is more effectively concealed than the lighter one. Releases of mixed populations of light and dark in a non-polluted area is followed by an increase in the proportion of light-coloured insects on subsequent recaptures, while the reverse happens in smoke-blackened areas. Direct observation shows that insect-eating birds, such as robins, which feed on these moths find it easier to pick out the colour form which contrasts most with the background. The moth's behaviour is such that each form selects a background most suitable for con-cealment. This kind of behaviour, which optimizes the effect of the colour-pattern, is also found in the caterpillars which have reversed colour shading. Instead of a dorsal light response, these insects have ventral light response which causes them to turn their darkly pigmented underside upwards. See also mimicry.   J.D.C.

CRYPTIC COLOURATION IN ACTION. Nobody doubts that many animals enjoy the advantages of a camouflage, or cryptic colouration, that makes them hard to be seen by predators. At the same time, no animal could survive or enjoy a full life if this 'cloak of invisibility' were in operation at all times. If no more, there must be some means by which members of a species recognize each other.

Such considerations have led to debate, even heated argument, among scientists and non-scientists. One that has often been de-bated is the value of the stripes of a zebra. It is customary to say that the stripes break up the outline of the animal's body and conceal the zebra when it is among tall grass, when

its stripes tend to resemble the shadows cast by the grass stems.

Sceptics point to the fact that many of a zebra's stripes are horizontal, unlike the shadows cast by vertical grass stems. They also remind us that in any photograph or film a group of zebras in the distance stand out, whereas unstriped dun-coloured gnus associating with the herd are hard to see.

The problem is not a new one. A century ago Francis Galton wrote: 'No more con-spicuous animal can be conceived, accord-ing to the common idea, than a zebra; but on a bright starlit night the breathing of one can be heard close by you, and yet you will be positively unable to see the animal. If the black stripes were more numerous he would be seen as a black mass: if the white, as a white one; but their proportion is such as exactly to match the pale tint which the arid ground possesses when seen by moonlight.'

William P. Pycraft, in *Camouflage in Nature* (1925) tells us that the stripes 'have a highly protective value, in spite of very emphatic assertions to the contrary . . . thus masked he (the zebra) escapes the eye of the prowling lion, at any rate so long as he remains motionless. For no one supposes that absolute immunity is secured by this 'mantle of invisibility'. It is effective just when it is needed; that is to say, when the wearer is at rest.'

A different view is adopted by Dr H. B. Cott, a leading authority on cryptic coloura-tion. In his book, *Adaptive Coloration in Animals* (1940), he says: 'In full sunlight and in open country, the zebra may be a con-spicuous enough object. But in the dusk, when he is liable to be attacked, and in country affording thin cover, he is one of the least recognized animals.' Cott shows, in his book, two rectangles side-by-side, of equal size, the one patterned with black stripes longitudinally on a white ground, the other similar but with a pattern of vertical stripes. These produce an optical illusion, the one with the vertical stripes appearing the larger. Cott uses these to demonstrate that the vertical stripes may alter 'the zebra's appar-ent size—and therefore distance—(so that) the stripes may cause a predator to misjudge its leap.'

If their stripes are so effective we have to explain why lions so often kill zebras when there are plenty of more conspicuous game

Swordgrass moth (top), even close to has un-canny resemblance to piece of stick; looper or Stick caterpillar of the Brimstone moth *Opistho-graptis luteolator* (left centre), sticklike even to the 'bud'; leaf-like Bush cricket *Tanusia brullaei* (centre right) of South America; Privet hawk moth *Sphinx ligustri* caterpillar feeding (bottom left); *Cilix glaucata* a moth that resembles bird droppings (bottom right).

occupying the same area, even the same habitat. There is also the anomaly that the quagga, a species of zebra living in South Africa, that became extinct at the end of the 19th century, was striped like a zebra on the front half of its body and coloured like an ass on the rear half.

Camouflage is of value only while the animal is at rest (when it has most need of protection) and under certain special circumstances, as in the zebra that seems to disappear at twilight—the optimum period for the lion to hunt. M.B.

CRYPTOBRANCHIDAE, largest of living amphibians and known as Giant salamanders. Their origin dates back to the days of the dinosaurs and they are only distantly related to other living salamanders which are mostly small and delicate.

The family contains two genera: the Asiatic genus *Megalobatrachus* containing two equally large species, the Chinese giant salamander *M. davidianus* and the Japanese giant salamander *M. japonicus,* and the American genus *Cryptobranchus* with but one smaller species the hellbender *C. alleganiensis.*

The Asiatic forms reach a length of over 5½ ft (167 cm) and there are references in ancient writings to much larger sizes. The hellbender female grows to just under 2½ ft (74 cm), the male to only 22 in (56 cm).

The Giant salamanders have maintained their primitive characteristics and their size. All are exceptionally grotesque and ugly, robust creatures with a flattened head as wide or wider than the body. The nostrils and eyes are small, inconspicuous and in the Japanese species further obscured by numerous fair-sized tubercules found on the head and body. The legs are sturdy but short with five stubby toes on the hindfeet and four on the frontfeet. From behind the head an undulated skin fold extends on each side of the body to the base of the tail, which is laterally compressed into a broad oval fin. The skin is slimy, dark greyish brown with irregular darker or lighter mottlings. When injured, they secrete white irritating fluid from pores on the back. The Giant salamanders have small teeth in both upper and lower jaws. The hellbender has four internal gill arches on each side of the head, and retains a single pair of gill openings. In the Asiatic species the number of paired gill arches is reduced to two and the gill openings are absent. The Chinese species has small, bead-like barbels below the chin.

Fossil remains of Giant salamanders are found over an extended area, including Europe. A large skeleton of an extinct central European species *Andrias scheuchzeri* was originally described in the 18th century as belonging to an antediluvian human child under the name *homo diluvii testis* 'man a witness of the deluge'. Today the range is much reduced, the three remaining species living isolated, far from each other. The Chinese giant salamander is found in the waters descending from the Himalayan Mountains into the western Chinese provinces of Chinkiang and Tungkiang and also in northern Kwangtung.

The most popular Chinese name is *Nei-yü,* mentioned as long ago as 600 BC. Occasionally it is also referred to as *Wah-wah yü.* Western science suspected its existence from the study of ancient writings and in 1869–70 Abbe Armand David, a Jesuit priest and naturalist, collected the type specimen. It differs little from the previously discovered Japanese species and at first was regarded as only a geographical race. Its legs and toes are proportionately longer, the skin tubercules are smaller, and arranged in pairs in rows. The largest specimen on record was collected near Kweiyangfu in 1923. It measured 5 ft 9 in (175·3 cm).

More than 1,000 miles to the east on the islands of Japan lives the Japanese giant salamander popularly called the *Sancho-uo.* It was introduced to western science in 1829 when Phillipe François de Siebold brought a living specimen to Europe, which lived 50 years in captivity. Its dermal tubercules are larger, single, and irregularly placed.

The hellbender is found in the Appalachian mountain region of the eastern United States and in a couple of smaller areas in the Ozarks.

All Giant salamanders need cool, well oxygenated water. Their habitat is restricted to limpid mountain streams and rivers with moderate current. They are totally aquatic, spending their days in a hollow dug under logs or rocks, usually solitarily. During the late summer breeding season the males find an appropriate nesting area upstream and prepare the site before they are joined by the females. The females lay a long garland of connected grape-sized eggs, each with a pea-sized nucleus surrounded by clear jelly. Fertilization is external. 200–600 eggs are laid by the Asiatic salamanders; 300–450 by the hellbender. In the hellbender, the female pushes the eggs onto the bottom to which they adhere. Several females may lay in one nest. The male then chases the females away and guards the eggs for some time. The male *Sancho-uo* reputedly winds the egg garlands around his body and aggressively defends them against potential predators during incubation. When the larvae hatch, in two to three months or in the following spring, the male abandons them. Their rate of growth is very slow.

The Japanese giant salamander young, for instance, are only 1¼ in (3 cm) long in four months, 4 in (12 cm) in a year and a half, and less than 8 in (20 cm) in three years. They do not reach sexual maturity for at least five years, perhaps much later.

Giant salamanders feed mostly on crayfish, but will eat almost any aquatic animal they can capture and swallow. They leave their underwater shelter after dark, and presumably return to the same place at the end of the hunt. In cold well-aerated water they can extract enough oxygen to stay submerged indefinitely. However, if the demand increases because of their activity or the oxygen level of the water is insufficient, they come to the surface and gulp atmospheric air. Captive hellbenders occasionally engage in a peculiar rocking motion to bring fresh water to their surroundings.

With the growing human population and increasing water pollution, the survival prospects of the Giant salamanders is poor. Both the Asiatic species are caught for human food. Some Chinese salamanders find their way to the Hong Kong markets, but otherwise their status is unknown. In Japan, the Giant salamanders are growing scarcer and are now under government protection. The hellbenders are not generally eaten, but they are accidentally caught by fisherman which usually results in a fatal injury. Even more serious is the threat to their habitat.

It seems that the Giant salamanders, whose size, ancient origin and discontinuous distribution inspired Karel Capek's early science fiction classic *War with the newts* in which these salamanders, challenging man for the possession of the Earth, are rapidly losing the war. See Giant salamander and hellbender. SUBORDER: Cryptobranchoidea, ORDER: Caudata, CLASS: Amphibia. E.L.-J.

CRYPTOCLEIDUS, one of the plesiosaur group of reptiles (see Sauropterygia) which first appears as fossils in rocks transitional in age between the Triassic and Jurassic periods and was extinct by the close of the Cretaceous. Every feature of the plesiosaur skeleton was perfectly adapted for free swimming marine life. *Cryptocleidus,* from the Upper Jurassic of Europe, exemplifies such features. The relatively small head with jaws beset with conical teeth, denoting a fish diet, was carried on the very long vertebral column. As in all plesiosaurs the limbs were modified as paddles with each digit lengthened, by the addition of accessory phalanges, so increasing the paddles' surface area. The powerful plate-like shoulder and hip girdles carried the extensive locomotive musculature. SUBORDER: Plesiosauria, ORDER: Sauropterygia, CLASS: Reptilia.

CRYPTODIRA, the most advanced group of the Testudines, able to retract the head within the exoskeleton by S-shaped bending of the neck in the vertical plane. The suborder includes all the tortoises and common turtles and terrapins. They are distributed throughout the tropical and subtropical regions and the warmer temperate areas.

CTENOPHORA or Comb jellies, exclusively marine and usually pelagic gelatinous animals, their distinguishing feature being eight rows of comb plates bearing fused cilia, 100,000 in each plate, which beat in a co-ordinated sequence and drive the animal through the water, mouth first. They used to be classified with the Cnidaria which they resemble in many ways, in the phylum Coelenterata, but now each has been given phylum status. They differ from the jellyfishes of the Cnidaria. Whereas members of the Cnidaria may exist in more than one form per species, i.e. the polyp and the medusa, there is no trace of this in the Ctenophora. The ctenophores are composed of two cell layers, ectoderm and endoderm, separated by mesogloea, the latter primarily a protein secretion as in the Cnidaria but extensively invaded by wandering cells and forming the bulk of the animal. Except for *Euchlora rubra*, ctenophores have no nematocysts but possess lasso cells or colloblasts, cells specialized for the capture of prey.

The best known of the 80 species is the Sea gooseberry *Pleurobrachia*, ¾ in (2 cm) long. Typically ctenophores are egg-shaped slightly flattened in one plane, so appearing oval in cross-section. At the pointed or oval end is a central mouth, while at the opposite, broader aboral end is a sense organ lying in a depression and composed of chalky particles supported on S-shaped cilia, as if on springs. If this sense organ is removed the movements of the comb plates becomes unco-ordinated and the animal loses the ability to remain vertical. On each side of a Comb jelly and between two of the comb rows, is a deep pouch from which a long retractile tentacle protrudes. This bears the lasso cells, with hemispherical heads containing adhesive granules which attach to passing prey.

The central mouth leads to a long pharynx opening into a central stomach from which a canal system branches into the mesogloea. From the roof of the stomach one canal leads to just below the sense organ where it divides into four excretory canals, two of which open to the exterior by small pores. From the oral surface of the stomach two canals travel towards the mouth parallel to the pharynx and end blindly near the mouth. A large canal runs horizontally from each side of the stomach giving off an inter-radial canal on either side and ending blindly at the base of the tentacles. Each inter-radial canal divides into two, so that four canals in each tentacular half lie meridionally under the comb rows. The function of this elaborate canal system is to ensure distribution of food materials round the body, the canals being ciliated. Small planktonic animals are caught on the outstretched tentacles, which contract and are wiped across the mouth so that food passes in. In the pharynx extracellular digestion occurs and the food particles enter

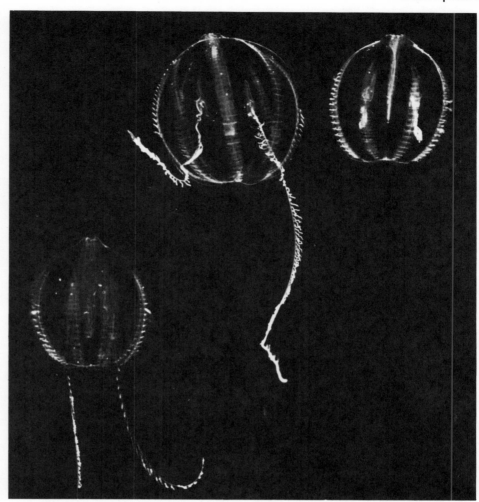

Comb jellies *Pleurobrachia pileus*, a kind of jellyfish distinguished by their comb plates.

the canal system to be circulated and taken up by cells lining the canals, with which digestion is completed.

The nervous system consists of a 'nerve-net' concentrated under the comb rows. Experiments involving removal of parts of the comb rows have shown that the beat of the comb plates is under nervous control. Ctenophores are luminescent and this luminescence seems to arise in the canal system below the comb rows. The animals luminesce only after being in the dark for some while and the way in which luminescence spreads when the Comb jelly is touched is suggestive of nervous propagation.

All ctenophores are hermaphrodite, the gonads being located on the walls of the canals underlying the comb rows. Generally fertilization is external, although a few species retain their young in brood pouches. Development of ctenophores is very different from that found in the Cnidaria. After fertilization cleavage or division into cells takes place. At the eight-cell stage, the cells are unequal in size, there being four large macromeres and four small micromeres. The small cells continue to divide evenly, but the

large cells continue unequal division producing large and small daughter cells. The small cells give rise to the ectoderm and these spread over the large cells which give rise to the endoderm. This type of cleavage is known as spiral and determinate, since the removal of any cells results in the adult lacking some component. The larva is known as a cydippid and resembles adults of one of the orders, Cydippida. In the other orders the larva changes in shape to give the adults.

The Ctenophora are divided into two classes: Tentaculata with four orders, Cydippida, Lobata, Cestida and Platyctenea, all possessing tentacles, and Nuda, with one order only, the Beroida, lacking tentacles.

The Cydippida show typical ctenophore characters, being globular in shape with two long tentacles. The genera include *Hormiphora* and *Callianira* as well as the Sea gooseberry. The Lobata, including *Bolinopsis*, are laterally compressed in the tentacular plane, the oral region is expanded in the opposite plane into contractile lobes, the tentacles are reduced as are four comb rows, while the other four comb rows are extended down the oral lobes. In place of the tentacles are processes with a ciliated edge from the oral ends of the reduced comb rows. These, termed auricles, are important in capturing food. Members of both these orders are more common in warmer waters.

The peculiarities of the Lobata are exaggerated in the Cestida, the third order, which are long and ribbon-like and found only in the warmer seas. The body is now elongated in the sagittal plane and four comb rows are very reduced, while the other four are very elongated. These are no longer used for swimming, the animals moving by undulation of the body. There are only two genera, Venus' girdle *Cestum* and *Velamen* (or *Vexillum*).

The Platyctenea have adopted a creeping habit and are flattened from above down. Examples are *Coeloplana* and *Tjalfiella,* not readily recognizable as ctenophores, because of their shape and because they are lacking comb rows, although they still possess sense organs. Their identity was in doubt until young cydippid larvae with comb rows were found in their brood pouches.

In the Nuda, the one order Beroida consists of thimble-shaped ctenophores compressed in the tentacular plane. They have a very large mouth and pharynx, the stomach lies closely under the aboral sense organ and the canals of the digestive system are much branched and lie close to the surface. Comb rows, extending most of the body length, are very obvious. *Beröe,* the principal genus, is worldwide and can grow up to 8 in (20 cm) in length.

The discovery of creeping ctenophores led to the suggestion that they formed a missing link between Cnidaria and Platyhelminthes, i.e. from a two-layered to a three-layered organization. Theories about the origin of the ctenophores ranges from the suggestion that they are degenerate Platyhelminthes via the Platyctenea, which seems very unlikely, to the idea that they diverged early from the original two-layered animals, possibly before the evolution of the Cnidaria.   S.E.H.

CUCKOOFISH, alternative name for the Cuckoo *wrasse, a foot-long inshore marine fish living around the coasts of Europe, noted for its vivid colours, particularly in the males, which are blue and yellow. It is especially sensitive to prolonged cold weather and sudden cooling of the sea may kill it, so the Cuckoo wrasse is seldom seen in winter. FAMILY: Labridae, ORDER: Perciformes, CLASS: Pisces.

CUCKOO FLIES, two-winged flies belonging to the families Ichneumonidae and Chrysididae, named for their habit of laying their eggs in the larvae or eggs of other insects. ORDER: Diptera, CLASS: Insecta.

CUCKOO-ROLLER, a single species of insectivorous birds inhabiting Madagascar and the Comores Islands and distantly related to the true rollers. About 17 in (43 cm) long, the cuckoo-roller resembles rollers in size and proportions but not in plumage, which is chiefly grey in the male, with coppery reflections in the upperparts and whitish-grey underparts. Females are quite different, being a little longer, rufous-brown, barred above and spotted below. Cuckoo-rollers feed on large insects caught mainly in the forest canopy, are vociferous and perform spectacular 'rolling' courtship flights above the forest. The clutch of white eggs is laid in a tree-hole, but little else is known of their biology. FAMILY: Leptosomatidae, ORDER: Coraciiformes, CLASS: Aves.

CUCKOOS, a family of birds, the Cuculidae the species of which show a considerable range of variation in size, shape, colour and behaviour, although the name is, for most people, associated with birds that leave their eggs in the nests of other birds which then rear the young. In fact only 47 of the 127 species in this family are brood-parasites. Cuculidae together with the turacos, family Musophagidae, form the order Cuculiformes.

Most cuckoos have zygodactyl feet, the outermost toe being reversed so that two are directed forwards and two backwards; relatively short legs, causing the bird to squat close to a perch; an elongated shape, a longish tail and a relatively large head and heavy bill. Some tropical species have bare, and often conspicuously coloured, skin around the eyes, and some have noticeable eyelashes. Some have a small, usually tapering crest on the back of the head and this can be erected to some extent. As a group they tend to be skulkers, keeping to the concealment of foliage, better known for their voices than for their appearance. A number of mainly terrestrial forms, usually larger, longer-legged and capable of running strongly, but with wings reduced in size and with poor flying power, have evolved independently in different groups of species.

The songs of cuckoos are unspectacular and are usually a monotonous repetition of a single call or of several notes. While the repetitive disyllabic call of the Common cuckoo *Cuculus canorus,* which has given the whole family its name, is hailed as a welcome sign of summer, the incessant calling of the Brain-fever bird *Cuculus varius* of the Orient, combined with a hot climate, is reputed to drive men nearly mad.

The principle food of cuckoos ranges from insects and small invertebrates in the case of smaller species to snakes, lizards, small rodents and birds taken by the larger terrestrial forms. A few species also eat fruit. The cuckoos are among the few birds that regularly eat hairy caterpillars which are unpalatable to most.

The typical parasitic cuckoos of the subfamily Cuculinae occur throughout the Old World from Scandinavia and Siberia to New Zealand, but are absent from the Americas. They vary in size from tiny sparrow-sized Glossy cuckoos to the giant Channel-billed cuckoo *Scythrops novaehollandiae* of northern Australasia, which is over 2 ft (60 cm)

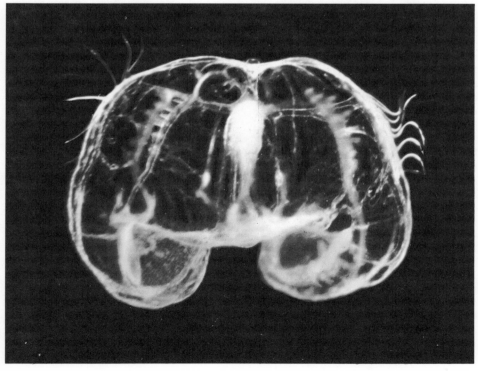
Young Comb jelly *Bolinopsis*. The comb plates can be seen in their early stages on either side.

Young Common cuckoo calling continuously for food, while its foster parents, Tree pipit *Anthus trivialis*, work laboriously to satisfy its enormous appetite.

ong. In general they have fairly long tails nd long narrow wings and are strong flyers. ome species migrate, the Common cuckoo f northern Europe travelling south to Africa n winter, while in the southern hemisphere ne little Shining cuckoo *Chalcites lucidus* reeds in Australia and migrates north over ne Pacific Ocean as far as the Solomon slands. The smallest species have plumages vith vivid iridescent green tints, and in one ase a glossy violet colour.

These cuckoos exploit a wide range of ost species. The koel *Eudynamys scolo-acea* parasitizes crows, the Great spotted uckoo *Clamator glandarius* uses magpies, ther cuckoos of the genus *Clamator* use abblers, typical cuckoos of the genus *'uculus* exploit a range of small songbirds, nd the smallest of the Glossy cuckoos, the 'iolet cuckoo *Chalcites xanthorhynchus*, ays eggs in the tiny pendent nests of sun-irds. These cuckoos lay an egg directly into ne nest of the host. Where the nest is domed r partially inaccessible the cuckoo either orces its way in or else clings to the outside f the nest and lays the egg so that it falls nto the nest. Only two or three seconds are equired in which to lay the egg. There is no ood evidence that any other method is ever sed. Usually only a single egg is laid in a

nest by any one cuckoo, and one of the host's eggs is removed and often eaten. The cuckoo will have observed the nest of the host for a period prior to laying and will usually deposit its egg during the time the host is laying its own clutch. The cuckoo's egg has a shorter incubation period than that of the host and so hatches a little sooner. Subsequently the young cuckoo grows much faster than the young of the host. The young cuckoo may simply supplant the other young by taking almost all of the available food, so starving them, and forcing them out of the nest as it grows. The young cuckoos of the genus *Cuculus* have evolved a more certain method. For the first few days after hatching the young cuckoo appears to be physically irritated by the presence of an egg or nestling touching it and will wriggle underneath it until the egg or nestling rests on its back. The little cuckoo then rears up against the side of the nest and heaves the egg or nestling out, continuing this until it has the nest to itself. The host parents returning with food appear quite indifferent to their ejected nestlings. The young cuckoo may grow to such a size that it bursts the nest apart. The conspicuously coloured gapes and begging calls of young cuckoos appear to be sufficient to stimulate their hosts to feed them.

In many instances cuckoos lay eggs that closely mimic those of the host in colour, pattern and, to some extent, in size. The eggs of the Black-and-white cuckoo *Clamator jacobinus* and some of those of the Violet cuckoo may so closely resemble those of the host in whose nest they are laid that it is very difficult to distinguish them with certainty. The evolution of such a close resemblance seems to have been aided by the tendency for a female cuckoo to lay eggs in the nests of the same host species as that in which she was reared. Some young cuckoos reared in nests of crow species which could harm intruding nestlings have a superficial resemblance to the young of their host. While the advantage of this to the cuckoo is obvious, the fact that several adult cuckoos have a strong superficial resemblance to birds in other families is less obviously advantageous. Some cuckoos closely resemble hawks and in some of these species the immature cuckoos also resemble the immature raptors. The Drongo cuckoo *Surniculus lugubris* resembles the drongo, whose nest it parasitizes, both in its black plumage and its shape.

The non-parasitic cuckoos of the subfamily Phaenicophaeinae are widespread, with a few species on each continent with the exception of Australia. They are slenderlybuilt skulking birds of forest and thickets. They build shallow cup-shaped nests in trees and incubate their own eggs and rear their own young. The Oriental forms tend to have boldly-coloured bills, bare facial skin and long tails. One species, the Scale-feathered cuckoo *Lepidogrammus cummingi* of the Philippines, has very specialized feathers over the crown of the head and on the throat, the barbs of each feather being fused towards its tip to form a flat black plate with a glossy surface.

The couas of the subfamily Couinae are restricted to the Malagasy region. Little is known about them. They are sociable and non-parasitic and they have evolved some mainly terrestrial forms which occur in more open country.

The subfamily Crotophaginae of South and Central America is small but specialized. It comprises only four species, three anis of the genus *Crotophaga,* and the Guira cuckoo *Guira guira.* The latter is a strange semi-terrestrial species with a perpetually loose-feathered, scruffy-looking plumage, extremely tame and rather stupid. These species are of interest as a link between the brood-parasites and the non-parasitic cuckoos. They are sociable nesters and a number of birds may share a single nest although at other times pairs may nest on their own. It seems likely that at such times some females pass over a part, at least, of their share in incubation and the rearing of young to other adults, and this may indicate the way in which brood-parasitism in cuckoos could have arisen.

Ani eggs are blue-shelled with an outer white layer, and on Guira cuckoo eggs this white layer is deposited as a complex network of ridges, like dried foam, with blue areas showing.

The Ground cuckoos of the subfamily Neomorphinae tend to be large birds, heavy-billed, with long tails, long strong legs and small wings, with reduced powers of flight. They are all American species save for two Oriental ones, and three of the species, from Central and South America, are brood-parasites, being the only parasitic cuckoos in the Americas. The swift-running roadrunners belong to this subfamily.

The final group, the coucals of the subfamily Centropodinae, resemble the Ground cuckoos in their general build and size, being large birds, mainly terrestrial or inhabitants of thickets and undergrowth. They are non-parasitic, building domed nests, and occur only in the Old World. See also anis, coucals and roadrunners. FAMILY: Cuculidae, ORDER: Cuculiformes, CLASS: Aves.

CUCKOO-SHRIKES, a family of birds probably most closely related to the bulbuls but having no affinity with either cuckoos or shrikes. There are 70 species in this ex-

Male Common cuckoo; the female is browner. Both look like hawks except for the bill and longer neck.

clusively Old World family, ranging from about 5–14 in (13–35 cm) long. The family includes the brilliantly coloured black and scarlet or yellow minivets *Pericrocotus,* which are described under a separate heading. Otherwise the family consists of about 60 species, usually sombrely coloured in various shades of grey or patterned in black and white. Most species have long graduated tails which, combined with their colouring, gives them a shrike-like appearance. This is reflected in several of their numerous vernacular names, e.g. cuckoo-shrike, wood-shrike and flycatcher-shrike. The scientific name of the family, Campephagidae, means 'caterpillar-eaters'. an appropriate description that is also recognized in the vernacular names caterpillar-shrike and caterpillar-bird. Other common names by which some species are known are greybird and triller. In most species the lower back and rump are characteristically covered with a densely matted patch of loosely attached feathers with stiff, spine-like shafts. It has been suggested that these feathers function as a defence mechanism, as do the loose feathers of pigeons and trogons.

Perhaps best typifying the family are the cuckoo-shrikes in the genus *Coracina,* which are predominantly grey, often with much barring, many species being alternatively known as greybirds. They have a wide distribution, occurring from Africa through much of southern Asia to Australia and the Solomon Islands. Exclusively arboreal, living in forest and woodland, they feed on small fruits as well as caterpillars and other insects.

The cuckoo-shrikes in the nominate genus *Campephaga* are found only in Africa. The males are glossy black, sometimes with a patch of brilliant red or yellow on the shoulder, while the females are mainly brownish with much barring. Sometimes included in *Campephaga,* but more usually in a separate genus *Lobotos,* are the two Wattled cuckoo-shrikes. They are peculiar in having fleshy orange lobes at the gape, which are particularly prominent in the male. These species rival the minivets in the brilliance of their plumage. The very rare Wattled cuckoo-shrike *L. lobatus,* for example, has a glossy green head, chestnut rump and underparts, green and black wings, and a black and yellow tail, while the Oriole cuckoo-shrike *L. oriolinus,* as its name suggests, is amazingly similar to a Black-headed oriole *Oriolus brachyrhynchus.* Both species of *Lobotos* are found only in West Africa. Species of *Campephaga* and *Lobotos,* like those of *Coracina,* are exclusively arboreal and feed on both small fruits and insects.

Another group of cuckoo-shrikes is composed of species of *Lalage,* usually known as trillers on account of their clear whistling calls. Males are boldly patterned in black and white, while females are duller and browner. The White-winged triller *L. sueurii* of Australia is unusual in having two moults each year, before and after breeding, the male assuming a plumage similar to the female's during the winter months. Like most other cuckoo-shrikes the trillers are essentially arboreal, though the Pied triller *L. nigra,* a common garden bird in Southeast Asia, occasionally drops to the ground while feeding. Trillers range from southern Asia to the Philippines, Australia and the islands of the western Pacific.

The other groups, the wood-shrikes *Tephrodornis* and the flycatcher-shrikes *Hemipus,* are also composed of species that are mainly black and white, with a southern Asian distribution. Both groups differ markedly from other cuckoo-shrikes in being almost exclusively insectivorous, and in hawking for insects on the wing. The small 5 in (13 cm) flycatcher-shrikes are particularly deserving of their name, being very flycatcher-like in their behaviour. The 7 in (18 cm) wood-shrikes have strongly hooked bills and feed on large insects such as dragonflies and cicadas.

Finally there are the three Asian and Australian monotypic genera, *Pteropodocys, Chlamydochaera,* and *Campochaera.* Of these three, the Australian Ground cuckoo-shrike *P. maxima* is unique in the family in inhabiting open plains. It perches on prominent vantage points from which it hawks for insects, but also forages on the ground where it runs strongly. It is about 14 in (35 cm) long and the largest member of the family. The black-breasted triller *Chlamydochaera jefferyi* also calls for comment in that, alone among the family, it is said to eat nothing but fruit. It is a little known species confined to the mountain forests in the interior of Borneo.

Cuckoo-shrikes build shallow rather frail nests, relatively small for the size of the bird. It is usually placed 20–30 ft (6–9 m) above the ground on a horizontal branch, and is built of fine twigs, roots, grass or moss, camouflaged with spiders' webs and lichens. The eggs are light green or blue, finely speckled with brown, and number two to five. In the majority of species both sexes build the nest, incubate the eggs, and rear the young, though in a few the female alone incubates. Although it forages so much on the ground, the Ground cuckoo-shrike builds its nest high in a tree, as do the rest of the family.

During the non-breeding season cuckoo-shrikes are prominent members of the mixed flocks of several species that are such a characteristic feature of tropical forests. Cuckoo-shrikes are basically sedentary, though White-winged trillers that live in southern Australia are migratory, as are the more northerly distributed of the minivets. FAMILY: Campephagidae, ORDER: Passeriformes, CLASS: Aves.   M.P.L.F.

CUCKOO WASPS, incredibly beautiful insects, brilliantly coloured in metallic green, blue and violet, and often not more than $\frac{1}{3}$ in cm) in length. In general appearance they resemble small bees, and this may be to their advantage for, as their common name suggests, they lay their eggs in the nests of bees and wasps and rely on these hosts to rear their young. FAMILY: Chrysididae, ORDER: Hymenoptera, CLASS: Insecta, PHYLUM: Arthropoda.

CUCUJAS, a name with various spellings for beetles *Pyrophorus* living in America, from the southern United States to Argentina, including the West Indies. Another name is fire-beetles, or even *fire-flies, the second of these being more strictly applicable to beetles of another family. Cucujas belong to the *Click beetles. They are large beetles readily recognized by two yellow spots near each hind angle of the thorax. When they spread their wings the light is seen as brilliant orange.

Cucujas have long been used as a source of illumination. A few of them in a bottle give sufficient light for reading print. The local South American Indian women fasten the beetles to their clothing or put them in their black hair, for social gatherings, such as dances, to add to their charms. W. H. Prescott, historian of the conquest of Mexico, records how the Spaniards when besieged in 1520 mistook the lights in darkness for an army with matchlock muskets. FAMILY: Elateridae, ORDER: Coleoptera, CLASS: Insecta.

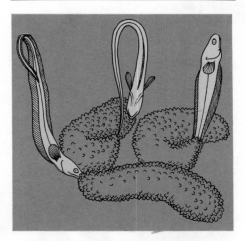

The cucumberfish *Carapus apus* shown entering and leaving a holothurian.

CUCUMBERFISHES, also known as pearlfishes, elongated marine fishes, related to the cods that live inside Sea cucumbers. In England they are often called fierasfers, derived from their former scientific name meaning 'shining beasts'. The most striking feature of these fishes is their habit of entering any small crevice tail first. Some species are very particular and *Carapus bermudensis* will only live in one species of Sea cucumber, while others, such as *C. homei,* will live in any shell or Sea cucumber. Although Sea cucumbers are hollow a certain strategy is required in converting the animal into living quarters. When a young cucumberfish finds its host it searches for the anus and pushes its way in. As the fish becomes larger it tends to enter the Sea cucumber tail first. In many other associations between two animals each

partner gains something from the relationship and it is because of this advantage that the association has evolved. In the case of the cucumberfishes, the host seems to gain nothing and may even suffer unintentional damage to its organs. Some cucumberfishes are not above nibbling at their hosts while inside. *Carapus apus* from the Mediterranean is believed to spend its entire life inside the Sea cucumber, presumably feeding on its host. This may not do as much damage as might be thought since the Sea cucumbers have great powers of regeneration.

The eggs of the cucumberfish float at the surface and the young fish do not closely resemble their parents. While still young they search for a suitable home. The body of these fishes is naked and in some species the pelvic fins are lacking. One of the largest species *Echiodon drummondi* reaches 12 in (30 cm) in length and is found in British waters. FAMILY: Carapidae, ORDER: Gadiformes, CLASS: Pisces.

CURASSOWS, the common name for a family of forest-dwelling birds (Cracidae), ranging from southern Texas, throughout Central and South America to Uruguay and Argentina. There are 44 species but only one, the Plain chachalaca *Ortalis vetula* goes as far north as southern Texas. Curassows are most numerous in the tropical part of their range.

They are large birds, the largest being almost of the size of a turkey. The smallest are the chachalacas of the genus *Ortalis* of which there are ten species. In many features they resemble pheasants. Their plumage is mostly glossy and either black, brown or olive-brown and in most of the species the sexes are alike. Some, such as members of the genus *Crax* with seven species, have a crest of curly feathers on the crown, while others like *Mitu* and *Pauxi* have bizarre looking and colourful helmets on the base of their bills or skulls. Their bills are short, often with a brightly coloured cere, their wings are rounded, the tails are long and flat and they have strong feet. Their flight is heavy but fast and direct even through a dense forest.

All curassows are birds of the forest where they live partly on the ground and partly in the trees. In trees they run fast over thick branches. Some of them are more or less gregarious. They feed on leaves and fruits.

The nests of curassows are small in comparison to the size of the birds. They make open cup nests of dead sticks, often lined with fresh leaves, in trees and shrubbery frequently quite near the ground and seldom at a great height. The eggs are white and the clutch consists of only two or three eggs. The nestlings which hatch with well-developed

Crested curassow *Crax alector* of the forests of the Amazon Basin.

wing feathers, leave the nest soon after hatching.

The name chachalaca is derived from their cackling alarm note, but the common call of, for instance the Guianan chachalaca *Ortalis motmot,* is a loud rhythmical note sounding like 'Wákăgŏ, wákăgŏ' and is one of the most characteristic calls of their habitat in the early morning.

They prefer dense shrubbery to the real rain forests and shun civilization. The numbers of all species are diminishing constantly in much of their range, and at least one species is already believed to be extinct. Overshooting for the pot by prospectors and people living and working in the forests, the building of roads which makes their habitat more and more accessible, but above all the clearing of the tropical forests which is taking place at an ever increasing rate all over Central and South America are all contributing to the decrease in numbers. Only the setting aside of large areas of primaeval forests as reserves can save many species from ultimate disappearance. Some South American countries have made a start but much more will be necessary. The chachalacas seem less threatened than most species as they often live in secondary growth and even in overgrown wasteland. The larger forest species vanish as soon as the forests are cleared and they cannot live in cultivated forests of introduced trees. Curassows thrive in captivity but they are difficult to breed. FAMILY: Cracidae, ORDER: Galliformes, CLASS: Aves.   F.H.

CURLEWS, eight species of wading birds of the genus *Numenius* distinguished by long downcurved bills and characteristic call-notes. Their plumage is largely cryptic, with mottled brown upperparts, but most have a white rump, conspicuous in flight. In the Palearctic, the large curlew *N. arquata*

Curlew, recognizable by the down-curved bill.

breeds in wet meadows and on moorlands in the temperate zone, while the smaller whimbrel *N. phaeopus* replaces it at higher latitudes (and altitudes), where it has a discontinuous circumpolar distribution. Whimbrel are absent from north central Siberia, where the Little or Pygmy curlew *N. minutus* breeds, and from northeastern Canada, where the now almost extinct Eskimo curlew *N. borealis* occurs. Further south, in the temperate zone of the North American continent, the whimbrel is replaced by the ecological counterpart of the European curlew, the larger Long-billed curlew *N. americanus*. In the marshy steppes of Asia the Slender-billed curlew *N. tenuirostris* breeds. This species rarely reaches Europe except on passage.

Most species show strong migratory habits. The populations of the European curlew mostly move southwest in autumn, to winter in the British Isles and Iberia; some reach Africa and Southeast Asia. The whimbrel has a migration pattern which has been termed 'leap-frog' migration, since it breeds to the north of the European curlew, e.g. in Iceland, but winters well to the south, on the coasts of western and southern Africa. Other breeding populations of whimbrel reach southern South America during the northern winter, and the Pygmy curlew winters in Australasia. Curlews are birds chiefly of sandy and muddy (rarely rocky) shores of rivers and lakes outside the breeding season, but some, like the whimbrel, are largely confined to the sea coasts.

The distribution of the curlew has altered

Common European curlew in East Pakistan. Curlews migrate southwards in autumn, some reaching North Africa, others going to southern Asia.

considerably in some European countries in this century, as a result of changing agricultural practices. Reclamation and drainage of marshy fields and moorland, and afforestation of the latter, have led to local decreases, while conversion of forest to grassland in some parts of Scandinavia has led to increases there. The whimbrel's chosen habitat, marshy tundra with or without low shrub vegetation, has been affected much less by the hand of man, so the bird's numbers have probably altered little.

The curlews feed on a variety of small organisms living on or close to the surface of the soil, including insects and crustaceans, but also take many seeds and berries. The significance of the curved bill in obtaining food is not known. Those species which stay to winter in the temperate zone may be forced to move to coastal areas in winter if their inland feeding grounds become frozen. The curlews breeding in Scotland and northern England are partial migrants, some wintering close to their breeding areas, while others move to western Ireland, where the ground close to the Atlantic seaboard is rarely frozen. FAMILY: Scolopacidae, ORDER: Charadriiformes, CLASS: Aves.   P.R.E.

CUSCUS, name given to any of at least six species of *marsupials of the genus *Phalanger,* resembling monkeys in appearance. The affinities of the cuscuses, which have a tropical distribution from the Celebes Islands east to the Solomon Islands, appear to be with the Brush possums; their ecological counterpart in tropical and temperate regions of Australia and adjacent islands. Cuscuses are arboreal animals with rounded heads, small ears, large eyes, dense soft fur and a long prehensile tail, the terminal portion of which is without fur. The head and body of full grown animals of the larger species is over 2 ft (60 cm) in length and the tail is only a little shorter.

The Bear cuscuses (*P. celebensis, ursinus*) are large, brown to black animals found only in the Celebes and adjacent islands. As in all the other phalangers the cuscuses have three incisor teeth on each side of the upper jaw and the anterior lower pair of incisors enlarged and bent forwards (procumbent). A pair of canine teeth are always present in the uppper jaw. In the Bear cuscuses the third upper incisor is enlarged and the canine is reduced in size, a dental condition approaching that of the larger kangaroos. No colour differences between the sexes occur in the Bear cuscuses and white individuals are unknown.

The so-called Grey cuscuses include a multiplicity of colour phases ranging from pure white, through various shades of grey, to chocolate brown or even distinctly reddish (*P. orientalis, gymnotis, vestitus*). The pure white phase is restricted to the male only. This is the most generalized and widest ranging group extending from the Celebes and Timor, through New Guinea, eastward to most of the Solomon Islands and southwards to Cape York on the Australian mainland.

The Spotted cuscuses (*P. maculatus, atrimaculatus*) include forms in which both sexes may be pure white. Other forms are, by marsupial standards, brightly coloured and spotted in a variable and irregular, non-symmetrical fashion; a rarity amongst wild animals. The Spotted cuscuses range from New Guinea to Cape York, the Moluccas and other islands near New Guinea but not to the Celebes or Solomon Islands. Except on certain islands northwest of New Guinea, female cuscuses appear to lack the spotted pattern. FAMILY: Phalangeridae, ORDER: Marsupialia, CLASS: Mammalia.
G.B.S.

CUSHION STARS, starfishes not necessarily closely related but all having a body form rather like a five-cornered cushion. The Common cushion star of western European shores is *Asterina gibbosa,* but the name may also be used more widely to refer to other species of similar general shape: *Porania* and *Hippasteria* have been so named in Britain, and *Pteraster* in North America. In details of body structure, development and mode of life they differ from one another, but *Asterina* may be considered as a particularly common and well-known example.

It is a small starfish, some 2 in (5 cm) in diameter, of almost pentagonal shape, its body produced into five very short, stumpy arms. The upper surface is slightly swollen, the lower surface flat. The upper or dorsal surface is covered with overlapping scale-like plates, carrying small spines in groups of four to eight and also, but less abundantly, simple pedicellariae (pincer-like structures) between the spine groups. On the lower or oral surface, the central mouth is surrounded by five grooves which extend radially to the ends of the arms, each groove being flanked on either side by a series of suckered tube-feet. Between these grooves the regular overlapping plates, which are imbedded in the skin, bear spines, fewer in number but slightly larger than those of the upper surface. The fairly thin edge of the animal is formed of small, mostly indistinct, marginal plates of calcite. In life, Cushion stars vary from olive-green to yellowish or brownish-red.

This Common cushion star is widely distributed in western European seas, and the Mediterranean, and it also extends down the west coast of Africa to the Azores. In Britain it occurs along the south and west coasts, but not usually along those of the North Sea. Although recorded down to depths of some 400 ft (125 m), it is mainly a littoral species which dwells on or under stones, but may be found on shell gravel in deeper water. It feeds mainly on molluscs but also eats worms and brittlestars.

When breeding, the female is generally accompanied by two or three males. The eggs are not shed at random into the surrounding

Cushion star *Culcita schnideliana,* a five-cornered cushion-shaped starfish seen (above) in dorsal view and (below) from the underside showing the five ambulacral grooves meeting at the mouth.

water but deposited in small groups, typically attached to the undersurfaces of stones. They are very yolky and quite large (0·5 mm in diameter) and adhere by their surface membranes. The fertilized egg develops into an embryo which escapes from the egg membrane in a few days. Usually a starfish larva passes through two different stages of development in turn, named the bipinnaria and brachiolaria, but in *Asterina* the bipinnaria stage is always omitted, and the embryo either develops directly or, in some species, metamorphoses to the adult form after spending some ten days as a free-swimming larva of brachiolaria type. In British seas breeding usually takes place in May-June, but may occur earlier, April-May, in the Mediterranean. It has been claimed that this Cushion star behaves as a male when young and small and as a female when older and larger, but this lacks confirmation.

The Common cushion star moves slowly, $\frac{3}{4}$–2 in (2–5 cm) per minute towards moderate light but away from strong sunlight, and upwards against the force of gravity, when kept in captivity. See echinoderms. ORDER: Spinulosa, CLASS: Asteroidea, PHYLUM: Echinodermata. E.P.F.R.

CUSKEELS, elongated marine fishes related to the cods and the cucumberfishes. The cuskeels have long bodies with the dorsal and anal fins running the entire length of the body. The pelvic fins are under the head and are reduced to two barbel-like structures on the chin. They probably serve a sensory function since they are trailed along the bottom as the fish swims and may indicate the nature of the substrate, availability of food, etc. Most species are less than 12 in (30 cm) long although the South African kingklip *Genypterus capensis* grows to 5 ft (1·5 m). In spite of its slimy and unprepossessing appearance, this species is considered to be a delicacy. It is caught in trawls from depths of 1,500 ft (500 m). Like their relatives, the cucumberfishes, many of the cuskeels stand on their tails or enter crevices tail first. FAMILY: Ophidiidae, ORDER: Gadiformes, CLASS: Pisces.

CUTICLE, non-cellular outer surface of the body in some animals. This is produced by an underlying layer of cells called the epidermis and it is a particularly prominent feature of the nematodes and arthropods. Annelids also have a cuticle, but it is very thin and delicate.

Many parasitic flatworms, like the tapeworms and flukes were once thought to be covered with a 'cuticle' but recent electron microscope studies have shown that the outside 'epidermis' or 'tegument' is a highly specialized living layer secreted by cells whose nuclei are embedded into the underlying parenchyma below the basement membrane. In all parasitic forms, this layer probably has an important excretory function (by reverse pinocytosis) and also absorptive functions (by pinocytosis). This latter role is of particular importance in the tapeworms which lack a gut and so rely on food ingested through the tegument. The tapeworms are unique in that their tegument is folded into small projections (microvilli) which have hardened tips. It is thought that this arrangement may serve to keep the animal away from the wall of the host's gut and so facilitate movement of food past the parasite's tegument.

The arthropod cuticle is built on a different principle. Here protection is achieved by a series of rigid plates, but in order to allow movement these plates are joined by flexible membranous regions. The whole is rather like a suit of armour. All arthropods have a cuticle of this type and it will suffice to describe the cuticle of insects in detail, although there are some minor variations in crustaceans and arachnids.

The insect cuticle is laid down by the epidermis so that it covers not only the whole of the outside of the body, it also lines the fore-gut, the hind-gut and the tracheal system. In addition, there are places at which the cuticle becomes deeply inflected into the body to form points for muscle attachment and support or protection for organs.

The structure of insect cuticle varies over the surface of the body. Hard parts, called sclerites, are separated by regions in which the cuticle is flexible or membranous so allowing the sclerites to move. Sometimes, although there is still membrane between them permitting movement, the sclerites articulate with each other at one or two points so that they make very precise movements. In other cases the sclerites are not separated by membrane at all, but are joined together by a special kind of cuticle called resilin. This has the properties of an almost perfect rubber, storing energy when it is stretched and returning to its original shape as soon as the tension is released. A large pad of resilin is present at the base of the wing of the locust, and probably of other insects, where it forms a hinge ideally suited for the rapid up and down movements of the wing since, unlike any ordinary hinge, there is no friction.

The insect cuticle consists of an inner region up to about 200μ or more thick covered by a delicate outer layer, the epicuticle, only $2-3\mu$ thick. The inner part is made up of characteristic proteins and a polysaccharide, *chitin. The rigidity of the cuticle depends on whether or not the proteins are linked together to give an inflexible structure. When cuticle is first laid down at the time of the *moult it is soft and the insect, by pumping blood into the various regions of its body, can expand and stretch the new cuticle. The most spectacular instance of this is the expansion of the wings at the final moult to adult. Subsequently the proteins become linked together to form the rigid sclerites. This process does not take place through the whole thickness of the cuticle, but only in the outer parts immediately beneath the epicuticle. Thus the cuticle of a sclerite comes to consist of three major regions: epicuticle, hardened exocuticle and unhardened endocuticle. In the soft parts between the sclerites only epicuticle and endocuticle are present.

In some insects, at least, more endocuticle

is added after the moult and the chitin fibres are laid down differently in light and darkness so that daily growth layers are visible with the polarizing microscope. By cutting sections of the cuticle and counting the numbers of layers it is possible to tell the age of some insects, such as grasshoppers, but only up to the time when cuticle deposition stops.

On the outside of the chitinous cuticle is the epicuticle which contains no chitin. The bulk of the epicuticle is formed by a mixture of substances, including proteins and lipoproteins, which are known collectively as cuticulin. Outside the cuticulin is the wax layer. Wax consists of long molecules of various alcohols, paraffins and other substances and it is believed that in the inner layer of the wax these molecules are all lined up side by side to form a kind of palisade all over the outside of the cuticulin. Because the layer is only one molecule thick it is called a monolayer and it is thought that this is the layer which makes the cuticle waterproof because the spaces between the wax molecules are too small for water molecules to pass through. Outside the wax is a thin layer of a substance called cement which forms a varnish-like protective layer over the whole surface.

Running through the cuticle at right-angles to its surface are fine tubes called pore canals, $1 \cdot 0\mu$ or less in diameter, which are thought to contain extensions from the epidermal cells. Pore canals are extremely numerous with an estimated density of 1 million per square millimetre in the cockroach. It is believed that they make it possible to transport cuticular material out from the epidermal cells to the surface of the cuticle.

When it is first laid down the cuticle is colourless but it usually darkens as it hardens. This is, in part, due to the changes in the proteins which effect hardening, but it also involves the development of dark pigments. Some parts, however, remain completely transparent. This is true of the cuticle over the eyes and that forming the wings of many insects. The microscopic structure of the cuticle sometimes results in the production of

physical colours, such as the metallic greens and reds of many insects and the iridescence of insect wings.

The cuticle has several functions. It provides support for the body and protection from enemies. The hard, jointed appendages enable the insect to make accurate movements while using only small muscles, and by raising the body off the ground they allow the insect to move quickly. The cuticle forms the rigid wings without which flight would not be possible. Modifications of the cuticle form sense organs, while the wax layer in particular reduces water loss to a minimum.   R.F.C.

CUTLASSFISHES, and their close relatives the hairtails, ribbon-like oceanic fishes related to the swordfish, mackerel and tunas. The elongated, highly compressed body suggests a resemblance to a cutlass. The dorsal fin is long, the anal fin short and there is either a very small tail (cutlassfishes) or the body tapers to a point (hairtails). The jaws are large and have sharp, widely-spaced teeth, some of which may be fang-like. The frostfish *Lepidopus caudatus* is one of the cutlassfishes.

Trichiurus lepturus is a hairtail that reaches 5 ft (1·5 m) in length. It is widely distributed throughout the Atlantic, western Pacific and Indian Oceans and although it normally lives in deep water it is found in shallower waters off Japan and South Africa where cold currents well up. It is silvery in colour with the anal fin consisting of isolated spinelets. There is not much flesh on it but what there is has a good flavour and the species has some importance in fisheries in India. Several common names are used for it, including snakefish, bandfish and ribbonfish. *Aphanopus carbo,* another member of this family, is an elongated black fish caught in the temperate deep waters of the North Atlantic. FAMILY: Trichiuridae, ORDER: Perciformes, CLASS: Pisces.

CUTTLEFISH *Sepia officinalis,* marine mollusc related to the squid and octopus, having a well-defined head with two large

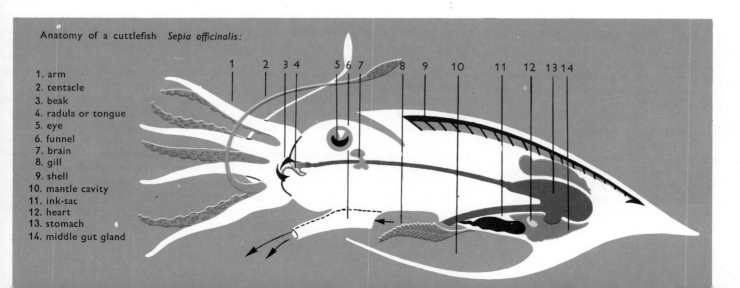

Anatomy of a cuttlefish *Sepia officinalis:*

1. arm
2. tentacle
3. beak
4. radula or tongue
5. eye
6. funnel
7. brain
8. gill
9. shell
10. mantle cavity
11. ink-sac
12. heart
13. stomach
14. middle gut gland

eyes, and eight arms and two retractile tentacles encircling the mouth. The head is attached by a short neck to the body which is supported internally by the cuttlebone. This structure not only acts as a support, it is also a buoyancy mechanism enabling the cuttlefish to remain on the bottom or swim freely at any depth. The cuttlefish is a coastal animal and, like all known cephalopods, is a predator.

Modern cuttlefishes appeared some 21 million years ago. Their descent was almost certainly from a belemnite-like forebear. The order Sepioidea contains four families. The cuttlefish belongs to one of these, the Sepiidae, which is characterized by having a dorso-ventrally flattened body and a large calcified and horny internal shell, the cuttlebone.

The family Sepiidae is confined to the Old World, none of its members being found along the shores of North or South America. The cuttlefish is found in the northeast Atlantic, the Mediterranean, the North Sea and the English Channel. About 100 species of the family Sepiidae are known. They are found in tropical and temperate seas but rarely in colder waters. The cuttlefish inhabits coastal regions in water of 16–390 ft (5–120 m) depth. In summer it generally remains in water of 32–65 ft (10–20 m) depth. During the autumn and winter it migrates to deeper water returning again to shallow waters in the spring.

Along the length of each of the eight arms are four rows of stalked suckers. There are also two very long retractile tentacles, which when fully extended capture prey on a terminal pad, bearing stalked suckers. The pad has several rows of suckers the central row having five particularly large ones. These tentacles are normally retracted into two pockets which lie close to the mouth between the base of the third and fourth arms. The head is broad and somewhat flattened. The eyes are situated on either side of the head so that the animal can see both in front and behind, with a horizontal visual field of 360°. The eyes are large and have a single lens which throws an image on to the retina, showing in this and in other ways considerable similarity to the vertebrate eye.

The mouth found at the centre of the arms has an upper and a lower beak surrounded by a circular lip. The beaks are chitinous and resemble those of parrots, except that in the cuttlefish the upper one fits into the lower one. Inside the mouth is a tooth-bearing ribbon, the radula, used in the transport of food particles to the oesophagus.

The shape of the body of the cuttlefish is determined by the presence of the cuttlebone. Below it the visceral mass is enclosed by the muscular mantle. The mantle forms a cavity, open at the front, beneath the enclosed viscera. The gills are suspended within the mantle cavity and a respiratory current of water is maintained by the mantle muscle.

Water is drawn into the cavity and then expelled through a median funnel. Contraction of the mantle muscle forces a jet of water through the funnel, strong enough to bring about a propulsive movement. The cuttlefish uses this jet to move rapidly. It also swims more slowly by means of an undulatory movement of the lateral fins. The current of water is also used to expel, through the funnel, the produce of the ink sac and the digestive, excretory and reproductive systems. All of these open into the mantle cavity.

Vision is very important during the courtship of the cuttlefish as both the male and

Cuttlefish seen from the front.

female display a zebra-like pattern. The pattern, less brilliant in the female, is produced by the chromatophores or colour cells of the skin. When the male approaches another cuttlefish the pattern intensifies and the left fourth arm, which is more prominently marked, is extended towards the other. If the other cuttlefish is a female the display is not returned and the arm will touch. The female may accept the male immediately, or swim away in which case the male will follow. The animals then face each other with their arms interwoven. They remain in this position for at least two minutes during copulation. In this time the spermatophores, or packets of sperm, are transferred to the female by the fourth left arm of the male, which has a reduced number of suckers near the base. During copulation this region forms a groove into which a spermatophore is blown by a jet of water from the funnel.

The female lays her eggs a few days after mating. Each egg is blown out through the funnel which is held between the fourth pair of arms. The female then 'embraces' a clump of seaweed, or other suitable projection, with all her arms while the egg is attached to the object. It is not known how this is achieved, but a number of eggs are attached in this way. One female can lay 200–550 eggs, depositing

them over a period of several days. She does not remain to care for the eggs as does the octopus. Each egg is elliptical, about $\frac{5}{16}$ in (8 mm) in diameter, and contains sufficient yolk for the development of the embryo. Hatching occurs about 50 days after laying. The young cuttlefish measure about $\frac{3}{8}$ in (10 mm) and immediately adopt a life on the bottom like the adults.

Some yolk remains at the time of hatching and is absorbed during the first two or three days, after which the young cuttlefish will attack moving Opossum shrimps *Mysis*. This response to prey is vital for its survival.

The mode of attacking *Mysis* follows the same pattern from the very first occasion that the prey is seen. A recently hatched cuttlefish in captivity will watch a live *Mysis* dropped into the tank for perhaps as long as 2 min. It will turn to face the *Mysis,* both eyes rotating towards the prey and when within about $\frac{1}{5}$ in (5 mm) the tentacles shoot out rapidly to capture it. Once the *Mysis* has been observed it is generally captured within 10 sec.

The attack of young and adult cuttlefish on prawns has been carefully analyzed. When a live prawn is introduced into an aquarium the cuttlefish will exhibit colour changes, erect the first and second pairs of arms and move the eyes and the head. The whole animal turns so that the prey lies in front of it. It then moves until the prey is within reach of the tentacles. These are ejected quickly and the prawn captured on the terminal suckers. Seizure of the prey takes only $\frac{3}{100}$ sec. The tentacles are then retracted so that the prey is brought close to the mouth and the horny beak bites the abdomen of the prawn and poison is injected. A crab is generally captured in a different manner, being 'jumped on' and held by the arms of the cuttlefish.

The cuttlebone consists of numerous thin plates each supported by pillars. Each of the chambers, which are laid down as the animal grows, contains gas spaces. The density of the cuttlebone can be changed by pumping liquid in and out of these chambers thereby altering the volume of the gas-filled space. Changes in the buoyancy of the cuttlefish accompany alterations in light intensity. At twilight the cuttlefish becomes buoyant and swims around until dawn, when it becomes slightly denser than sea water and settles on the bottom where it remains buried in the sand, except for its eyes. Thus concealed it can capture prawns or crabs that venture too close.

The cuttlefish has a rich repertoire of colour changes. Chromatophores in the skin are of three colours, orange, orange-red and brown-black. The intensity of the colour depends upon the degree of contraction or expansion of radial muscles, which are controlled by nerves from the chromatophore lobes of the brain. Changes in the chromatophores occur quickly in response to the

Cuttlefish swimming and showing striped colour pattern assumed when among seaweed (protective) and when courting.

environment, as observed through the eyes of the cuttlefish. The chromatophores are present in larger numbers on the upper surface of the animal than on the underside. A cuttlefish swimming amongst seaweed in a lighted aquarium has a striped pattern which breaks up its outline making it difficult to see. On a sandy bottom the cuttlefish will adopt the pattern of its background and then almost bury itself using the jets of water from the funnel and the undulatory movement of the fins to excavate the sand. Resemblance to the sandy bottom is enhanced by the erection of skin papillae giving it a rough appearance.

Another protective device is the ejection of ink, a substance known to artists for many centuries as sepia. The cuttlefish uses its ink to foil a predator, the cloud of ink distracting it as the cuttlefish escapes from behind this black suspension ejection into the water.

The brain of the cuttlefish, like that of other cephalopods, is large and complex. It surrounds the oesophagus and, protected by the cranium, is bounded on either side by the large eyes. The cuttlefish is capable of learning and will follow a food lure, such as a prawn, round a corner although the prey has disappeared from sight. If a prawn is placed in a glass jar the cuttlefish will only attack it on a limited number of occasions, having learned that the food is unobtainable. The brain is formed of many lobes and an animal in which the so-called 'highest centres' have been removed fails in some of these tasks and will show signs of temporary forgetting, for example it will no longer follow a lure round a corner. FAMILY: Sepiidae, ORDER: Sepioidea, CLASS: Cephalopoda, PHYLUM: Mollusca.
M.N.

CUTTLEFISH LURES. Normally pursuing their prey, cuttlefish do sometimes lie half buried in the sand and grab a shrimp, prawn or crab as it passes by. There is, however, one report of a cuttlefish luring its prey. In 1956, J. Wickstead, in the Singapore Fisheries Station, watched a cuttlefish hide among seaweed. It changed colour so that its body matched the seaweed and it pushed half out

the two long tentacles which it normally shoots out to capture prey, and the tips of these hung down limply and went white. The cuttlefish lazily waved these tips and from time to time a fish swam over to investigate. Although Wickstead failed to see the cuttlefish catch anything he regarded this as a deliberate attempt by the cuttlefish to lure prey to it rather than catching it.

CUVIER Georges, 1769–1832. A French biologist who is justly called the father of comparative anatomy and of paleontology. He was born at Montbeliard, but worked for most of his life in Paris at the Museum National d'Histoire Naturelle, where he published works on molluscs, fishes and fossil mammals and reptiles. In 1817 his most important work, *Le Règne Animal Distribue d'après son Organization,* was published. In it, Cuvier gave a classification of all animals based on the principles of comparative anatomy; that is, he saw that animals with many anatomical features in common could be grouped together into natural units. Cuvier believed that animal species were created individually, and that extinctions were due to what he called 'local catastrophies'.

After Cuvier's time comparative anatomy became the central theme of zoological studies. In England, Sir Richard Owen (born 1804, died 1892), starting a medical career heard Cuvier's lectures in Paris. He learned the value of comparative anatomy in animal classification when preparing catalogues of material in the collections of the Royal College of Surgeons in London. Later Owen was put in charge of one of the greatest collections of zoological material in the world —the Natural History section of the British Museum. Owen published on many anatomical topics and under his influence the study of extinct vertebrate animals, or vertebrate paleontology, was established in Britain.

In America, vertebrate paleontology had an added attraction; during the 19th century

the first discoveries were made of dinosaurs. Their collection was of great zoological interest, but had added romance in that they were to be found in the western states which were still unexplored and populated by hostile Indian tribes. Pioneers in this field were Edward Cope (born 1840, died 1897) and Othniel Marsh (born 1831, died 1899). Between them, these two men made many great finds of fossil dinosaurs and mammals; their contribution to vertebrate paleontology was immense, but was marred by their intense rivalry which ended in a bitterness almost unrivalled in the history of zoology Their work was continued in America by Henry Fairfield Osborn (born 1857, died 1935) who made collections of fossil mammals and who wrote extensively on their evolution.

The study of paleontology and comparative anatomy changed in emphasis after the Darwinian revolution. Scientists were no longer content to make classifications of animals, but strove to unravel their evolutionary relationships. In America, Alfred Sherwood Romer (born 1894), has worked on the evolution of extinct amphibians and reptiles, while George Gaylord Simpson (born 1902), has probably been the most imporant single influence in mammalian studies. In England, D. M. S. Watson (born 1886), has contributed extensively to studies of extinct fishes and amphibians as has E. Stensiö in Sweden.

Today, paleontologists and comparative anatomists are still concerned with the facts of evolution, but more importantly, their work contributes to a greater understanding of the mechanics of animal evolution. P.H.

CYCLES AND OSCILLATIONS, fluctuations in the numbers in animal populations from year to year. Most species oscillate within quite narrow limits and never become extremely abundant nor extremely scarce. Some species, however, oscillate wildly every so often, with times of extraordinary abundance followed by times of great scarcity. These are divided into the cyclic and the irruptive species. The difference between the two is that the time of great abundance of cyclic species occurs predictably and recurs at more or less regular intervals, whereas with the irruptive species peak densities occur sporadically, and with no warning. Both types of population explosion are a source of irritation to mankind, and for centuries scientists, philosophers and theologians have sought an explanation for these phenomena.

Oscillations resulting in population explosions are usually identified by mass migrations of animals away from the breeding sites. They occur mostly in the temperate, subarctic and arctic regions of the world, and usually only herbivorous animals take

Cycles and oscillations

part. It has long been thought that the explosion is caused by a sudden and unexpected failure of the food crop at a time when the populations are large as a result of breeding. In northern Europe the main irruptive species are birds that are specialized feeders on tree seeds; a resource notably fickle in its abundance. Recently it has been shown that some form of migration occurs every year, although normally the reproductive excess is absorbed in nearby areas that produced excess food. These irruptions tend only to be severe enough to trouble lands far away in exceptional years when reproduction has been unusually successful and failure of the food crop is total over great areas of land.

The best known European irruptive species are the crossbill *Loxia curvirostrata* which feeds on seeds of spruce and pine, and the Evening grosbeak *Hesperiphona vespertina* which feeds on the seeds of the Ash-leaved maple. It is interesting that related species with a less specialized diet do not show such marked population explosions. A noteworthy mammal, the springbuck *Antidorcas euchore* underwent incredible population explosions periodically in South Africa, before the European colonists reduced the numbers of the springbuck severely and substantially changed the habitat. Migrations over many hundreds of miles were undertaken in search of food, and frequently resulted in mass deaths. Some insects undertake spectacular migrations, the best known example being the locust *Locusta migratoria*. In this species a special migratory type is produced which differs from the parent type in that it is gregarious and seeks to maintain the closest contact with its companions. When the population density of migratory types is high enough the locusts fly away in a huge swarm, to land possibly some hundreds of miles away from the parent population. Breeding occurs, and widespread havoc is created by the appetite of the newly hatched insects. The invasion ends when predators and parasites take their toll, and the great horde is gradually destroyed and dissolved.

In all cases of sporadic violent oscillation resulting in mass migration, most of the migrants perish without returning to the parent population, but not quite all. A very few manage to overwinter in foreign parts, and may even breed with migrants from other populations. This role of pioneer, which is sometimes associated with a movement back to the parent population by the offspring of the emigrés, is a very important side effect of the explosion, resulting in extension of range as well as the introduction of new blood into the parent population. Although the settlement areas used by the emigrés may have their food resources devastated, the irruption and migration has

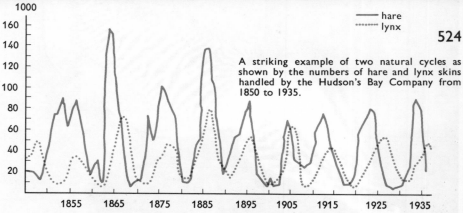

A striking example of two natural cycles as shown by the numbers of hare and lynx skins handled by the Hudson's Bay Company from 1850 to 1935.

served to offload the reproductive excess from the home site of the parent population, thereby conserving the food supply of the latter and guaranteeing the continued survival of the species in that region.

Two main types of cycles are recognized. First there is a three or four year interval between successive peaks of abundance, as shown by northern rodents, the Norway and Varying lemmings *Lemmus lemmus* and *L. trimucronatus*. Perhaps linked to this is a doubtful four year cycle observed in the voles *Microtus* spp. of temperate latitudes. The second main cycle type has peaks occurring every ten years. This is shown by the Varying hare *Lepus americana* and the muskrat *Ondatra zibethica*; both being North American species. Some birds of northern latitudes are also cyclic: the Ruffed grouse *Bonasa umbellus* of North America cycles each ten years, while the Willow grouse *Lagopus lagopus* of Europe has a four year cycle. In Britain the Red grouse *Lagopus scoticus* cycles every six or seven years but the cycles are not as regular as in the other grouse. It is interesting to note that this cycle is roughly intermediate in wavelength between that of the North American and north European grouse species. In general the cycles of Willow grouse and Norway lemming are parallel phenomena having the same years of great abundance, but in Britain the Red grouse does not fluctuate in phase with the voles.

The structure of a typical cycle during one phase of increase and decline may be described by considering the cycle of the Norway lemming. During the winter immediately following a peak of abundance the populations are small, and survival over the winter and breeding the following spring are poor, since the food supply (mostly mosses) is still unrecovered from the devastation of the year before. Due to the poor condition of the animals, contagious disease is still widespread, causing quite high mortality. During the second winter, however, survival is better, since the growing season of the year before has allowed the food plants to recover somewhat. The second spring shows animals in good condition and breeding success is high. The third winter and third spring are ones of further increase for the animals, and by now the valleys are refurbished with

mosses. If the fourth winter provides good conditions for increase (i.e. a deep and long lasting snow cover under which breeding can occur in the relative warmth), the population at the start of the fourth spring is already full, and some shortage of food may be felt. If the spring is warm and dry, breeding will continue at a high rate until the populations are overcrowded. Some individuals migrate to find new food so relieving the pressure on the food resources and this they do at the edges of the range. After a while, and usually before mid-summer, young, born in the original as well as the emigrant populations, have to travel great distances to obtain suitable food. These migrations cause widespread havoc to farmers and landowners, because behavioural changes associated with overcrowding make the lemmings sociable, and new found food is quickly eaten out.

The decline in numbers starts when the peak has been reached, and it is not the build up as much as the decline that has fascinated scientists for years. Predators undoubtedly act to accelerate the decline, but it seems unlikely that they initiate it. These animals, hawks, owls, foxes, cats, wolverines etc., react to the sudden increase in available food by faster and more successful breeding. As a result they oscillate in phase with their prey, but they reach their peaks of abundance about a year after that of the rodents. The best documented examples are the Snowy owl *Nyctea scandiaca* in northern Europe which fluctuates in response to population changes of its chief prey, the lemming, and the lynx *Lynx canadensis* in North America which similarly follows its chief prey, the Varying hare.

Epidemic disease has frequently been said to kill off the bulk of the animals. The occurrence of 'lemming fever' is closely correlated with peak lemming years. The disease is fatal to lemmings, but is rarely so to man. Tests of the blood of patients suffering from it suggest it is caused by *Bacterium tularense*. Most declines of cyclic species are associated with disease, but rarely is the same disease present in two successive cycles. In northern Labrador Arctic foxes die of a kind of encephalitis. This disease also causes the deaths of lemmings, and it appears that the foxes become ill through eating infected lemmings. Scientists working

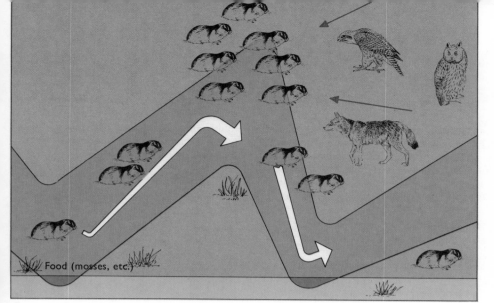

Fluctuations in the populations of the Norway lemming *Lemmus lemmus* over a three- or four-year period. As the food supply (green) begins to recover from the previous peak of abundance of lemmings, so the lemmings begin to increase in number, until dwindling food reserves, predators, disease and migration combine to reduce the population to its original level.

on the Varying hare detected a 'shock disease' that decimated overcrowded populations. The cause of this disease, which is only observed during peaks of population abundance, has not been established and nutritive deficiency has been suggested. These diseases are 'density dependent', for they are seldom found when the density of the populations is low. However, the diseases do not normally disappear from the population until two years (in lemmings), and four or five (in hares), after the peak of abundance has been reached. It clearly involves many generations that did not experience the overcrowding. Another confusing point is that the declines seldom start at the same degree of overcrowding as one would expect if disease, acting in a truly density dependent manner, served to trigger off the decline. The connection between disease and cycles is complex, therefore, and at the most can be said to be incidental and contributory, rather than a major factor in their initiation.

Without any doubt cyclic species interact with their plant food, and there is much evidence to suggest that rodents reach the limit of their food resources at the peak of the cycle, which is also the start of the decline. The continuation of a decline for several years after crowding has ceased is consistent with the fact that the species concerned invariably devastates part or all of its food supplies. A 2 oz (57 gm) lemming will consume 112 lb (50 kg) of vegetation a year. An experiment showed that a family of seven lemmings completely devastated 25 sq yd (21 sq m) of vegetation in two months, resulting in long term damage to the food resources.

Two main types of causal factors have been put forward to explain the regularity of cycles in nature. The first involves extrinsic causes, usually the weather, and the second involves intrinsic causes—usually an interaction between the animal and its food supply, of the sort already discussed. The possibility of an extrinsic cause acting as a 'master time' for biological cycles was discussed and considered for many years. Cycles were observed to be in phase with the cycles of abundance of sunspots, although its champions were unable to state clearly how the presence or absence of sunspots actually influenced the numbers of animals in populations. Later it was shown that the solar and terrestrial cycles became out of phase. The cycle of sunspots has a wavelength of about 11 years, but it is far more variable, with a range of 7–17 years, than the cycle of the Varying hare which lies between 8 and 12 years. Other strange physical phenomena have been purported to be the controlling factor of cycles, including a cycle of ozone abundance in the atmosphere, but so far there is little evidence in favour of this. Until further information is available on physical cycles in nature little can be added to the existing arguments.

The most feasible explanation for the cycle is that when climatic conditions are favourable, successful breeding allows a rapid build up in population density, almost logarithmic, until the food is in danger of being eaten out. The increased amount of social contact between individuals in the populations acts on some part of the nervous system and brings on the migratory habit. This habit is far from senseless, as it is supposed to be in the lemming, for it serves as a safety valve for the overcrowded population, and thereby conserves the food resources. Most migratory species become very sociable when they are out of their normal range, and this results in severe overgrazing and destruction of their newfound food supply. As the animals become poor in

condition, disease, which is normally kept suppressed in the population, takes a hold, and accelerates the decline. One school of thought maintains that the animals become more aggressive with increasing density, and the disruption to mating that this causes lowers the breeding rate. This school also holds that there is an increase in the frequency of occurrence of a gene for aggression, so that those few young that are born are more aggressive than their parents. When low densities are once more achieved, the frequency of occurrence of this gene is lowered, and breeding once more becomes successful.

We have seen, too, that the activities of predators can hardly be responsible for the control of the cycle. Predators have to be opportunists, increasing rapidly in numbers only when food conditions allow. Recent work in America has shown that carnivorous animals, eating a set number of rodents a day, lower the density of their prey populations more rapidly when the density is already low. Thus in a population of 100 rodents, a predator eating 1 rodent per day is taking 1% of the population a day. In a year of scarcity, when the population has, say, only 10 animals in it, the same predator eating the same amount of food per day is taking 10% of the whole. Before long it will no longer be profitable for the predator to hunt there any more, so it will move away or perish. If this event coincides with an improvement in the rodent food, then a rapid increase in rodent numbers occurs.

The one common feature underlying all cyclical populations is that they occur in regions of ecological simplicity. The paucity of species is a measure of the harshness of the environment, and under these conditions the food webs are relatively simple compared with conditions in temperate regions. In harsh conditions animals must have the ability to increase at a very high rate, if use is to be made of the short favourable periods, and if recovery is to be effected following climate induced catastrophes. In ecologically simple environments, the disruption of the mammal species affects the grouse because both eat the same type of food. The dependence of one species upon another is nowhere greater than in regions of ecological simplicity.

Migrations by cyclic species and irruptions by non-cyclic species have been shown then to serve the same function—offloading the reproductive excess on to uncolonized ground. Although much controversy surrounds the cause and control of cycles, the interaction between the animal and its food is sufficient to explain the phenomenon. The separate roles of disease and predators are little understood, but their effect would seem to be to accelerate the rate of decline of populations. Irruptions occur in areas of instability and often the species is a specialized feeder. When the food crop fails to develop, many individuals are forced to move away in search of more, or perish if they stay. Some species (e.g. the locust) appear to have adapted to the fickle nature of their food by the production of a special migratory phase or caste. In years of adequate food, the migratory generation moves only short distances, but it is always poised and ready to move large distances if necessary.

Cycles and oscillations serve to illustrate how precariously balanced and dependently interwoven are the life-histories of organisms in simple and unstable environments, and how a tiny tremor in the fabric of one population is amplified and accommodated for in some way by the seismograph of others.   D.M.S.

CYCLOPS, microscopic, somewhat pear-shaped freshwater crustaceans. While they all conform to the same general shape and structure, the detailed structure is variable, and this has given rise to much confusion in classification. Those who have wished to emphasize uniformity have followed the example of the late Robert Gurney in recognizing a single genus called *Cyclops* of which there are 46 species and subspecies on the British list alone: other workers, conscious that distinct differences are glossed over by Gurney's treatment, have used the name *Cyclops* to describe only one genus of cyclopoid copepod among several others. Those who have adopted the latter course, have nonetheless retained the basic name of *Cyclops* as a suffix, and have added prefixes such as *Acanth-, Mega-, Meso-* and so on.

The body of a *Cyclops* has two clearly defined parts, a bulbous anterior cephalothorax and a narrow posterior abdomen, a character which distinguishes it from that of a related group, the Harpacticoida. The first pair of antennae are no longer and often shorter than half the length of the body and have not more than 17 segments: in contrast the first pair of antennae in the related Calanoida are as long as the body and have not less than 17 segments. Unlike the eggs of both Harpacticoida and Calanoida, which are carried in a single sac, those of *Cyclops* are carried in a pair of sacs, one on each side of the abdomen.

Species of *Cyclops* are extremely widely distributed. Several are cosmopolitan and wherever there is a permanent body of fresh water some species may be present. In keeping with the greater variety of habitats around the margin of lakes or ponds, more species are usually found inshore than off-shore.

Eggs are carried until they hatch and an adult female needs to mate only once in her life. Thereafter she can lay a sucession of fertile batches of eggs (up to about ten) with no male present. After hatching, *Cyclops* passes through a series of naupliar and copepodid stages, shedding its outer chitinous skin, increasing in size and adding on appendages and segments, between each instar. There is much specific and individual variation in the number of eggs laid in each brood; it can be as high as 150 but is often lower. Few of those which hatch survive to become adult. Immature stages, though only $\frac{1}{16}$ of the size of the adults are at times much more numerous but because of their small size and transparency are not so easily seen.

Life-span from extruded egg to mature adult varies from two or three weeks to two or three years depending mainly on temperature and food. Growth rate is generally slower in the more advanced instars and in many

Cyclops, a one-eyed freshwater crustacean. The female carries two egg-sacs.

species the last two copepodid instars in particular are able to live for several months without moulting, sometimes under conditions of very low oxygen, often without feeding and occasionally, in some species, in a dormant state. Dormant copepodids of a few species form enveloping cysts, but most do not. Arrested development may be in summer for some species, winter for others, or extend over both seasons for yet others. The state is evidently a physiological one for although it may be ended prematurely by artificial changes in the environment, it cannot, once ended, be reinduced, by a return to the former conditions.

Cyclops, whether they are large or small species, have essentially the same kind of mouthparts, for grasping and chewing. Large species tend to feed more on animals than plants and vice versa, but there is no sharp distinction between the two. Organisms considerably larger than themselves, such as aquatic insects and the fry of fishes may be attacked and damaged.

Cyclops may harm fishes indirectly by harbouring larval stages of certain parasitic tapeworms which when eaten by a fish burrow through the gut wall where they form cysts. Fishes with many cysts develop peritonitis and anaemia and die. ORDER: Cyclopoida, SUBCLASS: Copepoda, CLASS: Crustacea, PHYLUM: Arthropoda.   W.J.P.S.

CYCLOPS THE ONE-EYED. One of the most distinctive features of the copepod crustaceans, that is *Cyclops* and its relatives, is the single red or black eye in the middle of the head. As described under the heading copepods this is truly a single eye and not the fusion of a pair of eyes as in some other crustaceans. This single eye has given *Cyclops* its name, the original Cyclops being the one-eyed giants that Odysseus and his men met on their long journey home from Troy. It is thought that the legend of these giants is based on the discovery of elephant skulls in which there is a single nasal opening in the forehead.

CYNODONTS, advanced group of carnivorous mammal-like reptiles which flourished in the early Mesozoic and which lie close to, if not on, the direct line of evolution to the mammals. In nearly every feature of their anatomy the cynodonts show a close approach to the mammalian structure. The teeth were differentiated into incisors, canines and molars, and the latter in advanced forms were cusped for masticating food. In all a bony secondary palate separated the nasal passage from the mouth so that air could be breathed while food was being chewed. The limbs were underslung in mammalian fashion, a large departure from the sprawling gait of their immediate ancestors. Long ribs surrounded the thorax and a mammalian type diaphragm was no doubt present. Much evidence suggests that the cynodonts were in fact warm-blooded reptiles. Their remains are common in the Triassic rocks of southern Africa and South America. ORDER: Cynodontia, CLASS: Reptilia.

CYTOLOGY, the branch of biology dealing with the structure, functions and life-history of cells and their component parts. The word is used mainly in connection with work done with the light microscope, i.e. at magnifications of up to about 2,500 times. The electron microscope, with its much greater magnification and resolving power, has revolutionized our knowledge of cell structure and these studies might logically be considered to fall within the scope of cytology but they are generally distinguished, at least by workers in this field, as cell microstructure or fine structure.

DAB *Limanda limanda,* a small flatfish living in sandy bays along the coasts of northern Europe. The dab, which reaches 17 in (43 cm) in length, can be recognized by the sharp curve of the lateral line near the pectoral fin and the spiny margins of the scales on the eyed side of the fish (these are smooth on the blind side). The general colour of the eyed side is sandy brown, flecked with orange and black, while the blind side is white. Occasionally specimens are found

Dab, enormously abundant European flatfish.

which are coloured on both sides and the scales are spiny on the two sides as well. The dab is common round British shores and reaches as far north as Iceland. These fishes are inactive during the day but feed at night and are more easily caught then. The breeding season is from March to May, the eggs being pelagic and amongst the smallest of any of the European flatfishes (averaging 0·8 mm in diameter).

The Long rough dab *Hippoglossoides platessoides* is a close relative of the halibut. It is a smaller fish and has rough-edged scales on the body but an almost straight lateral line. It is found on both sides of the Atlantic and is common at depths of 120–480 ft (40–160 m). FAMILY: Pleuronectidae, ORDER: Pleuronectiformes, CLASS: Pisces.

DABCHICK, name given to members of the genus *Tachylaptus.* Until recently they were included in the genus *Podiceps.* Freshwater diving birds, dabchicks include the

Least grebe *P. dominicus* of South America and tropical North America; the Little grebe *P. ruficollis* which is widespread in Europe, Africa and Asia; the Australian Black-throated little grebe *P. novaehollandiae;* Delacour's little grebe *P. rufolavatus,* and Hartlaub's little grebe *P. pelzelnii* of Madagascar; the New Zealand dabchick *P. rufopectus;* and the Australian Hoary-headed grebe *P. poliocephalus.* Dabchicks are typically the smaller species of the family—the Little grebe for example is 10–11 in (25–28 cm) long—and they have fewer ornamental plumes than other grebes. FAMILY: Podicipedidae, ORDER: Podicipitiformes, CLASS: Aves.

DABOIA *Vipera russelii,* or Russel's viper, a very colourful adder found in India and southern Asia and on some Indonesian islands.

DACE *Leuciscus leuciscus,* a small carp-like fish common in the rivers of England and the continent of Europe. The body is silvery with the back dark, the lower fins often having a yellow or orange tinge. The dace grows to 16 in (40 cm) in length and closely resembles a small chub. The dace, however, can be distinguished by the concave edges to the dorsal and anal fins, those of the chub being slightly convex. The dace is a shoaling fish, usually found near the surface of the water where it

feeds on flying insects as well as insect larvae, worms and snails. FAMILY: Cyprinidae, ORDER: Cypriniformes, CLASS: Pisces.

DADDY LONG LEGS, name most commonly referring to craneflies. Harvestmen are also sometimes called Daddy long legs because of their very long legs, and occasionally some long legged spiders are given the name. See craneflies and harvestmen. ORDER: Diptera, CLASS: Insecta, PHYLUM: Arthropoda.

DAHLIA ANEMONE *Tealia felina,* an anemone varying in colour from crimson and green less commonly to yellow and dull orange, with a broad, short body which is rough due to the presence of scattered greyish warts. Although common between tidemarks, the Dahlia anemone is much less well known than either the Beadlet or Snakelocks anemones.

It occurs in at least four varieties, three of which are offshore and deep-water forms. The variety found on the shore, generally at low-tide levels, is difficult to find because it covers itself with gravel which adheres to the very rough body. It is common round the coasts of Britain and extends north to Norway and the Faroes and south to the Atlantic coast of France. Two of the offshore varieties may be seen in very deep rock

Dace, European freshwater fish, valued as a sports fish, but too small and bony for eating.

Damselfishes

Dahlia anemone of European coasts.

cracks where they are never exposed at low tide and are of variable colour. A circumpolar variety is also known which does not occur as far south as the British Isles. This lacks the rough body and is viviparous, in contrast to the other varieties in which fertilization of the ova and development of the young anemones occur in the sea. FAMILY: Actiniidae, ORDER: Actiniaria, CLASS: Anthozoa, PHYLUM: Cnidaria.

DAMSELFISHES, small tropical coral-reef fishes related to the perches. The damselfishes, which are often very brightly coloured, are mostly small and rarely exceed 6 in (15 cm) in length.

The Three-striped damselfish *Dascyllus aruanus* of the Indo-Pacific.

One of the few that grows larger, and also one of the few to be found outside the tropics, is the garibaldi *Hypsyops rubicunda* from the Pacific. This fish is a brilliant orange in colour and grows to 12 in (30 cm). The garibaldi is one of the many fishes that are capable of making noises by clicking together the pharyngeal or throat teeth. Many of the damselfishes exhibit a strong territorial behaviour, each fish having its own particular cranny in the coral and guarding this jealously. Members of the genus *Dascyllus* live in shoals and when danger threatens the

whole shoal seems to disappear into the coral. Several species of *Dascyllus* are imported into Europe for aquarists.

The remarkable clownfish is discussed elsewhere.

The damselfishes are among the most colourful of the inhabitants of the coral reefs. The Cocoa damselfish *Eupomacentrus variabilis* from Puerto Rico, which does not exceed 3 in (8 cm) in length, is rich blue on the upper-part of the head, shoulders and front of the dorsal fin and a lemon yellow fading to lime green on the edges of the fins. In the Bicolor damselfish *E. partitus* the front half of the body is black and the rear part lemon to white, with a clear-cut division between the two colour zones. The Sergeant major *Abudefduf saxatilis* occurs in all tropical seas. As well as having a wide distribution it also has a very wide dietary range, feeding on anything from algae to anemones and from sea-slugs to fishes. FAMILY: Pomacentridae, ORDER: Perciformes, CLASS: Pisces.

DAMSELFLIES, dragonflies of the suborder Zygoptera which, although resembling other dragonflies structurally and ecologically in all important respects, can be recognized by their more delicate build and by their possession of similar fore and hindwings stalked at the base. The larvae, which are aquatic, are distinguished by having external gills. Compared with other dragonflies, they are weak flyers. Some of the commoner species in

The West Indian damselfish *Chromis coerulens*.

Britain (e.g. *Coenagrion puella, Enallagma cyathigerum*) look like pale blue needles as they hover low among the vegetation along the edges of ponds and canals. See dragonflies. SUBORDER: Zygoptera, ORDER: Odonata, CLASS: Insecta, PHYLUM: Arthropoda.

DANIOS, small tropical carp-like fishes belonging to the genera *Danio* and *Brachydanio* and very popular with aquarists. The danios are slim, lively fishes, often brightly coloured and usually with two pairs of barbels. They are found in shoals in the rivers of southern India, Burma and the Indo-Malayan Peninsula.

The Pearl danio *Brachydanio albolineatus*, of India and Sumatra, is so called because of the beautiful pearly iridescence of its pink or grey-green body. It grows to 2½ in (6 cm) in length. The zebra-fish *Brachydanio rerio* has horizontal blue and gold stripes along the flanks, reaches less than 2 in (4·5 cm) and is found in eastern India. The Spotted danio *B. nigrofasciatus* of Burma is slightly smaller and has a light brown stripe along the flanks bordered above and below by thin blue stripes, with a number of blue spots on the lower half of the body. One of the largest species is the Giant danio *Danio malabaricus* of Ceylon and western India. It grows to nearly 5 in (12 cm) and has a much deeper but compressed body. The back is a slate blue-grey and there are three or four steel-blue

Damselflies *Calopteryx virgo* mating. These are small delicate dragonflies commonly seen around ponds.

stripes along the flanks which become fainter towards the tail.

Danios are easy to keep in an aquarium and are also easy to breed. Occasionally other species are imported, but the four listed here are the most popular. FAMILY: Cyprinidae, ORDER: Cypriniformes, CLASS: Pisces.

Danio aequipinnatus of southeast Asia.

DAPHNIA, the small crustacean properly known as the *Water flea, although this name is sometimes used for other small freshwater crustaceans.

DARKLING BEETLES, a large family of terrestrial beetles which vary widely in general appearance, although most species are dark brown or black. They range in size from a few millimetres to 1–2 cm in length. Many live under bark, while others such as the *Flour beetle, have become serious pests of stored products. Darkling beetles are well represented in the faunas of hot deserts where they are often the dominant group of ground beetles. FAMILY: Tenebrionidae, ORDER: Coleoptera, CLASS: Insecta, PHYLUM: Arthropoda.

DARTERS, a group of aquatic birds related to the cormorants (Phalacrocoracidae) and sometimes placed in that family although more usually in one of their own (Anhingidae). The common name used in America is anhinga, a Brazilian word which has also become the generic name. Popular alternatives include Water turkey (in America) and snakebird, the latter from the swaying of the long slender neck.

The different forms replace each other geographically and some taxonomists regard them as constituting a single species, *Anhinga anhinga*; commonly, as here however, they

are grouped into four species. They have a pantropical distribution, including some subtropical areas. The anhinga (*A. anhinga*, in the restricted sense) is found in the Americas from the southern United States to northern Argentina; the African darter *A. rufa* in the Middle East, through most of Africa south of the Sahara and in Madagascar; the Indian darter *A. melanogaster* in southern Asia east to the Celebes; and the Australian darter *A. novaehollandiae* in New Guinea and Australia.

Darters resemble attenuated cormorants. The body is elongated and the neck very markedly so, the wings and tail are long, the head is small and the bill is long and thin but with no terminal hook. Including bill, neck and tail the birds are nearly 3 ft (1 m) long. All four toes are connected by a web. The plumage is for the most part black or dark brown, with a few lighter markings and with pale areas below from the chin downwards. The sexes are only slightly dissimilar, but in the breeding season the male has white tufts on the sides of the head and neck.

They live near lakes, slow-flowing rivers and calm estuaries. The birds are highly adapted to an aquatic life. They often swim on the surface with the body deeply sub-merged, and they go under without any jump. The food consists mainly of fishes, caught by underwater pursuit. Among the anatomical differences separating darters from cormorants is a kink in the neck due to a conformation of the cervical vertebrae by which the bill becomes a 'triggered spear', the head being suddenly thrust forward as the neck is straightened. Indeed fishes seem to be speared on occasion, but commonly the prey is brought to the surface between the mandibles, tossed in the air, caught in the gape and swallowed.

Although clumsy in taking-off from the surface of the water—preferring to launch themselves from a perch—and in alighting, darters are strong fliers. They also glide and on occasion soar. They show a preference for waters with wooded shores and com-monly perch on trees, or on partly sub-merged logs, often with the wings extended to dry. They also roost and nest in trees gregariously and are often found with other species as well. In Africa an association with the small Longtailed shag or Reed duiker *Phalacrocorax africanus* is particularly com-mon. The nest, in a tree or bush near and often overhanging the water, is a platform of sticks, sometimes bulky. The three to six eggs are pale blue or green under a chalky outer layer. The young are hatched naked but grow a pale down plumage while in the nest. Both parents incubate the eggs and tend the young. FAMILY: Anhingidae, ORDER: Pelecaniformes, CLASS: Aves.   A.L.T.

DARTERS, small freshwater perch-like fishes found in North America. They derive their common name from their habit of darting between stones. They occur only in the temperate parts of North America to the east of the Rocky Mountains and about 95 species are known. They are bottom-living forms and some have surprisingly bright colours compared with most freshwater fishes of temperate waters. They lack swim-bladders and have two dorsal fins, the first spiny and the second soft-rayed. The darters are carnivorous, feeding on small insect lar-vae and tiny crustaceans. The entire body is scaled in most species. Their spawning habits vary widely: some bury their eggs in sand or gravel, others carefully guard the eggs and still others simply scatter the eggs and leave them. The Johnny darter *Etheostoma nigrum* spawns in the spring, the female depositing the eggs on the underside of stones and the male aerating them and guarding them in a most ferocious manner for a fish of only $2\frac{1}{2}$ in (6·5 cm).

The Eastern sand darter *Ammocrypta pel-lucida* has a row of scales only along the midline. It is sand-coloured and translucent and like most darters is secretive, burying itself in the sandy beds of streams with only

The anhinga, underwater javelin-thrower with a trigger in its neck.

its eyes and snout protruding. It reaches 3 in (7·5 cm) in length. Most darters live in clear shallow streams but *Etheostoma fusiforme* lives in murky, swampy waters and has been found in estuaries. The Log perches are the largest of the darters. *Percina caprodes* grows to 6 in (15 cm) and the flanks are marked by dark vertical bars which gave rise to the alternative name of zebrafish.

Although darters are common and wide-spread over a large part of the United States, their small size and secretive habits have meant that they are rarely seen unless especi-ally looked for. FAMILY: Percidae, ORDER: Perciformes, CLASS: Pisces.

DARWIN, Charles Robert, 1809–1882. He was a British naturalist and the most import-ant biologist of all time. Son of Robert Darwin, highly successful physician, and grandson of Erasmus Darwin, naturalist, ec-centric and philosopher, as well as physician, Charles Darwin was the fortunate possessor of qualities and recipient of experiences which, when integrated, were to result in his grand synthesis concerning evolution by natural selection: *The Origin of Species* (1859). The Darwinian theory of natural selection has become the most solid of foundations upon which to build the fabric of our knowledge of the organic world. As with

all great works some aspects of Darwinian theory may be found wanting in the light of new discoveries, but it is amazing how few mistakes Darwin made and how elaborately his theory has been confirmed by subsequent investigation.

Darwin had an undistinguished early career, though even in childhood he showed the beginnings of a deep interest in natural history and qualities such as perseverance which were to serve him well later. His mother died when he was eight and he attended a local boarding school for seven years—a period which he considered an educational blank and in which his enormous potential remained completely unrecognized. Before he was 17 he was sent to Edinburgh to read medicine but found the instruction, entirely by lectures, intolerably dull: 'Dr Duncan's lectures on Materia Medica at eight o'clock on a winter's morning are something fearful to remember.' Accord-ingly, after two years his father suggested that he should become a clergyman and he went to Cambridge in 1828 to study to this end. In his autobiography he notes 'Con-sidering how fiercely I have been attacked by the orthodox it seems ludicrous that I once intended to be a clergyman.' And again: 'It never struck me how illogical it was to say that I believed in what I could not under tand and what is in fact unintelligible.' Also, unfortunately: 'During the three years which I spent at Cambridge my time was wasted, as far as the academical studies were concerned, as completely as at Edinburgh and at school.' However, while at Cambridge he developed a passion for collecting beetles, an activity which gave him first-hand knowledge of the variety of forms in a single group and the ways in which these forms are grouped together in natural assemblages of different degrees of similarity. He also made the acquaintance of a number of eminent men, such as Henslow, Professor of Botany, who added to his already considerable knowledge and understanding of natural history. Thus, when through Henslow he was offered the place of naturalist on the voyage of the *Beagle* around the world he was well-qualified to fill the position.

The voyage of the *Beagle,* from December 1831 to October 1836, was the most important event in Darwin's life for it enabled him to study in the greatest possible detail the teeming flora and fauna of tropical forests, the puzzling coral formations of warm seas, the geological strata of many countries, and the unique inhabitants of isolated oceanic islands such as the Galapagos. Any lesser man would have been overwhelmed by the wealth of information presented and recorded, but Darwin's ability was such that he was able to concentrate fiercely on whatever was in hand and to compare all relevant data without losing sight of the wood or the trees.

The idea of evolution by means of natural selection probably came to Darwin during the voyage of the *Beagle,* being reinforced—not initiated as is usually said to be the case—by his reading in September 1838 of Malthus' *Essay on Population.* Certainly, the early *Ornithological Notes* written during the voyage show that he was searching for

an evolutionary concept, though to begin with, like many others he did not have the clarifying and crystallizing idea of natural selection. In July 1837, in the midst of numerous other labours, he opened his first notebook concerning the variations of animals and plants. It was not until June 1842 that he wrote the first brief abstract (35 pages) of his theory, such was his caution and his determination to avoid prejudice. This abstract he expanded to 230 pages in the summer of 1844. In the following years he continued to collect and collate information until in 1856, on the advice of Sir Charles Lyell, he began an extensive sketch of his views. This, although only an abstract, was on a scale three or four times as extensive as that of the *Origin,* but was only half completed because in the summer of 1858 he received an essay from A. R. Wallace in the Malay archipelago containing the same basic theory as his own. Darwin was quite prepared to give Wallace priority—although he himself had been working for over 20 years on the subject—but his colleagues persuaded him otherwise. The result was that part of his 1844 abstract, together with a letter he had sent to Asa Gray in 1857 outlining his 'species theory', and Wallace's essay, were read before the Linnean Society, and published in the *Journal of the Proceedings of the Linnean Society, Zoology,* August 20, 1858.

The *Origin of Species* was begun almost immediately, Darwin abstracting his previous lengthy abstract and completing the work in $13\frac{1}{2}$ months. It was published in November 1859 and had an immediate, and continuing, sales success. It is not, however, a very readable book, and its original success must be in part due to the enthusiastic *Times* review (actually written by T. H. Huxley) and the controversial nature of its contents. Of the most outstanding importance, it is

read by relatively few biologists, yet its basic ideas are simple—so simple that T. H. Huxley was moved to remark 'How stupid of me not to have thought of that!' The simplest things, however, are often the most powerful, and require the greatest genius to first perceive them.

Simply stated, Darwin's theory is as follows: 'Animals reproduce excessively prolifically, yet their numbers remain relatively constant—therefore there must be a struggle for existence. Animals also vary, no two being exactly alike, and the struggle for existence is based on these variations.' The more one is familiar with animals in their natural environment the more one is able to appreciate the power of this general statement.

We must remember also that Darwin made a considerable number of other major contributions to natural science. His work in botany, geology, and soil science ranks amongst the best, and his monograph on the barnacles is still the major contribution to our knowledge of the group. Also he was an ecologist and ethologist before these terms were used in their present designation for those who work on the inter-relations of organisms or on their psychology. And he was a first-class experimenter. To do Darwin justice is impossible; we yet await a scientist of sufficient competence.

P.M.D.

DARWIN'S FINCHES, a group of sparrow-like birds confined to the Galapagos archipelago (13 species) and Cocos Island, 600 miles (960 km) northeast of the Galapagos (a single endemic species). Although the original stock is unknown, they probably arose by speciation within the islands after the colonization of the islands by a single species, probably a finch. The group provides the best avian example of adaptive

Darwin's first diagram, drawn in 1837, shows how a number of species could have descended from a common ancestor at the base of the tree (1).

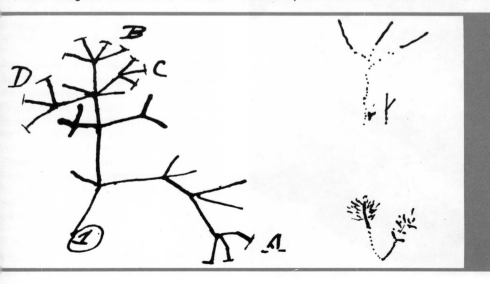

Darwin's diagram further shows how the extinction of some species (twigs ending blindly) results in increasing the gaps between the surviving species (twigs ending in cross-bars). This explains why the differences between species are unequal and how genera are formed from groups of species on one branch; 'Between A and B immense gap of relation, between C and B the finest gradation, between B and D, rather greater distinction'. Top right illustrates Darwin's statement that 'the tree of life should perhaps be called the coral of life, bases of branches dead so that passages cannot be seen'. Bottom right shows that 'fish can be traced right down to simple organisation. Birds not'. (First Notebook on Transmutation of Species.)

Dassies

radiation into ecological niches as this radiation has taken place so recently that some of the intermediate forms are still extant.

Superficially these birds are rather uninspiring, so like sparrows that it is great credit to Gould that he was able to interpret the skins correctly when he first described the group. Since then detailed studies by Swarth, Lack (see his book *Darwin's finches*) and Bowman have shown how interesting are these birds in the study of evolution. Historically they are important for the impression they made on Darwin during his short visit to the islands. To quote him, 'the most curious fact is the perfect graduation in size of the beaks in the different species of *Geospiza* (which include six species known as cactus- and ground-finches), from one as large as that of a hawfinch to that of a chaffinch'.

The *Geospiza* species feed on the ground and the different bills enable each species to deal efficiently with a different range of seeds so that on the larger islands, which have a range of different habitats, the various species can co-exist. The exceptions are the two species of cactus-finch, *G. scandens* and *G. conirostris*. These two species are restricted to islands with the Prickly pear cactus *Opuntia,* and as only one species is found on any one island, the slight differences in the bills may be insufficient to prevent severe competition between them, so that one species will always oust the other.

The other large group are the tree-finches *Camarhynchus,* the six species of which can be conveniently divided into three subgenera: *Camarhynchus* of three species which feed on largish insects and soft seeds,

Above: Map showing the Galapagos islands 600 miles to the west of Ecuador (South America). Below Four Darwin's finches and (centre) the Plush-capped finch *Catamblyrhynchus diadema* of Ecuador, bird of the type that probably crossed the 600 miles of ocean to settle on the Galapagos and give ris to a proliferation of species now known as Darwin's finches. Four of the species of Darwin's finche are shown here: (from left to right) Warbler finch *Certhidea olivacea* Albemarle Island (Isla Isabella Small ground finch *Geospiza fuliginosa* Barrington Island (I. Sante Fé), Medium ground finch *G. fort* Indefatigable Island (I. Chavez) and Large ground finch *G. magnirostris* Chatham Island (I. San Cristoba

Platyspiza with a single species eating buds, leaves and fleshy fruits and *Cactospiza* of two insect-eating species. Again there are marked differences in bill size and shape correlated with the different diets. The woodpecker- and mangrove-finches *Cactospiza pallida* and *C. heliobates* regularly use small twigs and cactus spines to prod out insects which they would otherwise be unable to reach. The two remaining finches, the warbler-finch *Certhidea olivacea* and the Cocos-

finch *Pinarolaxias inornata* have thin bil and eat mainly insects, although the latte species may also eat some nectar. Th warbler-finch is a superb example of cor vergent evolution as in outward appearanc and feeding habits it is exactly similar to true warbler. Its true relationships are onl shown by its internal structure and nestin habits.

There is no doubt as to the close relation ships of these birds or that they have arise from some common ancestor, but they ca hardly have speciated unless they had bee separated from each other geographicall Probably they became differentiated on di ferent islands and became so genetically an ecologically distinct that when they met late they remained separate and natural selectio favoured more divergence and the adaptiv radiation we now see. FAMILY: Fringillidae ORDER: Passeriformes, CLASS: Aves. M.P.H

DASSIES, mammals about the size of marmot yet showing definite links with suc animals as the elephants, rhinoceroses an tapirs. They were at one time placed with th ungulates, but they are now in a separat order, the Hyracoidea, which consists of tw genera and three species. In size and genera form they appear to have much in commo with the rodents, and yet their finer detail place them between the perissodactyl ur gulates and the elephants. The points the have in common relate to their skeletal an nervous structure.

One of the most remarkable features c these small animals is the feet. The forefee have four functional toes and a rudimentar

Geospiza fortis one of the Ground finches of the 14 species of Darwin's finches.

first toe, all of which have short nails in the manner of the rhinoceros. The hindfeet have only three toes, of which the inner has a curved claw. The other toes are similar to those on the front feet. The alimentary canal is unusual in having a supplementary caecum and the brain of the dassie is more akin to that of an ungulate than a rodent. The collar bones are not developed and the tail is short. The incisors of the upper jaw grow from persistent pulps and are curved as in rodents. They do not follow the rodent plan of ending in a chisel-like edge, but are prismatic and end in fine points. There is one pair of incisors in the top jaw, but those in the lower jaw number four and differ in being rooted. The outermost pair tend to lie flat and have trilobate crowns. The grinding or cheekteeth, separated from the incisors by a considerable gap, are seven in number and resemble those of a rhinoceros.

The dassie, Rock hyrax, Rock rabbit or coney, *Procavia capensis* is about the size of a rabbit, has a blunt head with small ears and is covered with soft brown fur. In the middle of the back is a yellowish white patch of hair that marks the site of the dorsal gland.

The dassie is found in Africa from Algeria and Libya through southern Egypt to the Cape Province of South Africa. It also occurs in southern Arabia and Syria. Dassies live in groups of 60 and more, making their homes in cliffs and on rocky hilltops. They are experts at climbing rocks and boulders.

They feed mainly on plants and fruits, but they will also eat lichens and seeds. Their feeding times are rigid and they will appear for this purpose in the early morning and the late afternoon. They also have the habit of using a communal latrine in their dens, and the excrement that collects here has a commercial value, as it contains an ingredient used in the manufacture of perfumes. They spend a large part of their day basking in the sun, but they also have to keep at least one eye open for predators such as leopards, hawks and eagles. When alarmed they either utter a whistling note or make a chattering noise. The litter of two or three young are born after a gestation period of $7\frac{1}{2}$ months (225 days). At the time of their birth the young are able to see and very soon after they are born they can follow the mother.

The Syrian hyrax *Procavia syriaca* is very similar to the Rock hyrax or dassie. This is the 'coney' of the Bible. The Tree dassie, or bosdas *Dendrohyrax arboreus* is a tree-dwelling hyrax which differs slightly from the dassie in that the fur is often longer, the coat may vary from a rich brown to a grizzled grey and the soles of the feet are entirely naked, allowing it to move with ease in the trees. It is found from South Africa northwards into the Belgian Congo, Tanzania and Kenya. In other respects it is very similar to the dassie. The cry differs in that it starts with a series of groans and culminates in a screaming wail. FAMILY: Procaviidae, ORDER: Hyracoidea, CLASS: Mammalia.

N.J.C.

Dassies or Rock hyraxes on their rock outcrop, ready to bolt into the crevices at first alarm.

DASYURE *Dasyurus quoll,* alternative name for the *Native cat of southeast Australia and Tasmania. See Marsupial cat.

DEAD MAN'S FINGERS *Alcyonium digitatum,* a typical Soft coral, drab yellowish-white in colour and shaped rather like a human hand. It is a colony of octocoralline *polyps which can be found in temperate waters, although most Soft corals prefer warm seas. The colony is a mass of mesogloea in which the polyps are embedded. Each polyp bears eight feathery tentacles and is very much elongated, the cylindrical tube-like body extending through the mesogloea to the base of the colony. It is connected to other polyps in the colony by tube-like extensions of the body wall which leave at varying places from the body. The skeleton consists of a mass of spicules, elongated spindles of calcium carbonate which are secreted by ectodermal cells and generally distributed through the mesogloea. As typical members of the phylum Cnidaria, the polyps catch their prey by means of *nematocysts on the feathery tentacles. See Soft coral. FAMILY: Alcyoniidae, ORDER: Alcyonacea, CLASS: Anthozoa, PHYLUM: Cnidaria.

DEALFISHES, a family of ribbon-like oceanic fishes related to the oarfish and the opah and usually found in deep water in all oceans. Although quite large, dealfishes are very fragile and it is often difficult to determine the exact form of the fins. In some species there are two dorsal fins, the first one consisting of a few elongated rays narrowly separated from the second long dorsal fin; in other species the two dorsal fins are united. The anal fin is missing, the pectoral fins are very small and the pelvic fins are reduced or absent. The most curious feature is the tail. Only the upper half is present and this sticks up like a fan at right angles to the body. The changes that occur in the fins during the development of the fish have been studied in the vaagmar *Trachipterus arcticus* of the North Atlantic. In the small larvae the first dorsal finrays are elongated into filaments several times the length of the body and the pelvic fins are also filamentous. As the fish grows, these filaments shorten and some of the pelvic finrays are lost so that only two or three are present in the adult. The tail of the young fish has the rays of the lower lobe elongated while the upper lobe is barely developed. Gradually the lower rays shorten and finally disappear while the upper lobe grows into the vertical fan-like structure found in the adult. The young appear to live in deep and calm water where the filaments are not liable to damage and can be used to support the fish by increasing its surface area.

The vaagmar is the dealfish occasionally washed up on European shores. It derives its name from Old Icelandic, meaning 'Sea horse'. It is found everywhere in the Atlantic and has even been recorded from New Zealand. It lives at depths down to 1,800 ft (600 m). The largest specimen washed ashore was 8 ft (2·4 m) in length. Few people have been fortunate enough to see this fish alive, but in 1966 an angler caught a specimen of 4 (1·2 m) at Marsden on the northeast coast of England. Another specimen of 6 ft 2 in (1·9 m) was measured and found to have a body depth of 14 in (35 cm) but a body width of only 3¼ in (8 cm). A related species *T. iris,* is found in the Mediterranean and the tropical southern Atlantic. A small form growing to only 12 in (30 cm) from South Africa and named *T. cristatus* may perhaps merely be the young of a known larger species.

Curious legends have been associated with dealfishes, although some of the stories may have been based in part on the oarfish. Several species in different countries are known as 'King of the herrings' and one species from the Pacific has been called *T. rexsalmonorum,* that is 'King of the salmon'. The Vikings believed that if anyone hurt one of these dealfishes it would drive away that important food fish, the herring (the fish in the legend may, however, have been the oarfish). Some tribes of American Indians on the American Pacific coast had a similar fable concerning *T. rexsalmonorum.* The basis for these legends has never been satisfactorily explained.

The dealfishes, together with the oarfish and opah, were formerly placed in the order Allotriognathi or 'strange jaws', an allusion to the curious method of jaw protrusion shared by these fishes. By depression of the lower jaw, the whole upper jaw is pushed forward, the mechanism being essentially the same in the deep-bodied opah as in the ribbon-like forms.

The dealfishes are all fairly rare and if any are found washed up on beaches they should be preserved if possible and a museum or other institution notified. FAMILY: Trachipteridae, ORDER: Lampridiformes, CLASS: Pisces.

DEATH ADDER *Acantophis antarcticus,* a dangerous *elapid snake that looks like an adder because of its short body. It lives in Australia and New Guinea, where there are no adders or vipers.

DEATH WATCH BEETLE *Xestobium rufovillosum,* a small wood-boring beetle related to the woodworm, about ¼ in (5– mm) long, dark chocolate-brown with patches of yellowish scales which soon wear off. The head, in common with all members of

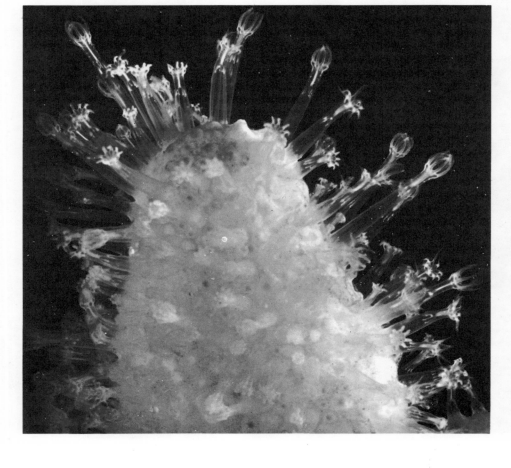

Portion of a colony of Dead man's fingers with polyps expanded.

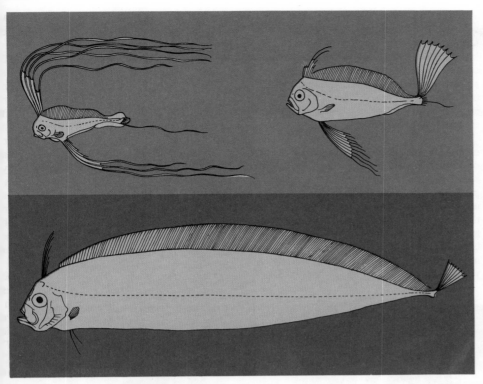

Vaagmar, the dealfish *Trachipterus arcticus* (below). In the small larva (left above) the first dorsal finrays and the pelvic fins are elongated into filaments, which shorten as the fish grows (right above).

its family, is deeply sunk into the prothorax, giving a hooded appearance, but unlike all other members its wing-cases are not marked with longitudinal grooves or striae. Although under favourable circumstances out-of-doors the length of its life-cycle may be as little as one year, when infesting interior woodwork this may take ten years or longer, depending on the state of fungal decay of the wood it is eating. The presence of wood-rotting fungi appears to be obligatory for the development of the beetle which usually emerges in April or May. It is seldom seen to fly. Perhaps the best-known feature of the Death watch beetle, however, is the tapping noise it makes, by both sexes striking the head, usually against the wood on which the insect is standing, and appears to act as a sexual call. The heavy incidence of attack by woodworm *Anobium punctatum* in the United Kingdom, amounting to some 10 million of the 17 million national stock of dwellings, tends to overshadow infestations by other woodboring insects in buildings. The Death watch beetle is, however, of great importance as a pest of historic buildings. It is to be found out-of-doors where the larvae inhabit pockets of rotting wood in pollard willows and in dying branches of over-mature oaks. Infestations by this species are almost entirely confined to buildings where large dimensioned timbers were installed at least 100 years ago and it seems virtually certain that Death watch larvae went into the buildings with the timber in the first place. There are no new infesta-

tions of Death watch beetle so that with progressive control, the number of viable infestations is decreasing. FAMILY: Anobiidae, ORDER: Coleoptera, CLASS: Insecta, PHYLUM: Arthropoda.   N.E.H.

DECAPOD CRUSTACEANS, term applied to the larger Crustacea, such as lobsters, crabs and shrimps which possess five pairs of walking legs. The ten-armed squids and cuttlefishes are also called decapods. Decapod simply means ten legs and it is therefore necessary, when talking about decapods, to indicate which we mean by adding 'mollusc' or 'crustacean' to the term unless the context is completely clear. Decapod crustaceans fall into two main groups: those that are largely swimming animals such as shrimps and prawns and those which are chiefly crawling, walking animals, that is the crabs, lobsters, crayfishes and Hermit crabs. ORDER: Decapoda, CLASS: Crustacea, PHYLUM: Arthropoda.

DEEP-SEA FISHES belong to a number of families which are not necessarily closely related to each other but which have independently evolved highly modified forms suitable to the rather extraordinary conditions of the deeps. Passing from the shallower waters of the continental slope into the deeper waters, one can see a transition in the fishes. Dr Lev Andriashev, the Russian ichthyologist, has suggested that there are, in fact, two distinct kinds of deep-sea fishes.

Those in the primary group are highly modified and seem to have evolved within the deeps, while those in the secondary group are less modified and appear to have evolved in shallow water, only later being forced into the deeper water, perhaps as a result of competition with other species. It was originally thought that the deeper waters of the world might harbour primitive relicts from the time when fishes first evolved. This has not proved to be the case, the deep-sea fishes being merely highly modified and specialized versions of quite advanced groups of fishes.

The deeps are usually taken to mean water below about 650 ft (200 m). No light penetrates to this depth and without light plants cannot grow. Animals living at this depth must, therefore, either feed on other animals (carnivorous) or, if small enough, browse on the detritus that filters down from above. A map of the world shows that two thirds of the earth's surface is covered by water of a depth of over 650 ft (200 m), so that the ocean depths represent a huge environment, but one that is very sparsely populated. Some shallow-water fishes, such as the cod *Gadus morhua*, are found below 650 ft but they are merely visitors. Conversely, many of the true deep-sea fishes regularly migrate every night towards the surface, descending again with the dawn.

Many problems confront the deep-sea fishes. Those that migrate vertically each day, sometimes as much as 5,000 ft (1,500 m), must overcome the great difference in pressure. Even cod trawled from a few hundred metres down will 'explode', the gut of the fish forced out of its mouth by the sudden expansion of the swimbladder as the pressure is decreased. Deep-sea fishes overcome this either by releasing air from the swimbladder as they ascend or they are species that lack a swimbladder. Most of the deep-sea fishes are small, with bone and muscle poorly developed, for there is little use in being swimmers in an environment which is almost uniformly cold and dark. Only when food or predators are near is it necessary to swim from one spot to another with any haste. Most of the deep-sea fishes are pelagic and only a few ever see the bottom. Below 2,000 ft (600 m) the fish populations become very sparse and the chances of meeting food or a mate are slender. To overcome this, various specializations have evolved.

The most striking of the modifications found in deep-sea fishes are the *light organs. The light may derive from colonies of bacteria contained in special glands (often covered by a transparent scale, sometimes tinted) or it may result from chemical actions under the control of the fish. In the Lantern fishes (family Myctophidae) the light organs are arranged in rows over the body, appearing as pearly spots the pattern of which

Deep-sea fishes

differs in each species. This suggests that the pattern is used by the fishes as a means of identifying members of their own species, both to avoid preying on their own species and to aid in recognizing a possible mate.

Light is also used by the ceratioid or Deep-sea anglerfishes to provide a luminous lure to attract prey. The first ray of the dorsal fin is enlarged and can be bent forwards so that a fleshy luminous bulb at its tip can be dangled in front of the mouth. Inquisitive fishes are then seized and swallowed. This fishing method is brought to perfection by another fish, *Galatheathauma*, which has a luminous flap actually on the roof of the mouth. It simply waits with its mouth open until a smaller fish swims inside.

In some deep-sea fishes the light organs are used to illuminate the darkness around the fish. A biologist on the research ship

William Scoresby watched an eel-like stomiatoid fish one night during a cruise in the Antarctic. The fish, which was about 12 in (30 cm) long, had powerful luminous organs that emitted a beam of blue light sufficient to illuminate the water up to 24 in (60 cm) in front. Any small shrimp-like animals caught in the beam were immediately snapped up.

The sparsity of animal life in the depths means that whenever food is encountered the opportunity must not be wasted, even if, in some cases, the prey is larger than the predator. The viperfish *Chauliodus* is unusual amongst fishes in that the head can be thrown upwards to increase the gape of the mouth and thus enable the fish to swallow larger animals. Its long, thin teeth—a common feature of deep-sea fishes—help to prevent the prey from escaping during the act of

swallowing. In the Black swallower *Chiasmodon niger* the gape of the jaws is enormous and the stomach is distensible, so that this species can swallow and accommodate fishes that are actually twice as large as the predator itself. The speed with which the jaws are snapped shut is obviously important. In the stomiatoid genus *Malacosteus* much of the walls and floor of the mouth are missing; presumably this allows the jaws to be snapped shut extremely quickly, the jaw encountering much less resistance to water than if membranes were present.

Deep-sea fishes live in water below 650 ft (200 m) where no light penetrates. Without light plants cannot grow and these animals must therefore feed on other animals. Opposite: One of the Snaggle-toothed fishes *Astronesthes*; top left: Juvenile Deep-sea anglers; bottom left, Deep-sea angler; top right: *Anoplogaster*; bottom right: viperfish.

Deep-sea fishes that migrate into the upper waters tend to have fairly large eyes, while those that remain in the very deep waters have eyes that are reduced or even absent. Vision is important to fishes that recognize their prey or mates by their light organs. In the giant-tails (family Giganturidae) the eyes are tubular and project from both sides of the head, giving the fish binocular vision, a rare feature in fishes. The deep-sea salmonid *Opisthoproctus* has tubular eyes that point upwards. In the family Ipnopidae the eyes in some species are merely enlarged retinas under a greatly flattened cornea, sometimes with luminous patches near the eyes. In the genus *Idiacanthus* the eyes of the young are set on the ends of stalks but are normal in the adults.

The *lateral line organs, sometimes referred to as the organs of distant touch, are normally in canals below the skin, with small pores communicating with the outside. In some deep-sea fishes, such as the Gulper eels, the lateral line organs are on stalks, presumably for greater sensitivity. Other deep-sea fishes have greatly elongated bodies and thus very long lateral line canals down the flanks. This may increase the sensitivity of the organ.

Breeding in deep-sea fishes is obviously extremely difficult to observe and deductions must be made from specimens brought to the surface. Examination of Deep-sea anglerfishes shows that their breeding habits are unique amongst the vertebrates. The specimens brought to the surface were dumpy, with a large mouth fringed with pointed teeth and, depending on the species, ranged in length from a few inches to almost 3 ft (1 m)—and they were females. It was then noticed that some of the larger ones had one or more small tubular and fleshy appendages hanging from the body and on investigation these proved to be the males. The males, which are slim with small mouths and chisel-like teeth at the front, are free-swimming only until they meet a female. They then bite into her skin and eventually their bodies fuse with that of the female and each male becomes parasitic on the female. The male loses its alimentary tract and sense organs and a placenta-like connection keeps him supplied with nourishment from the blood of the female. Eventually, the male degenerates into a sac of testes hanging from the female. The only free-swimming males found have been immature and presumably those that fail to find a female must die. Spawning takes place in summer. The eggs float to the surface but after hatching the larvae slowly sink again to the depths and the sexes begin their different patterns of development.

The deep-sea fishes provide a spectacular example of the way in which animals can become adapted to an apparently adverse environment. The increasing depth at which underwater observations can be made will help to resolve many puzzling features in the biology of these fishes.

DEER, ruminants, most of which carry bony antlers which are shed and renewed annually throughout life. They belong to the family Cervidae, which is a very extensive one consisting of no less than 17 genera, 40 species and over 190 subspecies.

Deer chew the cud and like other ruminants, including antelope, cattle, sheep and goats, are characterized by the absence of incisors or cutting teeth in the upper jaw. Instead of upper incisors, they have a callous pad against which the cutting teeth of the lower jaw can press. The normal dentition of all deer is either 32 or 34 teeth, depending on whether upper canines are present or not. In four genera, Tufted deer *Elaphodus*; the muntjac *Muntiacus*; Musk deer *Moschus* and Water deer *Hydropotes,* and in particular the last two, the upper canines of the males have developed into tusks which project from the gums to a considerable length. In the case of the Musk deer and Water deer, neither of which grow antlers, these tusks are the primary offensive weapons used when fighting other males, or in defence against a predator. Amongst the living Cervidae, the Musk deer and the Water deer stand apart from the remainder in their lack of antlers, although on the small Tufted deer of northeast Burma and southwest China, the antlers are, as its name suggests, hidden by tufts of hair, and, apart from the reindeer or caribou, genus *Rangifer*, the females of all deer are generally also lacking in antlers. On occasions the females of some species, such as the Roe deer, will grow small antlers. The male muntjacs have both small antlers and tusks, either of which can be used as offensive weapons, though the latter are generally employed, particularly against a predator.

The largest deer, with a shoulder height of up to 90 in (229 cm) is the Alaskan moose, whilst the tiny pudu, genus *Pudu*, of South America, with a shoulder height of only some 14½ in (37 cm) is the smallest. The lower Andes is the home of the pudu, of which two species *Pudu pudu* and *P. mephistophiles* are recognized, the latter, the more northerly species, consisting of two races. Pudu bucks, rufous brown in colour, have small spike antlers of 3–4 in (7–10 cm).

South American deer. Another small deer with simple spike antlers of from 3–5 in (7–13 cm) according to subspecies, is the brocket *Mazama*. This deer, the range of which extends from Mexico to Argentina, has a wide distribution in South America, occurring in every republic except Chile and Uruguay. Altogether some four species of brocket are recognized, which are again subdivided into 26 subspecies. All four species and 20 of the subspecies are found in South America, with a further race in the West Indies. The largest species in South America is the Red brocket *M. americana* which stands about 28 in (71 cm) high at the shoulder. The Dwarf brocket *M. chunyi* and some subspecies of the Brown brocket *M. gouazoubira* are little larger than the pudu with a shoulder height of 14–15 in (35–38 cm). The general body colour of the brockets is either red or brown according to subspecies, with the underside of the tail white.

Three other genera of deer which are restricted to South America are *Hippocamelus,* the huemul or guemal, of which there are two species; the Marsh deer *Blastocerus* and the Pampas deer *Ozotoceros.* Several subspecies of the White-tailed deer *Odocoileus virginianus* are also represented in the more northerly parts of South America.

The huemul, which stands about 36 in (91 cm) high at the shoulder, is a deer of the Andes range, the Chilean huemul *H. bisulcus* occurring in the Andes of Chile and western Argentina, and the Peruvian huemul *H. antisensis* in the Andes of Ecuador, Peru, Bolivia and extreme northwest Argentina, the two species being separated by a wide area thus preventing any interbreeding. Throughout most of its range the huemul often referred to as *taruca*, is scarce and seldom occurs below 13,000 ft (3,962 m). The males carry simple forked antlers of about 11 in (28 cm), but abnormal heads carrying more than four points do sometimes occur. The huemul of the southern Andes is dark brown, but turns greyish brown in winter. The northern form is lighter in colour.

The Marsh deer *Blastocerus dichotomus*, which stands about 44 in (112 cm) high at the shoulder, is the largest of the South American deer, and occurs throughout much of southern Brazil, Paraguay and northeastern Argentina, and perhaps still in Uruguay as well. Local names for this deer

Opposite: White-tailed deer, the most widespread deer in America, from Canada to Brazil.

Map showing distribution of deer, including introductions (e.g. New Zealand).

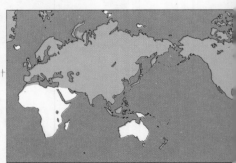

are *pantanos* and *Guazu pucú* deer. Eight is the usual number of points on Marsh deer antlers, but heads of ten or twelve points, or even more, are by no means rare. This deer, as its name implies, is fond of marshy ground and is seldom found far from water. Its colour is a deep rich red.

Considerably smaller than the Marsh deer is the Pampas deer *Ozotoceros bezoarticus,* of which three subspecies are recognized, the typical form *O. b. bezoarticus* in Brazil, *O. b. leucogaster* in Paraguay and adjacent areas of Argentina, Bolivia and Brazil and *O. b. celer* which is restricted to the pampas of Argentina.

Standing about 27 in (69 cm) at the shoulder, the Pampas deer is, without doubt, the most elegant of all the South American deer, and in many respects is rather similar to the Roe deer, particularly in the formation of the antlers, which normally bear six points. The general colour of its short, smooth hair is yellowish brown, with the insides of the ears and underparts white. The upper hairs on the tail are dark brown to black.

Pampas deer are generally found in small groups of 5–15, except during the fawning season when the doe becomes more solitary. As the name suggests, this is a deer of the open plains and it avoids, as far as possible, woodlands and mountainous country.

North American deer. The White-tailed deer *Odocoileus virginianus* is the most widespread deer in the American continent, its distribution extending from Brazil and Peru in South America northwards through Central America and Mexico into the United

Fallow deer fawn.

Fallow buck, typical park deer.

Sika deer stags, a species native to eastern Asia but introduced widely elsewhere.

States and southern Canada. In the United States it is resident in practically every state except Alaska, and possibly Nevada and Utah, although in both wanderers may occur in the extreme north. It is present in all the adjacent provinces of southern Canada, and also Nova Scotia. It is absent from Labrador, Northwest Territories, Yukon and Newfoundland. A recent estimate has put the White-tailed deer population of the United States at over 8 million. In 1965 over 30 million hunting licences were issued, of which a very substantial number were just for the White-tail. The race that frequents the Florida Keys—the Keys deer *O. v. clavium*—is, however, becoming scarce.

Throughout its entire range from southern Canada to northern South America no fewer than 38 subspecies are recognized, and since the range of many of these overlap, interbreeding has occurred widely. However, it can be said that the larger forms of White-tailed deer are to be found in the north and the smaller in the south. Thus the shoulder height of bucks from the most northern forms (*O. v. borealis, O. v. dacotensis* and *O. v. ochrourus*) will measure about 40 in (102 cm) as compared to the small White-tailed deer *O. v. margaritae* from Margarita Island, Venezuela which is only some 24 in (61 cm) high.

The White-tailed deer is so called by reason of its longish white tail which is raised erect as the deer bounds away when alarmed, thus acting as a danger signal to other deer. This deer is often referred to as the Virginian deer, but strictly speaking this should only apply to the subspecies of that name, the typical deer *O. v. virginianus* from Virginia.

In summer the general colour of most subspecies is one of reddish brown, with a whitish patch on the throat and inside the ears. This coat is replaced by a more sombre one of grey to greyish-brown in winter. Fawns are spotted.

Another deer belonging to the same genus as the White-tailed deer, and somewhat similar in size, is the Mule deer *Odocoileus hemionus,* which is found over a vast expanse of western North America and in a variety of habitats, from high mountains to plains and deserts. Its range is confined almost entirely to the western half of the United States extending northwards from central Mexico to southern Alaska, and the Great Slave Lake of Northwest Territories in Canada. 11 subspecies are recognized of which the typical deer *O. h. hemionus* has the greatest range. The type inhabiting the Northwest Pacific coastal areas, *O. h. sitkensis,* is generally referred to as the Blacktailed deer or Sitka deer. The smallest Mule deer is *O. h. peninsulae,* found in lower Baja California, whilst the two insular types, *O. h. sheldoni* and *O. h. cerrosensis,* from the

The Mule deer, common in western North America, is found in a variety of habitats, from high mountains to plains and deserts.

islands of Tiberón and Cerros respectively, are not much bigger.

Typical Mule deer antlers consist of a main beam with a number of even forks sprouting from it as compared with the typical White-tailed deer antlers which consist of a main beam and simple upright spikes sprouting from it. In some heads, particularly those of immature animals or of malforms, it is, however, sometimes difficult to distinguish the antlers of the two species.

The Mule deer is fairly uniform in colour throughout its range, and distinctions between subspecies are not too well defined. Generally speaking, the winter coat is a brownish grey which changes to a rusty tan or red in summer.

The other three deer of North America: moose, caribou and wapiti (elk) have been dealt with in detail elsewhere. All these deer have their counterparts in the eastern hemisphere, in the elk, reindeer and Red deer respectively.

Roe and Fallow deer. The Roe deer *Capreolus,* with three subspecies, has a wide distribution in Europe and the Middle East and northern Asia, the typical deer *C. c. capreolus* being present in Scotland and England, and in almost every country of Europe as far east as the Ural Mountains in Russia,

beyond which it is replaced by the larger Siberian Roe deer *C. c. pygargus*. The former also occurs in Anatolia, Transcaucasia and northern Iran. In the Far East, the Siberian Roe deer is replaced by *C. c. bedfordi* of China and Korea.

The European Roe deer stands 25–29 in (64–74 cm) high at the shoulder, and an adult buck may weigh from 38–50 lb (17–23 kg), with exceptional beasts from Poland weighing as much as 80–90 lb (about 38 kg).

The full head of a buck should be six-pointed, although multipointed heads occur. The tail is not readily visible, although a small one is present. During the winter the doe develops a prominent anal tush—a tuft of long hair—which is sometimes mistaken for a tail. The summer pelage of a rich foxy red, changes to a greyish fawn in winter with a most marked white rump patch. In the Netherlands and elsewhere melanistic Roe deer occur.

The rut takes place during late July and early August. Due to delayed implantation, no development of the embryo within the uterus is visible until December. Thereafter development is fairly rapid and the young, frequently twins and occasionally triplets, are born from late April to early June.

The Fallow deer *Dama dama,* has a wide

distribution in Europe and the countries bordering the Mediterranean. It is the typical park deer, and at the end of the last century in England alone, over 71,000 Fallow deer were being preserved in parks. They have also successfully been introduced to Australia, Tasmania, New Zealand and North and South America.

Standing about 36 in (91 cm) high at the shoulder, the typical feature of the buck is the palmated antler. There are also more colour variations in Fallow deer than in any other wild mammal, and these include black, white, menil, cream, sandy, silver-grey and the normal Fallow deer which is spotted in summer, but has little or no spotting in winter.

The rut usually takes place during October, at which time the bucks make a husky rolling grunt.

Another species of Fallow deer is the Persian Fallow deer *Dama mesopotamica* which has always had a rather limited distribution, and occurs only in Iran, where its total population is probably less than 50.

Only slightly larger than the European Fallow deer and with spotted summer pelage, the antlers of the bucks are the main point of difference, the brow being very short, with a long tray point sprouting close to it. The

These diagrams show six stages in the growth of a set of antlers, in one season, in the Red deer stag, from the first appearance of antler buds to the shedding of the velvet. (Below) Names of different parts of an antler.

upper points never palmate to the same extent as those of the European Fallow deer.

Whilst there is little uniformity of pattern in the antlers of male deer in the multi-pointed species such as caribou, Red deer, moose, etc. the antlers of the Rusa deer, as well as those of the genus *Axis* are extremely regular in formation and, in adult males, are normally six-pointed.

Asian deer. There are four species of *Axis* deer, and a number of subspecies, the most beautiful of all being the chital or Spotted deer of India *Axis axis axis,* with a subspecies in Ceylon *A. a. ceylonensis.* A typical chital stag from Madhya Pradish, rufous brown and profusely covered with white spots in both winter and summer, will stand about 36 in (91 cm) at the shoulder. Chital are comparatively common, and herds of 100 or more animals can be seen at times.

This deer has been successfully introduced to other parts of the world, including the Hawaiian Islands.

Another deer of the same genus as the chital but with a wider distribution, is the Hog deer or para *Axis porcinus,* of which two subspecies are recognized. The typical race *A. p. porcinus* is restricted to Ceylon and the low alluvial grass plains of the Indus and Ganges valleys, where its range runs from Sind in the west, eastwards as far as Assam and Burma. Further south in Thailand and Vietnam *A. p. annamiticus* occurs.

Hog deer stags, yellowish brown in colour, stand about 27 in (68·5 cm) high at the shoulder and weigh about 80–100 lb (36–45 kg). The general build is low and heavy, with legs and face comparatively short.

The other two members of the genus *Axis* are the Bawean or Kuhl's deer *Axis kuhlii,* which is restricted to Bawean Island situated in the Java Sea between Borneo and Java, and the Calamian deer *Axis calamianensis* which is also restricted to a group of islands in the Philippines—the Calamian Islands. Both these deer have a close affinity to the Hog deer in size and appearance. Little is known of their biology.

Of all the species of deer in southern Asia, the sambar *Cervus unicolor* is not only one of the largest but also the most widespread, for its range extends from India in the west, through Burma and southern China, to Indonesia and the Philippines in the east. It has also been successfully introduced to the North Island of New Zealand. Throughout its range, 16 subspecies are recognized, the largest of which *C. u. niger* is found in India, this animal being similar, but slightly larger than the typical sambar *C. u. unicolor* of

This picture by Charles Knight is called 'Before the Dawn of History'. It portrays the Irish elk, an extinct species of deer famous for its enormous antlers. These are said to have brought about its downfall, but this is debatable.

Ceylon. A large sambar stag from Central Provinces will stand about 52–56 in (132–142 cm) high at the shoulder, and weigh about 600 lb (272 kg). With antlers normally bearing six points and measuring up to 50 in (127 cm) in length, this deer is a uniform dark brown, the calves, which are never spotted at birth, being the same colour.

The sambar of South China *C. u. equinus* is also a large animal, but the one found on Borneo and adjacent islands, *C. u. brookei,* is a slightly smaller beast. Eight insular races are represented in the Philippines, the smallest of which, *C. u. nigricans,* has a shoulder height of only about 24–26 in (60–65 cm) and occurs on Basilan Island.

Sambar occur at all altitudes from sea level up to about 10,000 ft (about 3,000 m) for their habitat is very variable, ranging from coastal forest and swamp land to agricultural fields and mountains. They are seldom far from water.

A deer with a similar antler formation to the sambar, but smaller, is the Rusa deer *Cervus timorensis* which is the most widespread species of deer in the Indonesian Archipelago in which some eight insular races are represented. It is by no means certain, however, that all these are indigenous to some of the islands, for it is known that a considerable importation of deer has taken place.

The largest member of this species is *C. t. russa* from Java, which has a shoulder height of about 43 in (110 cm), whilst *C. t. floresiensis,* one of the smaller representatives, is found on Flores. The typical deer *C. t. timorensis* also occurs on Flores, as well as on Timor, Hermit and Ninigo.

Dark brown in colour and with the largest antler seldom exceeding 27 in (68·5 cm) in length, this is a deer of the grassy plains, though persecution will make them resort to cover.

This deer has been introduced to New Guinea and New Zealand (North Island).

A deer of southern Asia which is becoming scarce is the thamin or Eld's deer—sometimes also called the Brow-antlered deer—*Cervus eldi* of which three subspecies are recognized: *C. e. eldi* from Manipur; *C. e. thamin* from Burma and Tenassarim; and *C. e. siamensis* of Thailand, Vietnam and also Hainan Island, all of which are rare.

Standing about 45 in (114 cm) high at the shoulder, the general colour of the thamin is reddish brown, lighter in summer than in winter. The most noticeable features of this deer are the antlers in which the brow and main stem (beam) of the antler form a more or less continuous bow-shaped curve, with a number of small jags sprouting from the upper surface of the outer tine of the terminal fork.

Another peculiarity of this deer is that the foot has been modified, enabling it to walk on swampy ground, which is its principal habitat in the Manipur valley. The deer cannot tolerate heavy forests or hills, and to a great extent it is a grazing animal, feeding largely on wild rice, as well as browsing on certain trees.

Another deer of Thailand, with unique antler formation, was Schomburgk's deer *Cervus schomburgki*. It appears to have become extinct between 1932–39. Standing about 40 in (102 cm) at the shoulder, and a uniform brown with lighter underparts, the striking feature of this deer was its complex antlers in which all the main tines were generally forked, resulting in trophies having as many as 20 or more points. Its last

Red deer stag roaring to warn off others. Note blood on antlers.

Male Reeves' muntjac, a deer also called Barking deer.

The chital, also called axis or Spotted deer, is the common deer of India and Ceylon, profusely covered with white spots.

stronghold appears to have been on the great swampy plains around Paknam Po in central Thailand.

A small deer which has a wide distribution in southern and Southeast Asia, ranging from India in the west to southeastern China and Formosa in the east, and to Indonesia in the south is the muntjac *Muntiacus*, which includes five species and 17 subspecies. Other names for it are Barking deer and Rib-faced deer. The latter name has arisen because the antlers, which consist of a short brow tine and an unbranched beam measuring about

Musk deer, persecuted for its scent glands.

3—7 in (7·6—17 cm) in length dependent on subspecies, are supported on long skin-covered pedicles which continue down the forehead as converging ridges. The cry of this deer is a loud, short bark, similar to that of a dog, and this is often repeated many times, thus earning it the name of Barking deer.

A feature of the muntjacs is that both sexes have canine teeth in the upper jaw, those of the bucks extending to about 1 in (2·5 cm). These canines are used for fighting.

An adult male Indian muntjac *Muntiacus muntjak,* of which there are a number of subspecies, measures 22—23 in (56—58 cm) high at the shoulder, the body colour being a deep chestnut in summer, slightly darker in winter. The muntjac of southern India *M. m. malabaricus* is the largest of the Indian muntjacs, whilst the muntjac of Burma *M. m. grandicornis* produces the more massive antlers.

In central, eastern and southern China three species are represented. Reeves' muntjac *Muntiacus reevesi,* which is sometimes referred to as the Chinese muntjac, has the widest distribution. It is smaller than the Indian muntjac, measuring only about 16—18 in (42·5 cm) at the shoulder. One of the rarest of the Chinese deer is the Black or Hairy-fronted muntjac *Muntiacus crinifrons* which occurs in Chekiang Province. It is a

large muntjac, with a shoulder height of about 24 in (61 cm).

Early in the century some muntjac were released in Bedfordshire by the Duke of Bedford. At first Indian muntjac were released but died out. Later Reeve's muntjac were liberated and at the present time this small deer has a wide distribution in central England.

Another small deer with antlers shorter than muntjac but supported from long pedicles, is the Tufted deer *Elaphodus cephalophus,* which derives its name from the crest of long and dense bristly hair crowning the summit of the head around the antlers, sometimes completely concealing them. Tufted deer also have small tusks similar to muntjac. Three subspecies are recognized, extending from Burma to southern China, including eastern Tibet.

Generally brown in colour, this small deer, which stands 22—25 in (56—63 cm) high at the shoulder, according to subspecies, inhabits mountainous country, where it may be found at up to 15,000 ft or more (about 4,570 m). When feeding, Tufted deer carry their tails high, and when bounding off their tails flop with every bound, displaying the

white underside in much the same manner as the White-tailed deer.

Musk deer. Two other small deer of central southern Asia are the Musk deer *Moschus* represented by three species, and the Chinese Water deer *Hydropotes inermis,* a typical feature of both being that the males are completely devoid of antlers. Instead, they are armed with long upper canine tusks, $2\frac{3}{4}$—3 in (7—7·6 cm) in length. On the does they are much shorter.

An adult Musk deer stands 20—22 in (53 cm) high at the shoulder, and although there is some variation in colour, generally it is a rich dark brown, mottled and speckled with light grey above and paler beneath. Its principal habitat is forest and scrubland at elevations of about 7,000—11,000 ft (about 2,120—3,350 m).

This deer is much hunted for its musk which is a brownish wax-like substance from a gland on the abdomen of the bucks, used extensively in the manufacture of perfume and soap. About 1 oz (28 gm) of it can be obtained from a single male. Unlike all other species of deer, the Musk deer possesses a gall bladder. It is a solitary deer, and seldom are more than two seen together.

Red deer hinds fighting. See also separate entry on Red deer.

The distribution of the three species of Musk deer is as follows: *Moschus moschiferus,* of which there are two subspecies, in northern India, from where it extends eastwards into Transbaikalia. Here it is replaced by *M. sibiricus,* likewise divided into two subspecies, one being an insular form, *M. s. sachalinensis,* restricted to the island of Sakhalin or Karufuto in the Sea of Okhotsk. The third species, *M. berezovskii,* is an inhabitant of Szechuan, China.

Chinese deer. Smaller than the Musk, the Chinese Water deer *Hydropotes inermis,* of which there are two subspecies, one in eastern and central China and the other in Korea, have an entirely different habitat, preferring reed swamps and grasslands close to a river to mountainous country. Standing about 20–21 in (about 51–53 cm) high at the shoulder with an extremely short tail, the summer coat of the adult is reddish brown, which as winter advances, becomes a dull brown faintly flecked with grey. Twins and triplets are common and up to five or six fawns have been recorded. When fighting, the bucks often make a 'chittering noise' by clicking their tusks.

Another deer of western China and eastern and northern Tibet is Thorold's deer or White-faced Tibetan deer *Cervus albirostris,* also known as Przewalski's deer. Standing about 48 in (122 cm) high at the shoulder, the general colour of this deer in summer is brown, which becomes lighter in winter. The nose, lips and chin are white to the throat, with a small white spot in the region of the ears. Its main habitat is the Tibetan high mountains, where it occurs up to about 16,000 ft (4,877 m). Nowhere in its range is it plentiful.

Without doubt, the most remarkable of all the Chinese deer is the Père David's deer *Elaphurus davidianus,* a species which no man, living or dead, has ever recorded seeing in the wild state. It was in 1865 that the French explorer, Armand David, first saw this animal inside the walled Imperial Hunting Park of Nan-Hai-Tsue near Peking. Before the close of the century, specimens of this rare deer had reached some of the European zoos, as well as Woburn Park in England. And not a moment too soon, for by about 1900, due to flooding in the Imperial Park, the wall was breached and the escaping animals were either killed off by the starving peasantry or by troops during the Boxer rising. By 1910, not only was the animal extinct in China, but also in the European zoos, and the only beasts that remained alive were those at Woburn. From these few survivors a thriving herd of over 300 deer has now been built up.

Its physical attributes are unique. Standing about 48 in (122 cm) high at the shoulder, it has an extremely long tail, wide splayed hooves somewhat similar to rein-

Père David's deer, a species saved at the brink of extinction.

deer, and strange looking antlers which appear to be worn back to front, with all major tines protruding to the rear. On rare occasions, two sets of antlers have been produced in a year.

During the summer, the general body colour is a bright red which in winter changes to a dark iron-grey with fawn shading. Gestation lasts about ten months.

An old Chinese name for this deer was ssu-pu-hsiang which means literally 'not like four', i.e. like, yet unlike the horse; like, yet unlike the ox; like, yet unlike the deer; like, yet unlike the goat. Another name is milou.

Another deer which is of oriental origin is the Sika deer *Cervus nippon.* Of all the species introduced to parts of Great Britain, Europe, New Zealand and elsewhere, this species, of which some 13 subspecies are recognized, has proved to be the most adaptable. In eastern Asia, its range includes Japan (six subspecies), Formosa, eastern China (three subspecies), Manchuria and Korea (two subspecies) and northern Vietnam and Annam.

The Sika deer are animals of medium size, varying in shoulder height from about $25\frac{1}{2}$ in (65 cm) in one of the Japanese forms to about 43 in (109 cm) in Dybowski's deer from Manchuria. Antlers, usually eight-tined, seldom exceed 26 in (66 cm) in length in Manchurian specimens, considerably less in Japan.

The summer pelage, apart from melanism in the small Kerama sika deer *C. n. keramae* from the Ryuku islands, varies from a rich chestnut red to a more yellowish-brown hue, dependent on the subspecies, and is liberally spotted, which has given rise to the name Spotted deer. In winter these spots, in some animals, are barely discernible. A typical feature of the sika group, except those of melanistic strain, is the white caudal disc which is fanned out when the deer is alarmed.

The breeding habits are similar to the Red deer with which this deer will interbreed on occasions. The rut call of the stags is a peculiar whistle which may change into a high pitched scream. The deer is fond of cover. FAMILY: Cervidae, ORDER: Artiodactyla, CLASS: Mammalia.   G.K.W.

DENDROBATIDAE, the Arrow-poison frogs of South America, characterized by having a pair of small plates at the tip of each digit. In other features they most closely resemble the true frogs (Ranidae) and are sometimes included as a subfamily of that group.

There are only three genera, *Dendrobates, Phyllobates* and *Prostherapis,* of small frogs with smooth skins, most of them brightly coloured and with a remarkable variation in the colours. *Phyllobates aurotaenia,* for example, is a vivid red with black markings.

Dendrobates trivittatus may be either completely black or spotted with white or brown or may have a vivid pattern of black and yellow stripes along its body.

The poison from which these frogs get their name is produced by small glands in the skin. Most amphibians have such glands as a protection against predators but the strength of the poison varies. In these frogs it is particularly strong. It is usually considered that the vivid colouration is associated with their poisonous skin, serving to warn predators, but the most brightly coloured specimens are not necessarily the most poisonous. Individuals of *D. pumilio* which are dark blue, and difficult to see in the dark forest, have eight times more poison in their skin than those which are bright red and very conspicuous.

The poison from the skin of *Phyllobates aurotaenia* has been isolated and is given the name of batrachotoxin. It acts on the heart and nervous system and one millionth ounce (0·014 mg) is sufficient to kill an animal weighing 14 lb (7 kg). This means it is about 250 times more powerful than strychnine or curare. Arrow-poison frogs are used by the Indians of South America as a source of poison for their arrow tips. The frog is held over a fire and the heat causes the glands to eject poison which is scraped off the skin. The

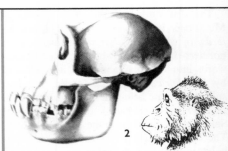

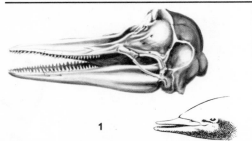

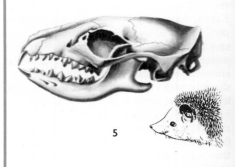

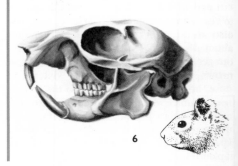

arrows are dipped in the poison and dried and birds and monkeys shot with such arrows are paralyzed almost immediately.

Many frogs in this family have an interesting method of caring for their tadpoles. In *Prostherapis trinitatis*, from the Andes, the 9–15 eggs are laid in moist places but not actually in water. The male remains by them and when the tadpoles hatch they climb onto his back where they stick to the skin and continue to develop. During the day the frog stays hidden on land but moves into pools at night. After about a week the tadpoles swim off and complete their development. Similar habits have been observed in the other genera of the family and in several other families of frogs as well.

Many Arrow-poison frogs have discs on the tips of their fingers and toes and are able to climb well but only a few have taken to a life in the trees. The majority live on the forest floor among the dead leaves and on the margins of streams and pools. FAMILY: Dendrobatidae, ORDER: Anura, CLASS: Amphibia.   M.E.D.

DENTAL FORMULA. Unlike other vertebrates, each species of mammal has a constant arrangement of teeth in the adult which may conveniently be summarized in a dental formula. The numbers of incisor, canine, premolar and molar teeth are indicated by the initial letter followed by a horizontal line with the number of teeth in the upper jaw of one side above it and the number in the lower jaw of one side below. At the end of the formula is given the total number of teeth of both sides. Some examples are: pig, $I\frac{3}{3} C\frac{1}{1} P\frac{4}{4} M\frac{3}{3} = 44$; man, $I\frac{2}{2} C\frac{1}{1} P\frac{2}{2} M\frac{3}{3} = 32$; rat, $I\frac{1}{1} C\frac{0}{0} P\frac{0}{0} M\frac{3}{3} = 16$.

DENTITION, collective word for the teeth. These are formed by the activity of the outermost layer of the skin, which folds in to form a continuous strand of tissue along the jaw. The exposed surface of the tooth is covered by the hard crystalline 'enamel'. Its main bulk is formed by a substance called dentine, which is very similar to bone except

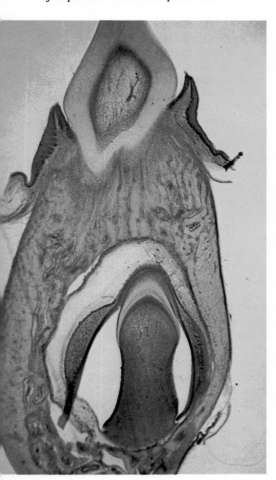

This photograph of a section through the lower jaw of a kitten of the domestic cat, shows a milk tooth at the top of the gum and a permanent tooth below awaiting its turn to erupt.

that it does not contain cells. The central 'pulp-cavity' of the tooth contains the nerves and blood-vessels. The root is attached to the jawbone by a substance known as 'cement'.

Teeth are normally present on the bones around the edges of the mouth. However, in bony fish, the fossil labyrinthodont amphibians (see below) and some reptiles, the bones of the palate are often also covered with teeth, which are usually small and conical.

In most vertebrates the teeth are periodically replaced. In sharks, new teeth appear inside the mouth and gradually move outwards around the edge of the mouth to come into use, so that a section through the jaw shows a whorl of teeth. Sharks and dogfishes have sharp cutting teeth and are usually carnivores or scavengers. Most of the other cartilaginous fish, the skates and rays, feed mainly on molluscs and have a flat 'pavement' of crushing teeth.

A variety of forms of teeth are found in the bony fish, perhaps the most remarkable being those of the parrotfishes, e.g. *Scarus*. These feed by breaking off pieces of coral

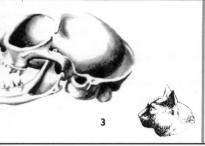

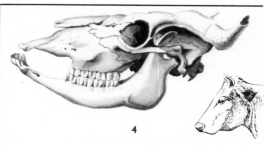

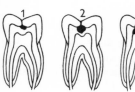

Types of teeth and skulls of some mammals. The dentition varies enormously between species, and is linked with the sort of food eaten. In 1. there are numerous teeth all alike, making what is called a homodont dentition, as in the fish-eating dolphin. The other sets of teeth are heterodont (with varying sorts of teeth): 2. those of an omnivore (eating plant and animal), like the manlike ape; 3. of a carnivore (flesh-eater), like a cat; 4. herbivore (plant-eater), such as cattle; 5. insectivore (insect-eater), as in the hedgehog; 6. gnawing animal (or rodent) represented by the squirrel.

and grinding them up to extract the soft polyps. Many rows of small teeth develop, but are fused together to form a pair of sharp-edged plates which look, and function, like the bill of a parrot.

Most of the fossil amphibians are known as 'labyrinthodonts' because the enamel surface is folded into the tooth in a complicated labyrinthine pattern. The teeth of living amphibians are quite small and do not show this feature.

In reptiles there are many generations of teeth, waves of tooth-replacement periodically passing forwards along the jaws. Each alternate tooth is replaced during the passage of one wave, while the intervening teeth are replaced during the passage of the next wave.

This process ensures that there is never a long, continuous gap in the tooth row.

Most reptiles are carnivorous or omnivorous and have simple pointed teeth, such as those of lizards. Snakes have long recurved teeth on both the marginal bones of the jaws and on the palatal bones; these help to hold the prey and swallow it by movements of the jawbones. In many snakes some of the marginal teeth are especially long and form fangs. In the poisonous snakes these fangs bear a groove or canal for the poison and are borne on one of the anterior bones of the skull, which can be rotated so as to bring the fangs into position for striking the prey.

Large numbers of round, conical teeth are used for impaling the prey in the fish-eating reptiles, such as the extinct ichthyosaurs and plesiosaurs, and in the crocodiles. A similar dentition is found in fish-eating mammals, such as dolphins and seals.

In some herbivorous dinosaurs, such as the hadrosaurs, several generations of teeth may be used at once, massed together so as to provide a large surface for grinding up the food. Perhaps because of the large amount of wear at the front of the mouth, the teeth here have been replaced by a horny covering (a similar feature is found in many artiodactyls).

In mammals the teeth in different regions of the mouth have become different in form and function. At the front of the mouth are the wide, chisel-like incisors; behind these is a pair of elongated, pointed canines, used for piercing the prey. Behind the canines, the cheekteeth become progressively larger and flatter, and are used for chewing the food. The mammals have also reduced the continual process of tooth-replacement found in reptiles, so that there are only two generations of teeth. The incisors, canines and anterior cheekteeth, or 'premolars', of the first tooth-generation are known as 'milk teeth'. These teeth are later replaced by the corresponding teeth of the second generation. In addition, the tooth-row is extended by the appearance of the posterior cheekteeth, or 'molars', of the first tooth-generation. The most posterior of these

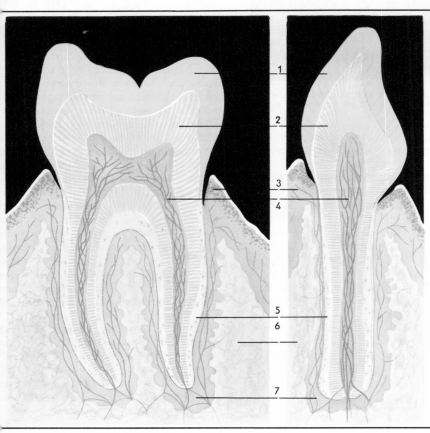

Section through a molar and an incisor tooth. Molars and incisors are fixed in cavities, or sockets (6), in the bone of both upper and lower jaws, and consist mainly of a tissue, the dentine or ivory (2), resembling bone. The visible part, the crown, is covered by a smooth but very hard layer of enamel (1). Under the surface of the gum (3) the crown of the tooth passes into the root (7) which is fixed in the socket by a bone-like cement (5). In the axis of the root is a narrow canal through which the tooth pulp (4), of connective tissue rich in capillaries and fine-nerve endings, penetrates to the centre of the tooth.

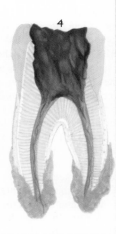

Tooth decay (caries): 1. early stage, 2. continuing tooth decay, 3. nerve cavity reached and toothache begins, 4. complete breakthrough with inflammation of roots.

appear last, and in man are sometimes known as 'wisdom teeth'.

Since the teeth of mammals are no longer being constantly replaced, the relationship between the opposing teeth of the upper and lower jaw becomes constant. The cheekteeth can now develop a complicated pattern of projections, or 'cusps', which fit into corresponding depressions in the opposing teeth. This provides a very efficient grinding apparatus.

Because the adult mammal has only one set of teeth, herbivorous mammals have special adaptations to ensure that their teeth are not worn out too early in life. This problem is especially severe for those which feed on grass, since this contains a lot of abrasive silica. Horses have overcome the difficulties in several ways. Firstly, all the cheekteeth are wide and long, providing as great a surface area as possible. Secondly, the enamel forms a complicated pattern of cutting edges on the crown of the tooth; these edges are supported by a special development of the cement. Finally, the crown of the tooth is extremely high, so that it can undergo a lot of wear before it is worn out. Elephants, which must eat a lot of food to maintain their great bulk, have solved the problem in a different way. Each of their teeth is so long, wide and deep that it occupies the whole side of the jaw. They can, therefore, only be used for a limited time, a new cheektooth moving down into position as the old one is worn down to little more than its roots and shed from the front of the mouth. The large tusks of elephants are enlarged incisor teeth.

The teeth have been lost and replaced by a horny beak in chelonians, birds and some extinct reptiles known as dicynodonts.

C.B.C.

DENTITION IN RODENTS. Rodents are gnawing animals: the name is from the Latin *rodo*–to gnaw. The incisors are used more especially for this so their edges are being constantly worn down. This is compensated by these front teeth growing continually at the roots. The rate of growth has been measured. In the Common rat the lower grow 5–6 in (13–15 cm) a year, the upper incisors just over 4 in (10 cm). This is about the same as in the larger European rabbit. The Pocket gopher holds the record relatively to its size with the astonishing 14·19 in (36 cm) a year for its lower incisors, the Guinea pig running it close with 10·2 in (26 cm). It is usually said this is why rodents are always chewing things other than food (rats gnaw concrete and lead pipes), to keep the teeth worn down. Even so, it is the habit of rodents to grind their teeth at odd moments throughout the day. They are sharpening (honing) them.

Should one or other of the incisors fail to make contact properly with its fellow the two will grow enormously, curve into the mouth and starvation ensues.

Although larger than a rat the porcupine's incisors do not grow as much. The upper incisors grow 2½ in (6 cm) a year, the lower 3½ in (9 cm). The chewing power is greater and the North American porcupine will gnaw glass bottles left by campers.

DERMAL SKELETON, those bony plates and scales which develop directly in the skin without being preformed in cartilage. They seem primitively to have consisted of an inner layer of compact bone, above which was laid down a layer of spongy bone. Above this lay another more compact layer of bone or, more usually, of the bone-like substance, dentine, found also in teeth. The surface was covered by a hard layer like the enamel of teeth, and was often subdivided into separate tubercles.

Garpike *Lepidosteus* has a primitive dermal skeleton of scales which are covered by a thick layer of ganoine.

Scales with this type of structure were present in most of the fossil crossopterygian fishes. In all living fishes, however, the scales have become very much thinner, so making the fish lighter and more flexible. The culmination of this process is seen in the teleost fishes, in which only a very thin flexible remnant of the deepest compact bone layer is retained. Since all bone has been lost in the cartilaginous fishes, these retain only the superficial enamel tubercles, now isolated as individual dentine-filled 'dermal denticles' which may be identical in appearance with the teeth.

In the fossil Agnatha and placoderms, large plates of dermal bone usually covered the surface of the head and of the anterior part of the body. Dermal bones form the operculum covering the gills in the actinopterygian fishes, and continue to contribute to the formation of the skull in all the vertebrates. However, the dermal plates covering the body are progressively reduced even in fishes, in which they finally form the dermal shoulder girdle. This forms the rear margin of the gill chamber and provides an anterior attachment for the muscles of the body; the skeletal elements to which the pectoral fin is attached are bound to its inner surface. In land vertebrates this dermal girdle survives only as the bones, running down the front edge of the shoulder girdle, known as the cleithrum and clavicle.

The ability of the skin to form bone is retained in most vertebrates. Bony elements often lie under the scales of lizards and in the skin of some crocodiles. Bony protective armour is found in many fossil reptiles, especially in the dinosaurs, and also in such mammals as the armadillos and their extinct relatives, the glyptodonts. The most extensive system of dermal bony armour is that found in tortoises and turtles, which consists of a dorsal carapace (fused to the vertebrae and ribs) and a ventral plastron, between which are apertures for the head, tail and limbs.

C.B.C.

DESERT FAUNAS, animals specialized for existence in areas with very little moisture. Although deserts are usually considered to be hot, dry sandy places, a precise definition is that deserts are places without accessible water. They therefore include some cooler parts of the temperate zones, such as the Gobi Desert of Asia, the Atacama Desert of Chile and the Great Basin Desert of Nevada. Hot and cool deserts are distributed, roughly as two broad bands around the earth, one about the Tropic of Cancer and the other about the Tropic of Capricorn. In addition, the cold polar region of Antarctica is considered as desert. The character of a desert will vary considerably from one part of the world to another, although all have one common feature, namely, they are very dry areas. A desert will develop where the amount of water evaporating into the atmosphere from the surface of the ground or from the vegetation exceeds the amount of rainfall, or where water is locked up as ice.

Some deserts, particularly those that are very hot or very cold, are barren wastelands, virtually uninhabitable. However, between these two extremes are desert regions in which enough moisture is present to allow animals and plants to become established and survive. These biological communities are well adapted to the rigours of desert life, and show many interesting specializations.

In order to survive in a desert, an animal has either to avoid the harsh conditions or tolerate them. Many examples of 'avoiders' can be found among desert birds which, by virtue of their great mobility, can migrate to more suitable areas on the fringes of the desert during the driest part of the year; included here are many of the birds of prey,

Evolution of higher vertebrates has seen the reduction of the dermal skeleton in the interests of body flexibility (snakes, lizards, most bony fishes). The body armour of chelonians (tortoises, turtles) and armadillos (and their relatives the fossil glyptodonts) is highly developed.

such as owls, kites, falcons and Sparrow hawks, together with francolin, quail, Zebra finch and pratincole which often occur along water courses. Another way of avoiding unfavourable conditions is by burrowing in the desert soil, and this habit is shown by small rodents, such as the Kangaroo rats and gophers, and also by tortoises, snakes and lizards. The rodents often construct elaborate burrow systems beneath the roots of desert plants and most of these small animals are nocturnal in habit, remaining in their cool, humid burrows during the heat of the day. Snakes and lizards often inhabit abandoned rodent burrows and also seek shelter under rocks and in caves where they are joined by the Pack rat, a rodent common in the southwestern United States.

The shortage of free water in deserts places a severe restriction on the kinds of animals that can live there, and only those with high powers of water conservation can succeed. Particularly favoured in this respect are the reptiles and the arthropod insects and arachnids, for they have a relatively impermeable body covering and are also capable of converting metabolic wastes to uric acid, a highly insoluble substance which requires little or no water for its elimination from the body. Hence, these groups of animals are among the most common members of the desert fauna, and the ability to tolerate high temperatures and dry conditions is clearly shown by the many lizards, spiders, ants and Ground beetles which are active on the surface of the desert soil during the day. Many desert inhabitants can apparently live quite happily without drinking water, although some of these at least, such as the Pack rat, ostrich, Ground squirrel and Jack rabbit, obtain the water they need through eating the green leaves of desert plants, succulents or cacti. Other desert animals, such as the Kangaroo

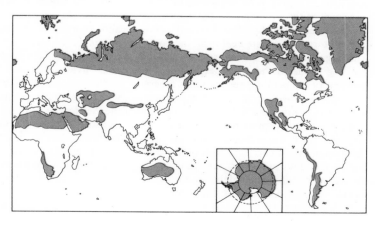

Map of world areas of desert fauna.

Camels and goats crossing the desert in Jordan.

rats, feed on dry seeds and are able to utilize the water produced when this food is chemically digested. These animals also conserve water by producing an extremely concentrated urine, in some cases as much as five times more concentrated than that of man. Special chambers in the nostrils condense vapour in the breath and the water from it is returned to the body.

In addition to water conservation, mammals living in hot deserts have to face the problem of overheating. The usual procedure to counter this tendency is to sweat, but this would normally involve a greater loss of water from the body than a desert animal could afford. Kangaroo rats have no sweat glands, and their only method of keeping cool is to secrete saliva over the fur covering the throat region. However, as many desert rodents are nocturnal in habit, they avoid, rather than tolerate, the consequences of overheating. In larger desert mammals, such as the Jack rabbits and camels, the problem is not so easily overcome for these cannot seek refuge in the soil. Jack rabbits shelter during the hottest part of the day in the shadows of rocks and under desert shrubs, and it has recently been suggested that the large ears of these animals, by having a very concentrated network of blood vessels, serve as radiators to dissipate heat from the body. The large bulk of the camel prevents it from utilizing shade in the open desert, and the problem of temperature regulation is a very serious one. However, the camel is superbly adapted in many ways for desert life. It can tolerate a wider fluctuation in body temperature than most warm-blooded animals, and this means that it can store heat in its body during the day and allow this heat to be dissipated by radiation at night. Although the camel can, and does, sweat, the amount of water loss incurred is slight and occurs slowly

over a long period. The camel can tolerate a far higher degree of dehydration (at least 27% of the body weight) than other mammals, and its drinking capacity is legendary. Contrary to popular opinion, the water is not stored in the stomach or the hump, but is dispersed through the body tissues.

In the cold, polar desert of Antarctica, the prevailing low temperatures and lack of suitable food make life impossible for terrestrial vertebrates, with the exception of certain marine birds, such as penguins, petrels, skuas, fulmars and terns. Under these conditions, only a few groups of small invertebrates, such as protozoans, nematodes, springtails and mites have become successfully established. These animals are adapted to the extreme cold and some, at least, remain active and can evidently breed at sub-zero temperatures. They feed mainly on moss, lichens and particles of organic debris. See polar faunas.   J.A.W.

DESMAN, an aquatic insectivore, of the mole family (Talpidae), resembling a very large shrew in appearance. Formerly they were widely distributed in Europe but are now represented by two very localized relict species: *Galemys pyrenaicus* in the Pyrenees and northern Portugal and *Desmana moschata* far away in the rivers north of the Caspian Sea. Both species lead very specialized lives, and are thus probably insufficiently adaptable to reinvade areas from which they were displaced by the ice ages of the Pleistocene.

Most of the mole family are specialized burrowers but the desman is highly adapted to its aquatic existence. Its hindfeet are powerful and have webbed toes, the forefeet are also wholly or partly webbed. All four feet bear fringes of bristles to increase their effectiveness as paddles. The tail is scaly

with sparse hairs and is used together with the feet for swimming. Desmans have long oily guard hairs which are water repellent and prevent the dense underfur from getting wet during swimming. This is a common arrangement in many groups of aquatic mammals but is not found in other members of the family Talpidae.

The snout is probably the most characteristic feature of the desmans. It projects well beyond the teeth and lower lip and is so long that it may be bent back on itself and licked with the tongue. It is flattened, tubular, has two grooves along its length and is only sparsely covered with short bristly hairs. It is very mobile and is frequently waved about in scenting the air. It is also used to investigate food and other items of interest by touch and smell, rather as an elephant uses its trunk. The nostrils are situated at the end of this snout and, as a further adaptation to aquatic life, they may be closed by small skin flap-valves. It has even been reported that the snout may be used as a kind of 'schnorkel', enabling the animal to breathe whilst its body is completely submerged. Eyes and ears are very tiny, and the desman relies very much on its snout and whiskers for investigating its environment.

Desmans live in burrows beside streams and rivers. An entrance tunnel is dug from water level up into the bank, often under tree roots. Fluctuations in water level may result in frequent changes of abode being necessary. Since they are more at home in water than on land, their diet is predominantly aquatic. Insects and their larvae, crustaceans and fish are eaten together with some worms and other terrestrial creatures. The large upper incisors enable the animal to kill large prey, while the snout is used a great deal for winkling out smaller creatures from under stones and other hiding places. Desmans are active throughout the day and night, do not hibernate and usually lead solitary lives.

The Russian desman *Desmana moschata* is the largest member of the mole family with a head and body length of about 8 in (20 cm). It is found beside water in southeastern Europe and central western Asia. It is reddish brown above, shading to grey below. The tail is flattened in the vertical plane forming an effective rudder and is about the same length as the head and body.

Strong scent glands around the base of the tail produce a powerful odour making the animal distasteful to most predators. Apart from the occasional bird of prey, the only animal that kills desmans on any scale is man, who formerly hunted them for their silky pelts.

The Russian desman prefers slow moving, muddy water around ponds and lakes, especially where there is plenty of rotting vegetation at the water's edge. Three to five young are produced in June, but little else is known about their breeding, and the presence of eight teats in the female even suggests that litters may be rather larger than at present supposed.

The Pyrenean desman *Galemys pyrenaicus* is similar to the Russian species, but only half the size with a head and body length of 4–5 in (11–13 cm). It also differs in having a proportionally longer snout, and a tail which is only flattened towards the tip. The fur is dark brown on the back, contrasting sharply with the pale grey underside. In certain lights the fur is iridescent.

Galemys lives in the Pyrenees in both France and Spain and in the mountains of northern Portugal. It prefers clean fast flowing water, in contrast to *Desmana*, and thus has a linear distribution along the banks of streams, although populations may be quite dense locally (79 being caught in one year along a 1¾ mile (3 km) section of river bank). Adults come into breeding condition in January or February and a single litter, usually of four young, is produced between March and July. The habits of this species, as far as is known, are similar to those of the Russian desman. FAMILY: Talpidae, ORDER: Insectivora, CLASS: Mammalia. P.M.

DEVIL RAYS, a family of large ray-like cartilaginous fishes whose 'devilish' reputation stems rather from their size and curious appearance than from their supposedly ferocious behaviour. They have the wing-like pectoral fins of the ordinary skate or ray and closely resemble the Eagle rays except that the mouth is much wider and is provided with a pair of appendages on either side which are used as scoops in feeding. The Devil rays are surface-living fishes (unlike the majority of bottom-living ray-like fishes) and they feed on small crustaceans and plankton. The mouth, which is terminal in

most of the species, is kept open as the fish cruises along and food is collected by fine sieve-like rakers before the water passes to the gills. Some species grow to an enormous size and there is a record of a specimen that measured 22 ft (6·6 m) from tip to tip of the pectoral fins. There are many records of these fishes leaving the water and sailing through the air, the resounding noise of their return to water having been compared with the sound of a cannon. A single species of the genus *Manta* is known from the warmer parts of the Atlantic and it is possible that it is this same species, *M. birostris,* that occurs throughout the Indo-Pacific region. Teeth are present only in the lower jaw, whereas there are teeth in both jaws in the genera *Mobula* (Atlantic and Indo-Pacific) and *Indomanta* (India), but only in the upper jaw in *Ceratobatis* of Jamaican waters. In some species there is a venomous spine on the tail similar to that found in the Sting rays. The Devil rays are all ovoviviparous and give birth to live young. One observation on a harpooned female off the coast of Florida records that an embryo was ejected into the air for a distance of about 4 ft (1·2 m), the embryo emerging tail first and instantly unfolding its large pectoral fins, which were more than 3 ft (90 cm) from tip to tip. However, this is probably not the normal method of birth. The Devil rays are very graceful swimmers and are favourite subjects for underwater films with an 'intrepid' skin-diver bravely swimming beside these huge but mostly harmless giants. FAMILY: Mobulidae, ORDER: Hypotremata, CLASS: Chondrichthyes.

DEVIL'S TOE NAILS, a local name in parts of England for fossil oysters of the genus *Gryphaea*. These are common in certain Jurassic deposits and because of their peculiar growth, one valve remaining small and flat while the other became much larger and strongly curved with marked growth ridges, resemble shed claws 2–3 in (50–75 mm) in length. ORDER: Eulamellibranchia, CLASS: Bivalvia, PHYLUM: Mollusca.

Devonshire cup coral.

DEVONSHIRE CUP CORAL *Caryophyllia smithii*, a member of a family of solitary corals. It is a True or Stony coral with a goblet or horn-shaped cup (theca) composed of calcium carbonate which is laid down by the cells of the animal. The *polyp, which lives above and in this cup, is whitish in colour with brown tentacles which can be seen when the animal is expanded. When contracted, the radiating ribs of the cup can be seen. This coral lives in temperate seas and may be found off the southwest coast of Britain. Like all corals it is carnivorous, feeding on small crustaceans which are caught by special stinging-cells or *nematocysts. It is attached to shells or rocks by the base of the cup. See corals, and Cnidaria. FAMILY: Caryophyliidae, ORDER: Scleractinia, CLASS: Anthozoa, PHYLUM: Cnidaria.

DE VRIES, H., 1848–1935, Dutch botanist and geneticist who originated the mutation theory and was one of the first to use the experimental method in the study of plant evolution. Discovering unusual forms of Evening primrose *Oenothera lamarckiana* growing as garden escapees in a meadow, De Vries carried out exhaustive breeding experiments as a result of which he postulated sudden discontinuous jumps or mutations as the basic means of evolutionary change. He was also one of those who rediscovered Mendel's work on heredity in 1900.

DHOLE *Cuon alpinus,* also called the Asiatic wild dog, known as a fierce hunter of great stamina. It weighs from 25–35 lb (11–15½ kg) and has a head and body length of 38 in (96 cm) and a tail length of 18 in (45 cm). It differs from most canids in having a reduced number of molar teeth in its lower jaw and a thick muzzle, both of which are adaptations to a strictly flesh-eating way of life. Distributed throughout the Oriental tropical and mountain forests, in Nepal, India, Malaysia and Sumatra, the dhole has rufous fur with a darker-coloured tail ending in a black tail tip. It lives in groups of 5–20 although large packs of several families and their young may have up to 40 members.

Mating usually occurs during the late winter, and males pursue the females whilst uttering a soft squeak. Like domestic dogs, they 'lock' or 'tie' during mating, and the litter of between four and ten cubs is born about two months later, from January to March. Mothers rear their offspring in caves or holes which are dug before the birth. Other pack members participate in guarding the young and bring meat back to the litter which is regurgitated to the pups after being chewed by the adults. Initially, the cubs are completely helpless and blind but at two weeks their eyes open and weaning starts when they are five weeks old.

When hunting, dholes display a certain degree of teamwork, with different individuals alternately chasing the prey and then resting. Favourite victims are Wild pigs, chital, Spotted deer, and muntjac which are attacked mainly on the muzzle and face or rump region and then pulled down. There are many myths associated with the hunting habits of the dhole because people are afraid of them. Packs are, for instance, reputed to attack and kill tigers, bears, and leopards and to kill many more victims than they can eat. Many of these beliefs are probably based on exaggerated stories or on episodes that occur rarely.

Within a pack, there seems to be a rank order with one male assuming the dominant position. The hierarchy ensures that relationships among pack members are peaceful; even pups are reputed to fight one another for several months until a leader or top dog emerges. Once it is chosen, when the cubs are seven to eight months old, conflicts within the litter cease.

Dholes are mainly active during the day, but the preferred time for a hunt is the early morning. While travelling through the forest, individuals communicate with one another by a whistling call, but they also howl, bark and whine, the latter especially when they are distressed. Undoubtedly, scent is important, both during hunting and for being kept informed of the location of other packs in the vicinity. Because of the size of packs, dholes require large territories to prevent them from reducing too severely the numbers of prey species. FAMILY: Canidae, ORDER: Carnivora, CLASS: Mammalia.   D.G.K.

DIAPAUSE, a state of delayed development in insects which lasts throughout a period of adverse conditions. In most parts of the world there are periods of the year when conditions are unsuitable for insects to continue their development. In temperate regions this is true in the winter when it is too cold. In the tropics there is often a dry season when development is restricted by a shortage of water. The insects are able to survive at these times in stages of development which are specially equipped to withstand the adverse circumstances. The strange thing is that in most cases the insects do not wait for the bad weather to come, but they prepare themselves for it beforehand. Now obviously they do not know that bad weather is coming, but it appears that the preparations against adversity and the delay in development which lasts throughout the unfavourable period have become fixed in the life-history in the course of evolution.

Diapause must be differentiated from quiescence in which development is temporarily stopped by adverse conditions occurring at that particular time, but is resumed as soon as conditions become suit-able again. Not only does diapause begin before the unsuitable conditions prevail; it may also continue even when the insect is exposed to suitable conditions for normal development.

Diapause occurs at a particular stage of development which varies with the species. The Vapourer moth overwinters in the egg; the Yellow underwing moth as a caterpillar; the dragonfly *Anax* as the last instar larva; and the Dagger moth as the pupa. In all these cases normal development stops throughout the winter and is not resumed until the following spring. Diapause in adult insects is rather different because they remain active, although they eat relatively little and no eggs are produced. Where diapause occurs in immature stages it is usually preceded by a period in which food reserves are accumulated, an obvious instance of preparation.

It is fairly easy to see how this could become fixed in the life-cycle in cases where it occurs in every generation as with the eggs of the Vapourer moth. Much more difficult to understand are those cases where diapause does not necessarily occur in every generation. For instance, in Britain some members of the population of the moth *Acronycta rumicis* have two generations in a year with a diapause only in the second. Somehow the insects of the second generation are informed of the approaching winter, but how? The moths must be able to perceive something about the environment which causes them to enter a state of diapause. In this and in many other cases the important factor seems to be day-length. This changes in a regular manner, the days getting longer in spring and shorter in autumn so that information about the length of day is all that is needed to warn of the approaching winter. Birds and mammals can perceive changes in day-length; insects probably cannot but they certainly are sensitive to the actual length of the daylight period. In the case of *Acronycta,* if the larva develops when the days are more than 16 hours long there is no diapause; if it develops when the days are shorter, as would be the case in autumn, then there is a diapause. The insects are sensitive to low light intensities so that, for instance, they are not 'fooled into thinking' that winter is coming by a period of cloudy weather in July. But it is odd that, at least in many cases, the eyes are not important in measuring the light period; possibly the light acts directly on cells in the brain through the cuticle of the head.

There is also the problem of what brings diapause to an end. It is not sufficient simply to return the insect to normal conditions such as a higher temperature. It seems that the species which overwinter in diapause really need a period of low temperature if they are to develop normally because if they are kept continually warm they often die. There is considerable argument about the effects of chilling; some people believe that there are certain chemical processes which only occur at low temperatures which must be completed before diapause can end.

Whatever the case it seems certain that a major factor in diapause is a failure of the insect's hormones to function in the normal way. A diapause in a pupa, for instance, is associated with the failure to release the brain hormone which normally causes the pupa to moult to adult. Similarly in adult diapause the hormone which controls the development of eggs is not released.   R.F.C.

DIAPHRAGM, a thin sheet of muscle and tendon which separates the chest and abdominal cavities in mammals and in reptiles belonging to the order Crocodylia. In mammals it is mainly muscular and takes an active part in respiration; in crocodilians it is largely tendonous and shows little active movement.

DIATRYMA, very large, long-extinct, flightless bird of North America. Similar fossils have been found in France and Britain. Diatryma and its close relatives must have constituted some of the dominant creatures in Eocene times, about 55 million years ago. *Diatryma steini* for example, from the Lower Eocene of Wyoming, stood about 7 ft (2·1 m) tall and, like its congeners, was very

Skeleton of the extinct bird *Diatryma* and (top left) reconstruction to show how the bird may have appeared in life.

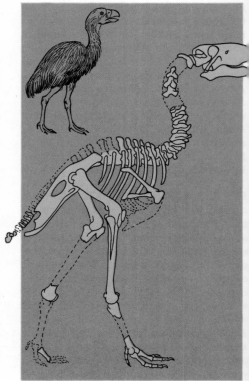

stoutly built. These birds were certainly built for running in spite of their bulk and were probably predatory. The head was as big as that of a present-day horse and had a massive, hooked beak. Members of the order Diatrymiformes have been found also in New Jersey and New Mexico. The group would seem to have been enabled to develop by the eclipse of the dinosaurs and by the fact that the contemporary mammals were small and primitive. The gradual development of the mammals may have been a factor in the decline of the diatrymids, the reversal of status being seen in the Oligocene which began some 40 million years ago. On the other hand, large predatory mammals and large flightless birds exist together today in Africa and South America. Perhaps the diatrymids were in fact too large and too specialized and were unable to obtain sufficient food of the right kind to support their bulk.

The Diatrymiformes has been placed near the Gruiformes, an order containing a wide variety of types including the present-day cranes, rails and bustards, as well as a number of other extinct giant birds such as *Phororhacos*. Diatryma therefore was probably not closely related to any of the large present-day flightless birds, the 'ratites', such as the ostrich. As far as we know, members of the two groups did not exist at the same time in the same place.

Diatryma therefore provides us with another example of convergent evolution: its skeletal modifications in connection with flightlessness are in many ways similar to those of the ratites and other groups of flightless birds. For example, in addition to the general reduction of the wings there is a great reduction of the uncinate processes (bone connections between adjacent ribs of flying birds providing a particular kind of mechanical strengthening). Also, the pelvic girdle was particularly strong and massive in connection with the running habit. Diatryma may even have used its feet and legs as weapons of offence or defence, as in the ostrich, which can kick effectively, and the Secretary bird, which pounds snakes with its outstretched foot. FAMILY: Diatrymidae, ORDER: Diatrymiformes, CLASS: Aves. P.M.D.

DIBATAG *Ammodorcas clarkei*, a long-necked, long-legged antelope superficially resembling a gazelle, especially the gerenuk. However, although it has gazelline face-stripes, it lacks facial or carpal glands, has a large bare muzzle, and has a tufted tail. The horns are short, forwardly concave, very like those of a reedbuck. In all, most modern specialists prefer to class the dibatag with the reedbuck and waterbuck in the Reduncini, rather than with the gazelles in the Antilopini.

A dibatag stands 31–36 in (79–92 cm) high, and weighs 60–75 lb (27–34 kg). The build is very slender, only slightly less so than the gerenuk. The colour is dark cinnamon, white below; the face is marked with white longitudinal streaks, with dark median and lateral stripes. The ears are rounded, the skull fairly short, not elongated and thick-boned like a gerenuk. In the field, the dibatag may be distinguished from the gerenuk by its ears, its more yellow colour, and its tufted tail which is held straight up when running.

The dibatag is found in Somalia, east of the Webi Shebeli river, and in eastern Ethiopia as far as 9° or 10°N. It lives in arid, thornbush country, in small groups of three to five individuals, or solitarily. When disturbed it bounds away with its head arched back and its tail swung forward above the rump. Little is known of its social behaviour, except that it mates in gazelle-like fashion, with the laufschlag (leg-beat) as the signal for the intention to mate, and the head held high, the male standing bipedally to copulate; this is a pattern common to gazelles and to the waterbuck group. FAMILY: Bovidae, ORDER: Artiodactyla, CLASS: Mammalia.   C.P.G.

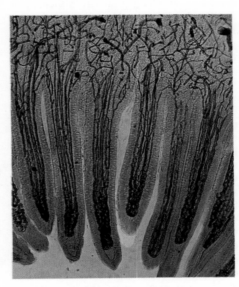
Photograph of the villi on the wall of the intestine which increases the digestive surface.

DIGESTION AND DIGESTIVE ORGANS. Digestion is the physiological process whereby animals break down their food, usually within a special alimentary canal, into simple soluble substances. These are then absorbed into the body and used either in the synthesis of new materials required for growth, regeneration and reproduction, or as sources of energy for these and all other life processes.

Digestive breakdown of the food is essentially a hydrolytic process, molecules of protein, carbohydrate and lipid undergoing hydrolysis by progressive addition of water molecules until they are split down to their basic constituents. Proteins are split into polypeptides and eventually down to amino acids, whilst carbohydrates (polysaccharides) are progressively hydrolysed to monosaccharides. It was originally thought that lipids were similarly split via di- and monoglycerides into fatty acids and glycerol and that these were then absorbed by the intestinal cells and resynthesized into triglyceride. The evidence now suggests, however, that in the mammal, at least, only a proportion of the lipid component of a meal is split in this way. The products of hydrolysis then combine physically with bile salts discharged from the liver to form an emulsification system which emulsifies the remaining lipid into tiny globules less than 0.5μ in diameter, and these then pass unchanged into the intestinal cells. Theories embodying the two concepts of lipid digestion are termed, respectively, the classical or lipolytic and the partition hypotheses.

The hydrolytic process is catalysed by organic catalysts, the digestive enzymes, produced by the alimentary canal and its associated organs specifically for this purpose, and it is the reverse of the process of condensation whereby living organisms build up proteins, carbohydrates and lipids from basic constituents. Any digestive reaction can be summarized in the equation:

$$AB + H_2O \underset{\text{condensation}}{\overset{\text{hydrolysis}}{\rightleftharpoons}} AOH + HB$$

As in the hydrolysis by peptidases (e.g. pepsin, trypsin, chymotrypsin, dipeptidases, aminopeptidases and carboxypeptidases) of the peptide bond within a protein molecule:

$$-CO-NH + H_2O \rightleftharpoons -COOH + -NH_2$$

Similarly carbohydrases (e.g. ptyalin, diastase, amylase) hydrolyse the glycosidic bond within carbohydrate molecules:

$$\ge C-O-C\le + H_2O \rightleftharpoons \ge C-OH + HO-C\le$$

And lipases hydrolyse ester type bonds within lipid molecules:

$$-C\overset{O}{\underset{O-C\le}{\big\langle}} + H_2O \rightleftharpoons -C\overset{O-}{\underset{OH}{\big\langle}} + HO-C\le$$

Each stage in the progressive hydrolysis of a food substance is catalysed by a different enzyme, so that the digestive enzymes exhibit specificity as regards the particular reaction hydrolysed. This is a fundamental property of all enzymes, but the digestive ones do not show the extreme specificity seen in those concerned with metabolic reactions. Rather, they exhibit group specificity and catalyse hydrolysis of several related substances, which is an obvious advantage in a process such as digestion where many different types of protein, for example, may be encountered. Apart from this important difference, the digestive enzymes resemble other enzymes, in that they are proteinaceous, thermolabile, act within closely defined pH limits and may require the presence of inorganic ions or organic co-enzymes before they can work at optimum efficiency.

The digestive enzymes are often secreted in an inactive form, particularly the peptidases, and require activation before they can catalyse digestive hydrolysis. Thus in the mammal inactive pepsinogen secreted by the chief cells of the peptic glands is activated in the stomach lumen by hydrochloric acid secreted by the oxyntic (parietal) cells of the glands. Once some active pepsin is formed, however, it itself activates further supplies of pepsinogen by a process of autocalysis. Hydrochloric acid continues to be secreted, though, and is concerned with killing and denaturation of the food, provision of optimal acidic conditions for peptic digestion and sterilization of bacteria which would otherwise break down the food along unsuitable pathways.

Secretion of a proteolytic enzyme in an inactive form is of obvious advantage in the prevention of autodigestion in the formative glands, and once the active enzyme is released digestion of the stomach wall is prevented only by copious secretions of mucus which line the stomach and are continually renewed throughout gastric proteolysis. A similar situation occurs in the mammalian intestine, where inactive trypsinogen secreted by the pancreas is activated in the intestinal lumen by enterokinase produced by the intestinal wall. The active trypsin released in this way, in addition to its digestive function, also serves to activate pancreatic chymotrypsinogen and, again, the gut wall is protected from attack by mucous secretions.

Digestion in most animals occurs in two distinct phases. The first phase is acidic and generally proteolytic with endopeptidases (peptidases such as pepsin which attack peptide bonds in the inner regions of the protein molecules) splitting proteins to polypeptides. This has the important secondary effect of breaking down cell walls and nuclear membranes, thus releasing carbohydrate and lipid constituents for subsequent digestion. The food is then generally moved on to another region of the digestive system (e.g. from stomach to intestine in the mammal) and the second, alkaline phase begins. Here, too, endopeptidases such as trypsin and chymotrypsin may still operate, but eventually progressive hydrolysis of protein molecules is completed by exopeptidases (carboxy- and aminopeptidases, and dipeptidases) which attack terminal peptide bonds and remove terminal amino acids from

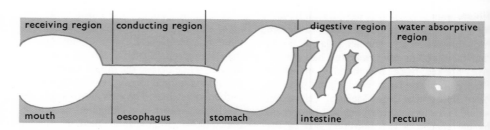

Schematic diagram representing a typical or generalized digestive tract of a vertebrate showing the receiving, conducting, digestive and water-absorbing regions and the organs included in each of these

polypeptides and dipeptides. Carbohydrate and lipid-splitting enzymes also operate in this second, alkaline phase of digestion.

The sequential secretion of the various substances concerned in digestion (enzymes, activating agents, acids, alkalis, bile salts and mucus) must necessarily be synchronized with the movement of food through the digestive system and with the particular stage of digestion already reached. In the mammal synchronization is achieved by nervous or hormonal mechanisms, or by a combination of these, depending upon the part of the gut concerned and the length of time food remains there. Thus in the mouth the salivary secretions, which are primarily lubricating in function but may also be enzymic, are under nervous control. In the stomach release of pepsinogen is controlled by nervous stimulation whilst release of hydrochloric acid is stimulated by the hormone gastrin, released into the blood stream by the stomach wall when this is stimulated by arrival of food down the oesophagus. Passage of acidic, partly digested food (chyme) from the stomach into the duodenum stimulates release of at least five hormones, which in turn stimulate production and release of materials concerned in intestinal digestion. Thus secretin causes the pancreas to produce the fluid and inorganic components of the pancreatic juice and the liver to produce bile which is stored in the gall bladder. Pancreozymin causes production of the enzymic components of the pancreatic juice, and cholecystokinin causes contraction of the gall bladder and discharge of the bile. Enterocrinin stimulates production of intestinal digestive juices and enterogastrone is antagonistic to gastrin and inhibits further production of acid in the stomach.

Systems for the control and co-ordination of digestive secretions in vertebrates other than mammals, and in invertebrates, have not been described in detail but there are indications that mechanisms similar to the mammalian one, but simpler and less sophisticated, are present.

Digestion in the mammal and most higher animals is extracellular and occurs in the lumen of the digestive system. In many invertebrates, however, at least part of the process is intracellular and follows phagocytosis of food particles by the gut

cells. Usually there is some initial extracellular breakdown, mechanical, enzymic or both, which reduces the particle size of the food to permit subsequent phagocytosis. This occurs in many coelenterates (hydroids, Sea anenomes and their allies), free-living flatworms, Nemertina (ribbonworms) and molluscs. Alternatively, the feeding mechanism of the animal may gather particles already small enough for phagocytosis and these, after preliminary sorting by ciliary mechanisms, may be phagocytosed directly.

Intracellular digestion is believed to be the primitive process, and in simple animals clearly has distinct advantages over the extracellular method. It is easier to control pH and enzyme concentration in a vacuole totally enclosed in a cell than in a simple saccate gut, which may be continuous with the external aquatic environment at the time of feeding if not continuously. Against this, however, is the disadvantage that different stages in digestion can only be separated in time, whereas extracellular digestion permits separation in space also, as the food moves along consecutive regions of the gut. Also, intracellular digestion requires that each digestive cell should be able to produce the full complement of digestive juices, whereas an extracellular process permits division of labour amongst different regions of the gut, and the development of anatomically separate multicellular glands such as the liver and pancreas the secretions of which can be conveyed from a distance into the gut by simple ducts. Finally, extracellular digestion permits ingestion of fairly large pieces of food, as opposed to the minute particles needed if digestion is to be exclusively intracellular.

All these factors, concerned with the evolution and facilitation of extracellular digestion, have given rise to the variety of digestive systems found in the Animal Kingdom. Basically, though, every digestive system can be regarded as an endodermal tube into which food enters through the mouth, which originates as an ectodermal inpushing, the stomodaeum, and eventually connects with the endodermal sac or canal. A gut of this type is found in coelenterates and flatworms, but from the Nemertina upwards a posterior ectodermal invagination, the proctodaeum, forms a second connection with the exterior, the anus. This permits one-way passage of food through the digestive system, and facilitates regional specialization of function and the separation in time and space of the different phases of digestion and absorption.

In vertebrates and most invertebrates five distinct regions can be recognized in the digestive system on the basis of functional homologies. These are: 1 a receiving region; 2 a conducting region which may also be used for food storage; 3 the digestive region proper, consisting of (a) a region of trituration and early digestion, (b) a region of later digestion and absorption; 4 a water absorbing region, where faeces are consolidated and conveyed to the exterior.

The receiving portion in most animals includes organs concerned with feeding and ingestion, such as the buccal cavity and pharynx, mandibles, jaws, teeth, radulae and salivary glands. Food may be mechanically or enzymically disintegrated here and the salivary secretions, primitively lubricant in function, may contain enzymes, poisons, acids, or in blood-feeders, anticoagulants.

The conducting region of the gut is usually a simple tube, the oesophagus, which links the pharynx with the stomach or equivalent region. In some instances, though, it expands into a sac-like storage region or crop, where preliminary digestion may occur by salivary enzymes swallowed with the food or by others regurgitated from the digestive region. Crops occur in a number of invertebrate groups, notably in the insects, and the birds.

The digestive region proper is generally divided into an anterior stomach, which is the region of trituration and early digestion (usually proteolytic), and a posterior extended intestine, in which digestion is completed and absorption occurs. Modifications of the stomach occur in a number of groups. In many arthropods, for example, an anterior portion becomes extremely muscular and forms a gizzard, where hard foods are crushed mechanically as well as softened and partially hydrolysed by digestive secretions. Seed-eating birds similarly possess a well-developed gizzard, and functionally homologous structures occur in rotifers, annelids and gastropod molluscs.

Extreme modification of the stomach is seen in ruminant mammals (e.g. sheep, oxen and deer), where it is subdivided into four chambers. The first chamber, or rumen, is greatly enlarged, contains vast numbers of symbiotic bacteria and ciliate protozoa and acts as a fermentation chamber where the *symbionts break down the cellulose which forms the bulk of the food. Rumen contents are periodically regurgitated into the mouth, thoroughly chewed (the process known as 'chewing the cud') and then reswallowed. The food may be returned to the rumen for further breakdown, but eventually is passed through the next two chambers (reticulum and omasum) to the fourth stomach or abomasum. This is glandular and corresponds to the single-chambered stomach of other mammals. Here other components of the food are digested, and also symbionts carried onwards from the rumen. These form a significant proportion of the proteinaceous content of the ruminant's diet, having multiplied and grown in the rumen using energy derived from the splitting of cellulose, and having synthesized protein partly from inorganic nitrates. Inorganic nitrogen cannot normally be utilized for protein synthesis by animals, but once synthesized into amino acids and proteins by symbionts it becomes available to the host when the symbionts are eventually digested.

The stomach in invertebrates is often supplemented by digestive diverticula, blind ending endodermal tubes the lining cells of which may be secretory, phagocytic or absorptive. Examples are the caeca found in polychaete annelids, the digestive glands of lamellibranch, gastropod and cephalopod molluscs, the pyloric caeca of asteroid

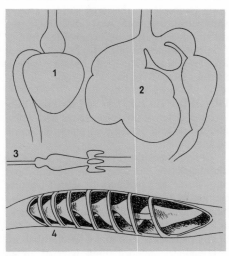

Different types of digestive system: 1. gizzard of some birds, 2. multiple stomach of ruminants (e.g. cattle, deer, etc.), 3. oesophagus, enteric caecae and intestine of some insects, 4. intestine of a shark, with spiral valve.

echinoderms, the digestive tubules or hepatopancreas of crustaceans and the enteric or gastric caeca of many insects.

The region of later digestion and absorption is generally an elongated tube, the intestine, confluent anteriorly with the stomach region. Since absorption is one of its primary functions it generally shows modifications which increase the internal surface area. These include various inward foldings of the lining such as the typhlosole found in earthworms and a few protochordates, the spiral valve of the cartilaginous fishes and the folds of Kerkring in the mammal. Villi, tiny finger-like outpushings covering the inner surface of the intestine like the pile of a carpet, are a characteristic adaptation for absorption in the mammal, and also occur in other higher chordates. The absorptive cells covering the villi also show an increase in the surface area in contact with the products of digestion, the distal wall bearing numerous closely packed microvilli. The combined folds of Kerkring, villi and microvilli increases the internal surface area approximately 600%, resulting in the average adult man having an intestinal internal surface area of some 2,000,000 sq cm.

The microvilli are important in carbohydrate digestion as well as in absorption, acting as physical catalysts bringing amylases and carbohydrates into intimate contact and significantly increasing the rate of hydrolysis. This type of digestion is termed contact digestion, as opposed to luminal or cavital digestion in the intestinal lumen.

The intestine in many animals contains a rich microflora and fauna of symbiotic micro-organisms often important in digestion or in the synthesis of vitamins. In herbivores, for example, intestinal symbionts play a similar role to those of the rumen in ruminant mammals, breaking down cellulose which the host could not otherwise utilize. In the horses and their allies this occurs in expanded portions of the intestinal tract, the caecum and colon, but the process is not as efficient as in ruminants since the micro-organisms live posteriorly to the regions of enzymic digestion. Thus whilst the products of cellulose breakdown are available to the host, the symbionts themselves cannot be digested and their protein content is never made available to the latter and is eventually lost when they die and are voided with the faeces.

Invertebrates relying on intestinal symbionts as an integral part of their nutritional physiology include the termites or White ants, where flagellates in the hind gut digest cellulose, and many blood-sucking insects which rely on symbionts for synthesis of vitamins.

The final region of the digestive system is concerned with absorption of water from the residues of the meal, mainly that poured on to the food as the major component of the digestive juices, and this function is of prime importance in terrestrial animals. The region is generally termed a rectum and may show specialized areas of absorption called rectal glands, as in insects.

Extraction of water consolidates the faeces and these are eventually voided to the exterior through the anus.   J.B.J.

DIK-DIK, six species of small antelope (*Madoqua, Rhynchotragus*) found especially in eastern Africa from Ethiopia to northern Kenya with one species in southwest Africa. They are 21–27 in (53–69 cm) in head and

The Age of Reptiles, when dinosaurs were the dominant large animals, lasted 120 million years and ended 70 million years ago. With the aid of abundant

body length, stand 12–16 in (30–40 cm) at the shoulder and weigh 7–11 lb (3–5 kg). The males have short horns often partly hidden by a tuft of hair on the top of the head. They live solitary or in pairs, sometimes in small family parties, in dense undergrowth from which they race away, when flushed, on a more or less zigzag course. FAMILY: Bovidae, ORDER: Artiodactyla, CLASS: Mammalia.

DIMETRODON, or 'sail-lizard', famous North American Permian reptile that was an early member of the mammal-like reptiles. It was an active carnivore, some 12 ft (3·7 m)

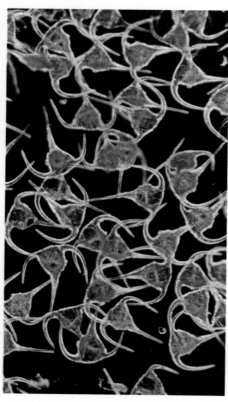

A swarm of dinoflagellates *Ceratium tripos* from the marine plankton.

long, with large jaws set with shearing teeth. The most spectacular feature was the presence of enormous upright, bony spines on the backbone which in life supported a membrane of skin. This adaptation is seen in several early mammal-like reptiles and would seem to be concerned with stabilizing the body temperature, the large surface area of sail permitting both heat absorption and radiation depending on external conditions. Complete skeletons of *Dimetrodon* have been found in North America. ORDER: Pelycosauria, CLASS: Reptilia.

DINOFLAGELLATES, a taxonomically isolated order of phytoflagellates with a few non-motile and filamentous plant-like representatives.

The exact position in the living world of the dinoflagellates has long been in doubt and may never be satisfactorily settled because the group as a whole links the animal and plant kingdoms. Some of the dinoflagellates are distinctly animal-like, others are distinctly plant-like, with many species that are intermediate and are often referred to as plant-animals.

The yellow-brown motile dinoflagellates have a prominent eyespot and two large chloroplasts or many small ones, with chlorophylls *a* and *c*, β-carotene and peridinin. They store starch and fat. Primitive forms are naked or have a simple cell wall of cellulose and pectin; advanced forms have a complex armour of sculptured plates, sometimes silicified and sometimes extended into wings and spines. All dinoflagellates have two flagella, one directed longitudinally and the other transversely. In primitive forms the flagella are inserted anteriorly; in advanced forms they arise laterally and lie in grooves. The longitudinal flagellum has a bilateral array of submicroscopic hairs, the transverse one, with only a single row of hairs, is fixed at both base and tip and undulates in a transverse furrow (girdle). The large nucleus divides by a

unique form of mitosis. Reproduction is mainly by fission; sexual reproduction is rare.

Dinoflagellates are important constituents of freshwater and marine plankton, sometimes producing 'blooms' in subtropical oceans, known as red tide, and poisoning large numbers of fish by the release of a toxic alkaloid. Other species form the symbiotic pigmented cells found in marine animals such as coelenterates and molluscs. In some cases the dinoflagellates are parasitic and eventually poison their host, and they may cause illness in man from infected shellfish. The aberrant dinoflagellate *Noctiluca is the cause of 'phosphorescence' in warm seas at night. The swollen cells (1–2 mm diam) contain luminescent bodies which discharge light (by oxidation of luciferin) when disturbed by wave or boat action.

Most dinoflagellates combine photosynthetic nutrition with the ingestion of solid food. The large armoured form *Ceratium* (0·001–0·007 mm) captures food by extending pseudopodia through the body furrows. PHYLUM: Protozoa.   G.F.L.

DINOSAURS. For 120 million years the land faunas of the world were dominated by two great orders of reptiles, the Saurischia and Ornithischia, which are commonly grouped together under the name Dinosauria (Gk *deinos*-terrible, *saurus*-lizard). The dinosaurs were a diverse group of reptiles for their habits were nearly as varied as those of the mammals today. There were, however, no marine or aerial forms. Many were fully terrestrial, adapted for fast running in the uplands, while others inhabited the lowlands and were semi-aquatic in habit. Although some were small and of delicate construction, among the dinosaurs we find the largest land herbivores and carnivores of all time.

The known record of dinosaurs extends from the Middle Triassic, some 190 million years ago, to the end of the Cretaceous, about 70 million years ago. The reasons for their

Gorgosaurus

Ornithomimus

Styracosaurus

Ankylosaurus

Corythosaurus

plant and animal fossils it is possible to reconstruct the landscape of those times together with its larger inhabitants.

final extinction are far from clear but the demise of so dramatic a group has over-shadowed, in the mind of the layman, the fact that for an immense span of time they were highly successful. The popular impression that they were a group of cumbersome monsters with a low state of mental organiza-tion, ill suited to a changing environment, and trapped in an ever increasing spiral of gigantism is far from true. In their loco-motory and feeding adaptations they out-stripped all other land reptiles and it is even doubtful if the tiny and more highly adapted mammals which existed throughout the Mesozoic – the 'Age of Reptiles' – played any significant role in their decline.

History of discovery. The years 1824–25 mark the beginning of dinosaur discovery and studies. In 1824 William Buckland, Oxford cleric, geologist and eccentric, de-

scribed the bones of a huge carnivore from the Jurassic rocks of Stonesfield outside Oxford. He gave the name *Megalosaurus* to these remains and suggested they belonged to a giant lizard. In the following year a Sussex geologist, but doctor by profession, Gideon Mantell, described the teeth of a massive herbivorous reptile from Sussex to which he gave the name *Iguanodon*. In fact, the first tooth of *Iguanodon* had been found by Mrs Mantell in 1822 but her husband delayed publication to search for more evidence to overcome the scepticism of his geological colleagues. This caution was understandable for the greatest anatomist in Europe, Baron Cuvier, on inspecting a tooth sent by Mantell had identified it as that of a rhinoceros.

The name Dinosauria for a new group of reptiles to include these and other discoveries was first used by Sir Richard Owen in 1842.

This name was valid until 1887 when Seeley, another noted British expert on fossil reptiles, recognized that dinosaurs comprised two quite distinct orders of reptile, of equal importance, which evolved independently along with crocodiles, pterodactyls, and birds from an ancestral group called *thecodonts. To these two independent dinosaur orders Seeley gave the names Saurischia and Orni-thischia and these names remain today. Although both orders evolved from a com-mon group in the Triassic their relationship to one another is not especially close. The distinction between the Saurischia ('lizard-pelvis') and Ornithischia ('bird-pelvis') is primarily based upon the structure of the pelvic girdle which articulates the hindlimbs. In saurischians the pelvic girdle of each side is a three pronged structure somewhat similar to the pattern in lizards, and hence the name for this order. In all ornithischians, however, the pelvis is a four pronged structure a pattern strikingly similar to birds – so much so that for a long time birds were thought to have evolved from ornithischians. A feature unique to ornithischians is the presence of a median toothless bone, the predentary, at the front of the lower jaw. In habit, the Saurischia includes bipedal carnivores (e.g. *Tyranno-saurus*), and quadrupedal herbivores (e.g. *Brontosaurus*). The Ornithischia also in-cludes both bipeds (e.g. *Iguanodon*) and quadrupeds (e.g. *Triceratops*) but all were herbivores. Both orders are found in the Triassic and both continued to evolve and diversify throughout the remainder of the Mesozoic.

The Saurischia was in many respects the more conservative of the two orders, its members preserving many of the anatomical features found in the thecodont ancestors. Two quite separate lines of saurischian evolution can be followed and the two groups which can be distinguished are called the Sauropoda and Theropoda, The sauropods, were all quadrupedal and plant-eaters and it is

Reconstruction of *Triceratops*, a three-horned extinct giant reptile.

Reconstruction of *Ceratosaurus* (left) and *Stegosaurus* (right), two well-known types of extinct giant reptiles.

in this group of dinosaurs (the *Brontosaurus* belongs here) that we see gigantism taken to the limits. They were small-headed forms and the greater part of their enormous length was accounted for by the extensive neck and tail. That they were lowland forms spending their lives browsing on the soft marshland vegetation is certain but to what extent they were amphibious is debatable, and we shall return to this question. The theropods were strikingly different from sauropods in their adaptations for all were bipedal and were the dominant predators of the Mesozoic.

Sauropods, as we have seen, were without exception plant eaters and in all but a few forms attained enormous size. From their skeletons it is possible to determine fairly accurately their live weight. *Brontosaurus*, for example, was just over 65 ft (20 m) long and in life would have weighed some 35 tons. In *Diplodocus* and *Brachiosaurus* the body length was 90 ft (28 m) but in the former where the body, judging by the skeleton, was slender and the tail very long the live weight was similar to *Brontosaurus*. In *Brachiosaurus* however the body was of massive construction and the tail short, and this dinosaur must have weighed 50 tons.

Problem of gigantism. This is a convenient time to discuss the problem of gigantism remembering that this phenomenom is not confined to the sauropods among the dinosaurs, and in fact is not confined to the reptiles. It has however been suggested by some experts that due to the excessive growth of the pituitary gland, which in part controls size, the dinosaurs were caught up in an inflationary spiral, unable to control their growth, and that this was one of the major factors causing their extinction. They became too big to move without an enormous expenditure of energy, and to nourish so large a body became increasingly difficult. As evidence it has been found that in some giant dinosaurs the bony recess in the braincase which housed the pituitary is large. One can,

however, argue that without a large and active pituitary dinosaurs could not have become very big, and, furthermore, that in many respects it is efficient to be big. To understand the reason why, it is necessary to consider the physical relationship which exists between the surface area and volume of a three dimensional object. A mouse has an enormous surface area relative to its volume but a large dinosaur has a very small surface area relative to its volume. This ratio is physiologically important for the following reasons. The large dinosaur with its relatively small surface area of skin would absorb heat slowly in the daytime and lose heat slowly by radiation in the cool of the night. It seems likely therefore that the largest of the dinosaurs had the benefit of a fairly stable body temperature unlike the small reptiles of their time and today. In mammals special adaptations of the skin and other organs have been necessary to stabilize the body temperature. The ratio of surface area to volume also has a marked effect on an animal's food requirements and again we can see how large size can make for efficiency. The small animal loses much of its metabolic energy by radiation through its large area of skin and must feed continually to compensate for this extravagance. The larger dinosaurs however did not need to do so although when they did feed a prodigious bulk of food would be required. A massive herbivorous dinosaur would need to have cropped a large area for its support. For this reason gigantism is never found in island species where pygmy races are often the rule.

It must be admitted that the advantages of gigantism are not obtained without some difficulty. With increased size great stresses are put on the body's internal scaffolding, the skeleton. When an animal increases in length its mass increases as a cube of the linear increase whereas the cross-sectional area of each supporting bone, and this determines their strength, increases by the square of the

linear increase. In other words as an animal gets bigger its weight increases at a considerably faster rate than that of the strength of the supporting skeleton. This factor imparts a limit to size but the evidence suggests that the sauropods, and other giant dinosaurs, although approaching this limit, functioned successfully without hindrance. It has always been assumed that the sauropods of necessity spent most of their lives in water dependent on the buoyancy for additional support. That some of their structural features are adapted for amphibious life is not denied but recent evidence suggests that sauropods spent as much time out of the water as in.

The sauropods. Being plant eaters and not requiring large jaws for predation the sauropods had disproportionately small heads. With so small and light a head they could afford the luxury of a very long neck. This enabled the sauropod to crop vegetation over a large ground area while the body was stationary and thus energy was conserved.

The small jaws were set with simple rather peg-like teeth which suggests a diet of soft riverine vegetation. The eyes and nostrils were set high on the skull which might indicate a semi-aquatic life. In *Diplodocus* there is a single common nasal opening on top of the skull which might have functioned as a snorkel.

The sauropod backbone was of massive construction for support of the viscera but the sides of each vertebra were ingeniously hollowed out to reduce their weight without loss of strength. Along the top of the vertebral column ran large ligaments to winch up the head and neck. The limbs were of pillar-like construction for support of the enormous body weight and terminated in elephantine feet with the toes embedded in great pads of tissue.

The origin of the sauropods can be traced back to a group of Triassic dinosaurs of world-wide distribution called prosauropods. It is often said that the sauropods are secondarily quadrupedal having evolved from bipedal ancestors. The shortness of the forelimb compared to the hindlimb has been cited as evidence for this theory. This feature is however typical of all dinosaurs and was present in their thecodont ancestors, the majority of which walked on all four legs. The recent discovery of large Triassic quadrupedal prosauropods, and their trackways, in southern Africa further suggests that the sauropods never passed through a bipedal stage of locomotion.

The sauropods, in terms of variety and numbers, reached their peak of development in the Upper Jurassic and by the Cretaceous were already in decline. It should however be stressed that fossil land vertebrates are rarer in Lower Jurassic and Lower Cretaceous times because throughout the world marine deposits predominate.

The richest fossil localities for sauropods are the Upper Jurassic Morrison and Tendaguru strata, of the western United States and Tanzania respectively. Rich Cretaceous deposits are found in Patagonia and Mongolia. Sauropod remains are not uncommon in Europe but the combination of poor rock exposure, a low erosion rate, and a declining stone-quarrying industry reduces the chances of discovery today. However there is one remarkable site in France for on a mountain slope outside Aix large numbers of complete and fragmentary sauropod eggs are found.

The theropods. The second group of the Saurischia is the Theropoda. Without exception all theropods were bipedal and the great majority were flesh-eating. Two separate groups of theropods can be distinguished and these are called coelurosaurs and carnosaurs.

The coelurosaurs were small for dinosaurs, *Compsognathus* from the Jurassic lithographic limestone of Bavaria was turkey-sized and the largest known coelurosaur had a maximum length of about 15 ft (5 m). They were delicately constructed and probably adapted for fast running in open country.

The coelurosaur skull was light and bird-like in construction. In the more primitive forms the jaws were set with sharp pointed teeth but in some advanced Cretaceous forms teeth were absent. It is likely that the toothed species fed on small reptiles and mammals and that the others had turned to an insect diet. The head was carried on a long and slender, upright neck. All the bones of the skeleton were thin-walled to reduce weight. The forelimb was quite well developed and in some Cretaceous forms ended in a three fingered hand with the thumb opposable for grasping prey. In all coelurosaurs the long and slender hindlimbs were adapted to give fast action and a long stride.

Coelurosaurs had a world-wide distribution throughout the Mesozoic but, for reasons not yet clear, their fossils are far more abundant in rocks of northern latitudes. One group, the ornithomimids ('bird-mimics'), from the Cretaceous of North

---

60
CRETACEOUS

Triceratops

Trachodon

Protoceratops

CERATOPSIA

Iguanodon

Ankylosaurus   Tyrannosaurus

100

Palaeoscineus

ANKYLOSAURIA

Camptosaurus

ORNITHOPODA   JURASSIC

Ornitholestes

Diplodocus

Brontosaurus   150

Stegosaurus

SAUROPODA

STEGOSAURIA   TRIASSIC

ORNITHISCHIA   THEROPODA

Coelophysis

SAURISCHIA

THECODONTIA
200

From a group of primitive bipedal reptiles, the Thecodontia, the Trias saw the development amongst others of two lines of dinosaurs, which differ amongst other things in the structure of the pelvis. In one group the pubic bone points backwards, as in birds, hence the name Ornithischia (bird-like pelvis). In the other it points to the front, as in most present-day reptiles, hence the name Saurischia (lizard-like pelvis). The Ornithischia were all herbivores and either bipedal or quadrupedal. *Stegosaurus* had spines on the tail and a row of upright dorsal scales; *Palaeoscinsus* and *Ankylosaurus* had scales like turtles; *Protoceratops* and *Triceratops* had neck scales and the latter also had three large horns. *Iguanodon* and *Trachodon* walked on their hindlegs and were shore animals, the latter also had a flat beak. The Saurischia developed on the one hand into enormous quadrupedal herbivores like the marsh animals *Diplodocus* and *Brontosaurus*, with their long necks, and on the other hand, into bipedal beasts of prey which used their frontlegs for gripping prey. The smallest of all dinosaurs, *Compsognathus*, the size of a domestic hen, belonged to this group, as did *Coelophysis*, 8 ft (2.4 m) long, which it resembled, and *Ornitholestes* 6 ft (2 m) long and *Tyrannosaurus* 50 ft (15 m) long.

Restoration of a scene in the distant past, showing the giant reptile *Diplodocus*, one of the sauropods.

America and Mongolia, is of particular interest. The ornithomimid skull and skeleton were extraordinarily ostrich-like in structure and ornithomimids no doubt led a very similar life to the ostriches today being adapted for fast running. When, as in this case, two quite unrelated groups of animals, by reason of their similar mode of life, develop the same kinds of anatomical features we call this phenomenom 'convergent evolution'. In some ornithomimids teeth were absent and these forms probably fed on insects. The skeleton of another ornithomimid, *Oviraptor,* was found in Mongolia beside a nest of dinosaur eggs. As the eggs belonged to a very different dinosaur, a ceratopsian, it is tempting to think that *Oviraptor* ('egg-robber') was an egg-eater and was trapped in the act.

Dinosaurs of Ghost Ranch. Of all regions where coelurosaurs have been found, none is more famous than Ghost Ranch in New Mexico. From a single site a number of perfectly articulated skeletons of the Triassic genus, *Coelophysis,* have been excavated. The skeletons of both young and old were tumbled together as witness to some local catastrophe. Cannibalism must have been rife for within

the skeletons of the larger specimens are found the dismembered fragments of the young. The Ghost Ranch locality is an exception because coelurosaur skeletons are rather rare, no doubt because the fragile bones did not preserve well.

The carnosaurs, the other theropod group, include the largest land-dwelling predators of all time for here belong forms like *Tyrannosaurus* with a length of 50 ft (16 m) and a weight of 8 tons. The massive hindlimbs supported the weight of the body, the skull was 4 ft (1·2 m) in length and was carried some 20 ft (6·1 m) clear of the ground.

One of the main features of carnosaur evolution was the progressive increase in skull size which was accompanied by the progressive reduction in size of the forelimb. The relationship between these two trends is easily explained for in carnosaur evolution the head took over completely the function of predation and the arms became unimportant in the seizure and destruction of prey. In the Upper Cretaceous tyrannosaurs where these two related trends are taken to the limit, the skull reached enormous proportions, and the forelimb was almost vestigial.

When we described the sauropods we

noted that because their heads were small and light they could afford the benefits of a long neck. In carnosaurs the situation is quite different for as the head increases in size for predation the neck must shorten for its carriage. In the tyrannosaurs the disproportionately large head was carried on a short neck of massive, compressed, and sometimes partly fused vertebrae. To offset in part the mechanical disadvantages of so large and heavy a head we find that in Cretaceous forms particularly the skull is a marvel of construction. Large openings were developed between the bones so that the whole structure of the skull is a system of columns and arches allowing reduction in weight without sacrificing mechanical strength.

Both the upper and lower jaws of carnosaurs were armed with serrated dagger-like teeth. The lower jaws were loosely hung from the skull enabling a large gape to the jaws. As in snakes, the two halves of the lower jaw did not meet in a bony junction to form a chin. This condition allows a gape in the horizontal plane so that large objects can more easily be swallowed.

The carnosaur vertebral column was pivoted on the fulcrum of the pelvis and a heavy and powerful tail was necessary to counterbalance the weight forward of the pelvis. When at rest the tail and hindlimbs would form a tripod.

The carnosaur hindlimbs were ideally adapted for bipedal locomotion with the upper bones, the femora, massively strong to carry the main limb musculature, and the lower leg long to increase the stride.

Carnosaurs are very rare in the Triassic and their derivation is obscure. In the Upper Jurassic the fragmentary remains of the European form *Megalosaurus* and its allies are found, and in North America complete skeletons of *Allosaurus* have been excavated. The giant tyrannosaurs are all Cretaceous in age, noted genera being *Tyrannosaurus* in North America, *Gorgosaurus* in Canada, and *Tarbosaurus* in Asia.

The Ornithischia is the second order of dinosaurs. Apart from the diagnostic pelvic pattern, already mentioned, many other features set apart ornithischians from saurischians. All were plant-eaters and the teeth tended to be set on the back half of the jaws and were often crowded together to form a file-like grinding surface. It would seem that unlike their herbivorous saurischian cousins they favoured a hard plant diet. The toothless fronts of the jaws were probably covered in horny pads. Although many members developed a bipedal mode of locomotion, the forelimb in these remained well developed and the dinosaurs at rest dropped down onto all fours. In many respects ornithischians were a less conservative group than the saurischians and show many unusual features of skull and armour. Although many were

Restoration of *Anatosaurus,* Duckbilled dinosaurs.

Antrodemus and *Diplodocus*, contrasting types of extinct giant North American reptiles.

large they never reached the gigantic dimensions of saurischians.

In the Mesozoic scene, particularly towards the end of the era, ornithischians made up the bulk of the dinosaur fauna and filled the same role as do the great herds of herbivorous mammals in Africa today. Moving in herds across the Mesozoic landscape they were alert for the approach of predators. Some forms with their horns or spiked armour were a match for all but the largest of carnosaurs, but others, without defensive armour, took to the water in times of danger.

Although common in Upper Jurassic deposits around the world, the order reached its peak of development in the Cretaceous. Only one or two skeletons have been found in rocks of Lower Jurassic age, a reflection of the predominance of marine deposits at this time, and only within the last few years have their remains been found in Triassic rocks.

Four groups of ornithischian dinosaurs can be recognized: the bipedal ornithopods, the quadrupedal stegosaurs with bony plates along the back, the quadrupedal and heavily armoured ankylosaurs, and the quadrupedal, horned ceratopsians.

The suborder Ornithopoda includes the earliest known ornithischians for their remains have been found recently in Triassic rocks in South Africa, South America, and China. All ornithopods were bipedal although the arm and hand structure shows that it could be used in locomotion. In the earliest members, like the Triassic genus *Heterodontosaurus* from South Africa, we find the primitive ornithischian tooth condition in which teeth are present on the front of the jaws. The next stage of dental evolution is found in Jurassic and Lower Cretaceous ornithopods like *Camptosaurus* and *Iguanodon* where leaf-like teeth are restricted to the back two-thirds of the jaws. The most

specialized type of ornithopod dentition is found in the Cretaceous hadrosaurs, or Duck-billed dinosaurs, where the back halves of the jaws are set with parallel rows of teeth crowded together to form a pavement-like structure for grinding hard plant material.

Mass death of dinosaurs. Perhaps the most famous of all ornithopods is *Iguanodon*, originally described by Mantell. This dinosaur reached a length of 35 ft (10·6 m), the hindlimbs being very massive, with three splayed toes on the foot, for support of the heavy body. A complex lattice of tendons ran along the back which helped to support the body when rearing up on its hindlegs. The hand was five-fingered, the outer two digits being weak and the thumb bone in the form of a long bony spike for defence. Iguanodont bones and footprints have been found in Europe, Asia, and Africa. The most remarkable occurrence of all was discovered in Belgium in 1877 when coalminers at Bernissart opened up at a depth of 1046 ft (322 m) a Cretaceous deposit filling a gully in the old Carboniferous landscape. A herd of *Iguanodon* had fallen into this gully and were entombed. Despite difficulties of excavation at this depth some 30 skeletons, many complete, were successfully removed to Brussels.

Not all ornithopods were large and one small form of particular interest is *Hypsilophodon*. This Cretaceous form found in England has a delicate skeleton about 4 ft (1·2 m) long. The structure of its hands and feet suggests an arboreal life, and if this is so then *Hypsilophodon* is the only known dinosaur to occupy this niche.

The hadrosaurs, or Duck-billed dinosaurs, were yet another ornithopod group and these were the most abundant ornithischians of the Upper Cretaceous, with a world-wide distribution. The Duck-bills take their name from the fact that the front of the skull and lower

jaw was drawn out into a large flat beak. Although bipedal when moving at speed, the presence of hoof-like ends to the hand digits clearly indicates that the hadrosaurs could walk on four legs.

We have already mentioned the complex tooth series in hadrosaurs but another remarkable skull feature is the development in this group of bony crests on the forehead. The North American genus *Corythosaurus* shows this character well. In the related genus *Parasaurolophus* an even more bizarre development was the presence on the snout of a long backwardly directed spur of bone passing over the top of the skull. When sectioned it is found that the nasal passage is carried back inside this to the apex and then turns forward along it to reach the throat region. Many suggestions have been made to account for the U-shaped nasal passage but none is convincing. The bone has no opening at its apex so the early theory that it functioned as a snorkel is discounted. That the long nasal passage could be used as an air store when *Parasaurolophus* submerged is unlikely because the storage area is so minute when compared to the estimated lung volume. The most recent theory is that hadrosaurs were far more terrestrial than has been previously supposed and that enlarged nasal passages were only concerned with the sense of smell. Warned of the approach of a predator, the hadrosaur took to the water.

The Upper Cretaceous rocks of Canada have yielded some superbly preserved hadrosaurs and in a few cases even the skin and much of the musculature has been fossilized. The skin was covered with small scales and extended between the fingers and toes as webs supporting the idea that hadrosaurs were at least semi-aquatic. The deep and powerful tail was possibly adapted as a swimming organ.

The Stegosauria was an even more strange group of ornithischians, their main diagnostic feature being the armour on the back. The stegosaurs were quadrupeds although the limb structure indicates that they were derived from bipedal ornithopods. The forelimb was very short in proportion to the hindlimb, and the back strongly arched so that stegosaurs stood high at the rump but low at the shoulders. The digits of both hand and foot ended in hoof-like pads. The head was disproportionately small and the brain kitten-sized. In stegosaurs however the spinal cord swelled out in the pelvic region to form an accessory 'brain' controlling locomotion.

The most obvious and remarkable feature of the stegosaurs was their armour which was confined to the upper surface of the body. In the best known form, *Stegosaurus* from the Upper Jurassic, the body was 20 ft (6·2 m) long and the neck, trunk, and tail carried a double row of vertical and triangular bony plates. The end of the tail was armed with four long, defensive spikes.

Restoration model showing head of a carnivorous dinosaur.

The earliest known stegosaur is a form found in England called *Scelidosaurus*. The remains come from a Lower Jurassic marine deposit, the carcasses having been carried to the sea by rivers at the time of death. Stegosaurs had a cosmopolitan distribution in the Upper Jurassic and Lower Cretaceous but none survived into the late Cretaceous.

Reptilian tanks. The third suborder of the Ornithischia is the Ankylosauria. These quadrupedal herbivores demonstrate the greatest degree of armour plating found in dinosaurs and with good reason have been called 'reptilian tanks'. Some reached a length of 20 ft (6·2 m) and in all the much flattened head and trunk was protected on its upper surface by a mosaic of bony plates. Typically the tail had a flexible armour of bony rings. In some the shoulder and tail regions carried long bony spines. With so heavy a body it is not surprising that the legs were very short and the feet broad.

The ankylosaurs were restricted to the Cretaceous, well known forms being *Polacanthus* from the European Lower Cretaceous and *Ankylosaurus* from the North American Upper Cretaceous.

The Ceratopsia is the remaining suborder of the Ornithischia and is the last dinosaur group to appear in the fossil record for no ceratopsian is known before the Upper Cretaceous. Here belong the rhinoceros-like horned dinosaurs with *Triceratops* the most famous genus.

Considering the group as a whole a number of evolutionary trends can be seen which continued throughout the Upper Cretaceous. The most important of these were: an increase in body size, enlargement of the head associated with increase in jaw length and the development on the skull of horns and a bony frill covering the neck, and a progressive reduction in limb length, particularly that of the back legs.

In the primitive ceratopsian, *Protoceratops* from Mongolia, the head relative to the body was of moderate size, and the skull carried an incipient facial horn but a well developed and fenestrated frill. A great deal is known about this little ceratopsian for their eggs and complete skeletons at all stages of growth have been collected. In *Triceratops* from North America the body reached a length of 25 ft (7·6 m) of which a third was accounted for by the head. In *Triceratops* there was a short nasal horn and a pair of long horns above the eyes. *Monoclonius* shows the reverse condition and in *Styracosaurus* there

was a long nasal horn and at least eight horn-like processes on the margin of the collar frill.

The skull frill served both to protect the vulnerable neck region and also to provide a large surface area for the attachment of the powerful jaw muscles. The front of the ceratopsian's jaws formed narrow turtle-like beaks but behind these were batteries of shearing teeth. The whole structure of the jaw apparatus suggests an unusually tough and fibrous plant diet and it seems likely that the ceratopsians cropped the hard fronds of palms and cycads.

Despite more than a century's research many problems remain unanswered, not the least of which is the cause of the dinosaurs' final extinction.

Why did dinosaurs become extinct

It is often difficult to explain why a group of animals becomes extinct, but when we consider the dinosaurs, which for so long a span of time were both varied and successful, the mystery is greater and we can only speculate wildly on the causes. In attempting to do so it is important to appreciate from the start that extinction in any group of animals can result from two different factors. In the first case, species in a lineage become extinct because in their evolution they are replaced by newly evolved forms – the ancestor being unable to compete with its descendant. This pattern of extinction is certainly found in the dinosaurs for there was a wholesale extinction of dinosaurs at the end of the Triassic when new and more highly adapted groups appeared.

The second pattern of extinction is seen when a group disappears without issue. This may be related to internal factors, or to changes in the environment. The final extinction of the dinosaurs at the close of the Mesozoic was probably the result of a whole series of events in the Cretaceous. This was a time of great mountain building and as the earth's crust gradually heaved up and crumpled some regions would be subjected to uplift, and others to compensating downwarping. In the regions of uplift the lowland swamps and sluggish river systems would drain and its vegetation wither. In the regions of downwarping the seas would flood the lower ground. The lowland herbivores and in particular sauropods and hadrosaurs would be the first to suffer and as they declined the food chain would be broken, for now the predators were denied their prey. A second feature of the Cretaceous was the gradual replacement of the palm and cycad forests by modern types of plants, the gymnosperms. The traditional food of hadrosaurs and ceratopsians was in short supply by the end of the Cretaceous and this factor alone might account for their extinction.

These are only partial answers to the problem but what does seem certain is that neither gigantism nor competition from mammals played any significant role in their demise. A further question which remains unanswered is why at the end of the Cretaceous not only the two orders of dinosaurs but the flying pterosaurs and both groups of quite unrelated marine reptiles, the plesiosaurs and ichthyosaurs, also became extinct. Perhaps we shall never know.

As Professor Colbert, our greatest living dinosaur expert, has said "when they died, they left their bones in the earth. Today one mammal, man, digs up these relics of the past and learns much from them and, at times, is confounded by them". J.A.

DINOSAUR DEMISE. The sudden extinction of the giant reptiles at the end of the Cretaceous will probably remain a mystery for ever. No single reason can adequately explain the extinction of not only the two orders of dinosaurs but also the aerial pterosaurs and the marine plesiosaurs, ichthyosaurs and others. According to W. Cuppy, 'the Age of Reptiles ended because it had gone on long enough and it was all a mistake in the first place'. This light-hearted statement draws attention to the fact that the giant reptiles had been successful for a very long time but lacked one essential for continued success – adaptability. It also suggests that there is little point in propounding theories without a sufficient framework of facts.

DIPLASIOCOELA, a suborder of frogs. The term diplasiocoelous describes the structure of the vertebral column. In the first seven vertebrae the spool-shaped centra have the anterior face concave and the posterior face convex and in the eighth vertebra both faces are concave. The members of the suborder usually have, in addition, a shoulder girdle which is firmisternal, that is, the two halves are fused down the mid-line.

There are four families: Ranidae, true frogs; Rhacophoridae, Old World treefrogs; Microhylidae, the Narrow-mouthed toads; and Phrynomeridae, a small African family containing a single genus. ORDER: Anura, CLASS: Amphibia.

DIPLOID. In the diploid condition the cell nucleus contains chromosomes in matching (homologous) pairs so that twice the *haploid number is present. It is the usual condition of all animal cells except the sex-cells (gametes). In man there are 23 different pairs of chromosomes so the diploid number is 46.

DIPLURA, a widely distributed order of about 400 species of wingless insects which, like the Protura and the springtails, are found mainly in well concealed habitats with constant conditions, such as in the soil, in rotting wood and beneath the bark of trees. They have no eyes but the head carries other important sense organs in the form of long, mobile, multi-segmented antennae. Like other primitive insects, the Diplura have small leg-like appendages of unknown function on the abdominal segments. At its hind end the abdomen carries a pair of movable appendages, the cerci, which in some forms (the Campodeidae) are many-segmented and antenna-like and in others (the Japygidae) are short, hard pincers used to catch prey. Some species have, at the tips of the cerci, the openings of a poison gland situated in the abdomen. The internal anatomy, including the reproductive system is, as far as is known, of a simple insect type. There are no external genital organs. Sperm leave the body of the male in a small sac of chitin called the spermatophore which is passed through a pore opening near the end of the abdomen. The spermatophore is deposited on the surface of the soil or on a piece of vegetation where it is later picked up by the female through her own reproductive pore and the eggs are fertilized within her body. The female lays batches of 10–20 eggs in cavities in the soil. The young are similar in appearance to the adults into which they grow and develop without a metamorphosis.

Two families, the Japygidae and the Projapygidae, are found mainly in the tropics and are predators of arthropods smaller than themselves. Some grow to as much as $\frac{3}{4}$ in (2 cm) long and populations of up to 1,500 individuals per sq yd (sq⁻m) have been found in pasture soils in West Africa. A species of *Japyx* living in the Mediterranean region shows a primitive form of territorial behaviour, which presumably ensures that each individual has an adequate supply of food. The third family, the Campodeidae, is found in both temperate and tropical regions and probably feeds indiscriminately on dead plant and animal material. Individuals are rarely more than $\frac{1}{5}$ in (5 mm) long and are found at densities up to 6,000 per sq yd (sq m) in some woodland soils. CLASS: Insecta, PHYLUM: Arthropoda. I.N.H.

A species of Diplura.

DIPPERS, rather wren-like songbirds of the family Cinclidae, and suborder Oscines. There are four species in one genus, distributed in western North and South America, northwest Africa, Europe and the temperate parts of Asia. They resemble wrens in their short wings and tail, copious plumage and type of nest, but are specialized for feeding in or under running water, with the tarsus long and sturdy and with stout claws for gripping the river bed.

The different species of dipper vary in size between a sparrow and a Song thrush, have thin bills and are predominantly grey or brown. Although the sexes look alike (and both sing), the dipper *Cinclus cinclus* of Europe can be distinguished in the hand by the greater wing length of the male, 87–95 mm compared with 84–92 of the female. In a recent study in Czechoslovakia a wing length of 90 mm was taken as the dividing line, with females invariably below this. Males are also heavier and a weight of over 60 gm is diagnostic except for females about to lay.

Dippers are confined to hilly and mountainous regions. Several races of the White-capped dipper *C. leucocephalus* inhabit the Andes. The range of the American dipper *C. mexicanus* extends from western Panama to Alaska and the Aleutians. The European dipper ranges from Britain eastwards to northwest Africa and central Asia, reaching 16,000 ft (4,920 m) in the Himalayas and nearly 17,000 ft (5,230 m) in Tibet. In Turkestan, the Himalayas and western China, its range overlaps with that of the Brown dipper *C. pallasii* which prefers lower, wider rivers and inhabits northern Asia eastwards to Japan. Within these ranges a certain amount of variation occurs between dippers from different areas and, because their habitat needs are specialized, the range is often discontinuous.

The breeding of the dipper has been studied in North America, Czechoslovakia and Britain. Nests are usually built on rock faces (including waterfalls), on man-made structures, for example on sluices, mills, culverts and bridges, and under overhanging banks and against tree trunks. The entrance is normally over water. Most nests are built at heights of 4–5 ft (1·2–1·5 m); 94 nests examined in Westmorland, in the north of England, were between 1½–20 ft (0·45–6 m). In Czechoslovakia dippers have nested in specially designed boxes which had no fronts.

The large nest is like that of a wren and usually fits into a roofed cavity which determines its dimensions. The measurements of nests not limited in this way are 7–10 in (18–25 cm) across, 5–9 in (13–23 cm) deep, and 6–9 in (16–23 cm) high. In Britain the outer shell of the nest is made of mosses. These are mostly gathered along the river bank although some aquatic mosses may be used. The material, collected by both cock and hen, is dipped into the river before use, presumably to make it work more easily into the shell of the nest. When the outer shell is completed an inner nest of dried grasses is added and finally a lined cup of leaves, which may be the work of the hen alone.

Nest-building begins as early as February and proceeds slowly. Eggs may be laid in mid-March but more usually in April. Later nests may be built in as little as nine days. Four or five thin-shelled white eggs are laid, sometimes three, rarely as many as seven. They hatch in about 16 days and the young are fed by both parents. Two broods are hatched in some years, perhaps those in which breeding starts earlier than usual.

Young dippers remain in the nest for about three weeks, and reach a weight of 2 oz (50–60 gm). From 14 days onwards they have a disconcerting habit of leaping out of the nest into the water if disturbed, and swimming away downstream. Their first plumage, which they begin to moult at nine weeks, is more mottled than that of the parent birds, and the white feathers at chin, throat and upper breast are tipped with dark brown giving a rather thrush-like appearance. They are fed by their parents until about five weeks old and then disperse. They can be distinguished from adults by the white tips of the greater wing coverts which persist until the following April, although in some cases they become much abraded.

The territorial habits of the dipper are striking and well known. Both sexes take up territories in winter, as well as in spring and summer. Because they are reluctant to leave those stretches of river or stream they can be chased to the end of the territory where they will double back over the observer's head, thus revealing the territorial boundary. Winter territories were found to be as little as 1,050–1,200 ft (320–365 m) long in North America where dippers are forced downstream by ice, but a distribution of one dipper to 2,100–3,300 ft (650–1,015 m) is more usual in Czechoslovakia and Scotland.

Summer territories also vary markedly in size, from about 1,200 ft (365 m) in Britain, and 1,650–1,950 ft (505–600 m) in Germany to nests $1\frac{1}{4}$–2 miles (2–3 km) apart in USSR. Territory size may be determined by the availability of nest sites, quite long stretches of some small fast flowing rivers and streams having no suitable sites.

Territories are defended by song, often delivered from favoured boulders near the margin of the territory and by ritualized forms of display. Dippers sing loudly so as to be heard above the rush of water and throughout the whole year except July and August. Both sexes sing and the song has been described as 'a very sweet rippling warble, somewhat wren-like in general pattern'. Display consists largely of bobbing up and down with wing-flicking, dropping into the water and swimming ashore during pursuit flight, and a form of upright posturing to display the breast colouring which is similar to that adopted by the robin. This is elicited by the approach of a male dipper, and probably serves to prevent him from attacking his mate. There is also a display flight, rarely seen, in which two dippers fly much higher than usual, at 50–100 ft (15–30 m), with loud and continuous song. Normal flight is directly along the watercourse and 1–6 ft (0·3–1·8 m) up.

Dipper feeding nestling.

Winter occupation of a territory may be by either sex or by both birds of a pair which remain to nest there the following spring. Some dippers stay for two or three years in the same territory, changing mates during that time, while others appear at widely scattered points as if unable to secure a permanent territory. Either male or female can be replaced with the original bird remaining the territory 'owner', and a missing bird, for whatever cause, is replaced within a few days in the breeding season. Young dippers, however, seldom succeed in establishing themselves by displacing older territorial birds and may be obliged to breed in less desirable areas.

The dipper's feeding habits have always aroused interest as an example of a passerine bird specially adapted to an unusual mode of life. There were early controversies as to whether it could walk under water and, if so, whether it could do so only against the current. More recently dippers have been filmed swimming under water and it can be shown that they do so by using their wings and not their legs. It is also quite easy to watch dippers walking upstream in shallow water searching for prey on the river bed, or swimming in slightly deeper water, but not usually more than 18 in (45 cm) deep, and diving from the surface. They will also plunge directly into the water from a river bank, a boulder or the margin of ice.

Their food mainly consists of the larvae of aquatic insects, and small aquatic molluscs and crustaceans. Small fishes are also taken but are not very expertly dealt with and they form, together with worms and tadpoles only a small proportion of the dipper's known prey.

A study of the roosting habits of dipper in northeast Scotland showed that they roosted regularly in girder spaces beneath metal railway bridges where they also nested. They preferred roofed cavities to other places, and dark places to light ones. This was more important than the choice between spaces over land and over water. The roost sites offered good shelter from wind and rain and were inaccessible to the rats, stoat, mink and otters which patrolled the river banks nearby and which, because of water noises, the dippers would not hear.

They flew upstream to roost, some birds passing through the territory of other dippers to reach their chosen sites. Some fighting and pursuit occurred near the roosts but strict territorial defence probably broke down at dusk as up to five birds roosted beneath the same bridge. The habit of flying upstream to roost may be linked with the greater abundance of rock faces in the higher reaches of streams and rivers. A roosting place affording security from weather and predators may be as important to dippers (and other species) as a winter territory. The average age of dippers in this study (and in a study of breeding in Czechoslovakia) was over three years, with a maximum of over six, but this was probably higher than for dippers which had not secured territories or roost sites.

FAMILY: Cinclidae, ORDER: Passeriformes, CLASS: Aves. R.H

DISCOGLOSSIDAE, a family of frogs the members of which are characterized by having a round tongue completely attached to the floor of the mouth that cannot be flipped out to catch prey. They also have ribs throughout their life. The family is confined to the Old World and there are four genera.

Four species of *Bombina* are known as Fire-bellied toads and occur in Europe and western Asia. When seen from above the true Fire-bellied toad *B. bombina* is a dull little frog with a grey warty skin but underneath it is vividly patterned with red. Fire-bellies spend most of the time in water. The Yellow-bellied toad *B. variegata* is the least discriminating and is found in any sort of pool or ditch throughout central and southern Europe. It hangs motionless in the water with only its snout and eyes above the surface and when disturbed can swim well, its toes being fully webbed.

The skin of Fire-bellied toads is poisonous, producing a white frothy liquid which irritates the mucous membranes. Just looking into a bag of freshly caught specimens causes

The wren-like dipper about to return to its nest with a beakful of food.

Midwife toad, a species in which the male alone cares for the offspring.

fits of sneezing and watering of the eyes. The bright colouration of their undersides is a warning associated with this poisonous nature. Since the colours are not normally visible from above, however, a Fire-bellied toad, when disturbed and unable to escape, arches its back and folds its limbs up over its body, revealing its bright colours to its attacker.

Fire-bellied toads leave the water at the approach of winter and hibernate in burrows. The breeding season is long, beginning in April or May and lasting for two or three months. About 100 large eggs are laid in water and are attached to stones or plants.

The single species of Barbourula, B. busuangensis, is similar to the Fire-bellied toads except that it is even more aquatic in its habits. The fingers, as well as the toes, are webbed. It is found only in the Philippines.

The Painted frog Discoglossus pictus is a small, very active frog with a smooth skin which varies in its colouration, the olive-brown ground colour being marked with dark bands or patches while a yellowish stripe down the middle of the back and reddish ones along the sides may be present. It lives in or near water and like the Fire-bellied toads, but unlike most frogs, is able to swallow its food underwater. Its breeding follows the pattern typical of most frogs; 300–1,000 small eggs are laid in water where they lie in a mass on the bottom. The tadpoles are able to leave the water after two months.

Frogs of the other genus in this family, Alytes, differ from the previous forms in that they live on land, either in burrows which they construct or in ones left by small mammals.

The Midwife toad Alytes obstetricans also has a very unusual method of breeding, the eggs being carried around attached to the hindlimbs of the male until the tadpoles hatch out. Pairing occurs on land and the female extends her hindlimbs to form a receptacle for the eggs. These are large and between one and five dozen are expelled in two long loops, each egg attached to the next by a tough elastic thread. The male fertilizes the eggs and then pushes his hindlimbs through the loops until the eggs are firmly wound round him. The female moves away and has nothing further to do with the development, while the male withdraws to his hole until the next night when he comes out to feed. He is not particularly hampered by his load and may repeat the procedure to add a second lot of eggs to the first. After about three weeks the tadpoles break through the egg capsules while the male is in water and swim off to complete their development. ORDER: Anura, CLASS: Amphibia. M.E.D.

DISCRIMINATION, an animal's ability to distinguish between two stimuli of a similar kind. A rat is unable to distinguish between different colours and is said to be colour-blind whereas human beings and monkeys are able to distinguish different wavelengths of light as colours. Thus animals have varying powers of discrimination for although dogs are almost colour-blind, they can distinguish between a large number of scents which cannot be recognized by the human nose.

It is possible to investigate experimentally an animal's ability to discriminate between two stimuli in a number of ways. The method most generally employed is to train the animal to choose between two stimuli so that if it makes the correct choice it is rewarded. The American psychologist, K. S. Lashley, designed an apparatus in which a rat had to jump off a platform and was given a choice of two doors, each with a pattern on it. If the rat made the correct choice of pattern it was rewarded with food; a wrong choice, however, led to the rat's jumping against a closed door and falling into a net, thus failing to reach the food reward. In order to avoid the rat developing a prefer ence for the left or right hand door, th position of the correct pattern was varied.

Using this apparatus, Lashley discovere that the rat could discriminate between large number of patterns; for example, could distinguish a circle from a triangle an an inverted triangle from an upright one.

Research on discrimination has show that the apparatus used should be appropr ate for the species of animal which is unde investigation. A large number of differer types of apparatus and different method have therefore been employed. A classi example of a discrimination experiment wa that in which the colour sense of honeybee Apis mellifera was investigated.

A bee was trained to feed at a dis containing sugar solution which was illum nated by a pure spectral colour. In th experimental situation the bee was given choice of two dishes, one of which wa illuminated by the colour to which the be had been trained and which contained suga solution and one which contained distille water illuminated by another pure spectra colour. If the bee was able to distinguish th two colours, it selected the colour to which had been trained. A series of experiment showed that bees can discriminate fou colours, orange-yellow (6,500–5,300Å blue-green (5,100–4,800Å), blue-viole (4,700–4,000Å) and ultra-violet (4,000 3,100Å). Thus the honeybee's ability t discriminate colours differs from our own whilst the honeybee can distinguish ultra violet light, which is invisible to huma beings, we can discriminate between seve other spectral colours. T.B.F

DISCUSFISHES, flattened disc-shaped fishes of the cichlid genus Symphysodo from fresh waters in South America. Thei common name aptly describes their shap but much more striking is their magnificen colour. There are four forms of the discu which appear to be referable to two species The Common discus Symphysodon discu grows to 8 in (20 cm) and occurs in th Amazon, the Rio Negro and connecte rivers. It is rare and expensive and is greatl prized by aquarists. The Green discus S aequifasciata grows to 6 in (15 cm) an comes from the Amazon; the Brown discu S. a. axelrodi is slightly smaller and is als from the Amazon as well as the Rio Urubu and the Blue discus S. a. heraldi is agair smaller and from the Amazon.

As in most of the Cichlidae, the parents lavish considerable care on the eggs an young. The eggs are guarded, fanned an mouthed by the parents. When hatched, th

The Green discus or Pompadour fish, of the Rio Negro and Amazon basins.

fry are picked up in the mouths of the parents and transferred to various surfaces where they remain attached by a short thread. It is remarkable that in the African genus *Tilapia* there is also a species, *T. zillii*, in which the larvae secrete a sticky thread from glands on the head by which they become attached to the substrate. The discusfishes go further, however, in their parental care. When the fry become free-swimming after about four days, they promptly make for their parents' sides where they start to feed on the secretions from special mucus cells in the skin of the parents and continue to do so for at least five weeks. Dr W. H. Hildeman recorded that the parents were adept at flicking their bodies and thus transferring the juveniles from one parent to the other. FAMILY: Cichlidae, ORDER: Perciformes, CLASS: Pisces.

DISEASE, a disorder or lack of health. It is often associated with infections but there are many contributory and interrelated factors which can cause illness. Apart from pathogenic agents such as parasites, bacteria, viruses and fungi, disease may be caused by hereditary defects, inadequate nutrition and stress. All animals, including man, are at risk to disease from the time of conception until death. The ageing process itself is associated with diseases which are markedly different from those which affect young animals. In man, ill-health has become a very personal matter and its presence may result in individual or family tragedy; in animals, on the other hand, disease may contribute to the survival of a species by controlling population numbers and eliminating strains which are ill-adapted to the particular environment.

In the wild, animals which suffer from hereditary defects or congenital deformities seldom survive to breeding age and the further distribution in the species of any genetic disability is therefore restricted. The process of ageing reduces the animal's fitness to forage and escape predators, it becomes more subject to stress, and it usually dies or is killed long before the diseases associated with senility in man appear.

Infectious organisms of one kind or another are present in practically all wild animals, but under natural conditions these acquire fairly early in life a degree of immunity to the infectious agents present in their particular environment. Overcrowding, shortage of food and water and other conditions of stress can, however, reduce resistance to infection and the animals may become susceptible to sudden outbreaks of endemic disease within their own communities. For example, most Arctic lemmings contain at all times within the body bacteria of the pasteurella group. When local populations of lemmings build up there is not only competition for territory and food but also a corresponding build-up of infection. The disease challenge is increased, and the animals' resistance is lowered. An epidemic or widespread outbreak of disease in the lemming community then occurs. Many individuals die but the strongest survive to continue the species under less crowded and more advantageous conditions.

All animals are more susceptible to those diseases with which they are not normally in contact. The effects of the sudden introduction of an alien disease to an animal community is well illustrated by myxomatosis. This is a virus organism endemic among American Cottontail rabbits, and in them it is a mild infection which causes lumps in the skin. The Cottontails recover, however, become immune and suffer no great harm. When infected Cottontail rabbits were first introduced into Australia the disease proved deadly to the introduced European rabbit and reached epidemic proportions. Artificial and illegal introduction of the disease to wild rabbit populations in the UK produced similar results and the recovery rate was probably less than one per cent. Yet there is no disease known which will kill all of a species. The European rabbits are becoming adapted to myxomatosis, acquiring an immunity and again increasing in numbers.

Although the domesticated animals (dogs, cats, sheep, goats, cattle, pigs, horses etc.) live a protected life, albeit often in large numbers and overcrowded conditions, they are particularly susceptible to infections from other domestic communities and also from wild animals unless preventive precautions are taken. Modern methods of quick travel and communication have increased the danger of introducing alien diseases to both animals and human beings.

Rinderpest or cattle plague is an endemic virus disease of wild ungulates and under conditions of stress, in certain species such as buffaloes, may reach epidemic proportions. When this occurs any buffalo or domestic cattle contact in marginal pastoral areas spreads the disease rapidly through the more susceptible cattle population and a high mortality results.

In parts of north, central and east Africa, the movement of cattle as a result of exploration, trade and wars increased rapidly during the latter part of the 19th and early 20th centuries and periodic rinderpest epidemics of continental magnitude occurred. Effective vaccines have now been developed to give immunity to susceptible stock in the rinderpest areas but rigid veterinary control is still necessary to prevent the introduction of the disease to countries such as, for example, the UK.

Another virus disease which is endemic in certain wild carnivores and in types of bat is rabies. In man the disease is known as hydrophobia and the symptoms follow a terrifying and inexorable course to death. Wild animal vectors of the disease include jackals, skunks and foxes. Infected animals lose all fear of other animals or man and, in this state, will at times bite indiscriminately. The saliva of the rabid animal contains the infection which passes into the wound of the victim. In the latter the disease may take as long as six months before symptoms develop.

In the UK there is no known wild life reservoir of rabies but cases have occurred in imported dogs during a six-month quarantine period, and on occasions even after release from quarantine. Rabies has also occurred in imported monkeys and in imported cats and other carnivores. A vaccine against rabies is available but no vaccine provides one hundred per cent protection, and in countries where the wild animal population is not involved the control of importations is the normal method of control.

Apart from diseases transmitted by the movement of animals, intensive methods of husbandry have resulted in diseases which are of little importance in wild animals but assume great significance in domestic stock. When, for reasons of economy, land shortage or labour difficulties, animals are crowded together and fed an artificially compounded diet various conditions of ill-health appear. Close proximity to each other encourages an exchange of harmful parasites and bacteria and the ground or housing accommodation becomes heavily contaminated. Disease occurs and the profit of the farmer disappears unless remedial action is taken. For example, there are some 250 million broiler chickens reared each year in the UK but this operation would be quite impossible without the constant use of drugs such as coccidiostats to suppress protozoal infections, and certain antibiotics to encourage growth and to keep harmful bacteria in check.

Large concentrations of animals in close confinement are also particularly susceptible to the quick spread of virus diseases such as foot-and-mouth in cattle, swine fever in pigs and fowl pest in poultry.   W.N.S.

DISPERSAL AND DISPERSION, phenomena of populations influencing the spacing of individuals. Dispersal is the movement of larvae or young into or out of the population area and dispersion is the pattern of occupation of the habitat by the species, and includes the process by which this is brought about. Although a population of animals may traditionally have occupied a certain habitat or physical site for long periods of time, the composition of the population will change continually; as some individuals move away, others move in to replace them. Most populations have a constant inflow and outflow of individuals or their reproductive products. Dispersal is concerned with this constant movement, and

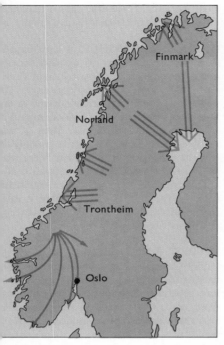

Emigration, one of the three aspects of dispersal, is well shown by the movements of the Norway lemming *Lemmus lemmus*, whose irruptions probably form the basis of the Pied Piper fable.

also with the changes in the birth and death rates that are associated with the movement. Dispersal is commonly discussed under three headings: emigration, or a movement away from the population; immigration, or a movement into a population; and migration, a seasonal movement away followed some time later by a return. There are two main ways by which dispersal can take place. It can be independent where the animal uses its own locomotory powers such as flying, walking, burrowing or swimming; or dependent, where it uses wind, erosion or attachment to floating objects to effect movement. The environmental features bringing about dispersal are little known, but seem to be connected with population pressure. Thus there is frequently a dispersal phase following reproduction or following natural disaster decreasing a population's available habitat.

Emigration frequently occurs after the breeding season when there are too many individuals in the population. Usually this occurs before the young have reached sexual maturity, although some early developers may successfully usurp their parents and remain within the population area. The emigrés will have to find suitable habitats for survival, and once ecesis, or successful establishment of invaders, is secured, ecological succession can take place. Climatic and soil conditions are of primary importance in establishing ecesis. There are many barriers to dispersal—rivers, mountain ranges and other stretches of unsuitable habitats fre-

quently prevent widespread dissemination of a species. However, land-living insects have been found high in the air above Spitzbergen having been transported 800 miles (1,300 km) over sea by wind. Small wingless forms are frequently blown great distances by the wind, and tiny helpless marine organisms are carried as plankton at the mercy of the wind and water. Transport by local violent air disturbances, such as hurricanes and tornadoes, can explain the occurrence of fish in land-locked ponds and stream systems. Mass emigrations, or population irruptions, occur quite commonly amongst arctic and sub-arctic herbivores. In Europe, two species showing such tendencies are the Norway lemming *Lemmus lemmus* and the crossbill *Loxia curvirostra*. Leaving aside the question of cycles of abundance (see cycles and oscillations) the irruptions of lemmings are caused by good early spring breeding resulting in too many individuals competing for a limited food supply. The emigration is merely an expansion of range enabling a greater proportion of young to survive than would be possible without this mass movement. The massed young have to move further down the hills towards the valleys. Here the extremely high densities are found, and in their efforts to cross water barriers in search of unoccupied habitats, they are drowned in large numbers. These observations, uncritically reported, have given rise to the fable about the suicide marches of lemmings, which can be seen to be nothing more than an emigration from an overcrowded population.

Immigration into a population is the result of emigration from others. Usually immigrating individuals are juveniles. Immigration is important since its agency allows mixing of strains and the exchange of genes. Population genetics and speciation are closely connected with this form of dispersal.

Migration is the most complex form of dispersal. Some species migrate annually long distances, e.g. the Arctic tern *Sterna macrura* that flies annually from northern polar and temperate latitudes to southern polar latitudes. Eels *Anguilla anguilla* breed in the Sargasso sea off Bermuda, travel to Europe as elvers, and return some years later to the Sargasso to spawn. Pacific salmon hatched in tiny head streams find their way, as adults some years later, back to the exact spot of their own hatching to spawn. The means of orientation and navigation of such long distance dispersers is as yet little understood but in general birds appear to navigate by the sun by day and by the stars at night. Fishes appear to respond to extremely low concentrations of dissolved scent chemicals after finding their way to the right general area by using heavenly bodies for navigation.

Some mammals, such as wildebeest *Connochaetes taurinus,* live in dense aggrega-

tions while others, such as lions *Felis leo,* are very thinly distributed. This is called dispersion, and in all cases the pattern observed is the product of a complex form of social behaviour. The correct spacing of individuals is of the greatest importance to the success of populations and ultimately the survival of the species. Observed dispersion patterns: random, non-random or clumped, are carefully controlled by a special spacing behaviour.

Carnivorous animals obtain the correct spacing such that competition for food will not occur, by competing for territories. The maintenance of these areas is frequently effected by scent which is produced in specialized glands and set at boundary posts. A bird displays from vantage points within its territory, and its often gay colours and shrill song serve to advertise its occupation of a particular area.

Dispersion patterns all serve to prevent over-exploitation of resources. These are preserved by the limitation of the population effected in a variety of ways. Competition in nature for a particular resource is never direct—it is always for a convention. Thus herbivorous animals living in aggregations establish *dominance hierarchies that determine, through conventional competition, which members of the society shall be permitted to breed and rear young. Often there is a breeding reserve of sexually mature individuals that will only breed if permitted breeders die or are killed.   D.M.S.

DISPLACEMENT ACTIVITIES, patterns of animal behaviour which appear to have no direct relevance to the situation in which the animal finds itself.

If two Herring gulls *Larus argentatus* are fighting over a patch of territory, the owner may suddenly ignore its rival and begin to pull at the grass, making sideways flicks with its head. Grass-pulling can therefore be described as a displacement activity in this context where it seems irrelevant, though it has a definite function during nest-building.

The occurrence of behaviour patterns which seem out of context are common in situations where an animal is subjected to two conflicting motivations. In the example described, the tendency of the gull to leave its territory to attack the opponent is balanced by a tendency to remain in its own territory. Since the gull cannot do both, it shows displacement activity.

The term 'displacement' was originally used by the Dutch ethologist, Niko Tinbergen, who suggested that the two types of behaviour which were in conflict were thwarted so that 'nervous energy' was displaced into the channel of a third behaviour-pattern, the displacement activity.

Today most scientists do not accept this explanation of displacement activities; in the first place serious doubts have been cast on the validity of models of behaviour which incorporate the concept of 'nervous energy', secondly, more recent work, stimulated by Tinbergen's original discovery, has indicated that other explanations can be applied.

Some of the displacement activities which have been described are more relevant to the situation than was at first supposed. For example, displacement preening or grooming has often been described in situations of conflict between approach and flight. It is quite likely that in this situation, however, sweating and hair-erection which are physiological effects associated with fear might stimulate the animal to groom itself.

C. H. F. Rowell's experiments on chaffinches *Fringilla coelebs* in conflict situations showed that wetting the feathers increases both normal and displacement preening so that both are influenced by the same environmental stimuli. Displacement drinking which often occurs during fighting in a number of species of bird may be a result of the dryness of the throat which is a physiological effect of fear.

Another explanation of displacement activities, know as the 'disinhibition hypothesis', suggests that in a situation in which two behaviour patterns with high orders of priorities are in conflict (for example, during a fight, the conflicting motivations being fight or to flee) they may be replaced by a third pattern, the displacement activity, which is normally inhibited.

Although some of the displacement activities which have been described closely resemble a normal behaviour-pattern, there are many cases in which the displacement activity is only an incomplete version of the normal pattern. A Jungle fowl *Gallus gallus* during a fight may peck at, but not eat, a grain of food. Terns *Sterna* spp., which are incubating eggs, may make brief and ineffective preening movements before flying to attack a territorial intruder.

In social interactions the behaviour of one individual influences that of another and it is well known that displacement activities may function as signals. Courtship, for example, in many species, contains behaviour-patterns which may have arisen as displacement activities. This is shown by the fanning behaviour of the male Three-spined stickleback *Gasterosteus aculeatus* which aerates the eggs in its nest by fanning water towards them with the pectoral fins. During courtship, however, the male stickleback commonly shows displacement fanning unconnected with the aeration of eggs. This example is interesting for in this case fanning is an activity which normally has a well-defined function but which has been incorporated into a situation in which its original function is in no way relevant. The Dutch ethologist, P. Sevenster, who studied this behaviour found that factors such as the amount of carbon dioxide in the water, which influence the rate of 'genuine' aeration fanning of the nest also influence displacement fanning in courtship in the same way.   T.B.P.

DISPLAY, a set of actions constituting a method of communication by showing off conspicuous physical features, such as the tail of the peacock or the teeth of a carnivore. Display may also include the ritualized performance of certain actions, such as bowing during courtship display or the uttering of certain sounds. The three main types of display are: the threat display, to warn off rivals, the territorial display to indicate ownership of a territory, and the courtship display preceding mating.

DISRUPTIVE PATTERN, a form of camouflage in which conspicuous, and generally irregular, markings distract attention from the animal's natural outline making difficult to pick out from its background.

DIURNAL BEHAVIOUR, a term used describe the activities of animals movi about by day and resting by night (Lat *diurnalis*, from *dies* meaning day). Th opposite is *nocturnal behaviour and at o time it was customary to think of animals either nocturnal or diurnal. Then it wa realised that some are active mainly twilight and again at dawn, and these we said to be crepuscular. The situation is no more complicated since it has been found th some of the smaller animals have a dai rhythm of alternating activity and rest every or 4 hours. See circadian rhythm.

DIVERS, fish-eating diving birds of t family Gaviidae, also known as loons. Th naming of this group, although there are on four generally-recognized species (some s three, some five), has been subject to co siderable change. The scientific name of t family was, for some time, Colymbidae, least in Britain and Europe, although Amer can ornithologists used this name for th grebes. As general agreement could not b reached as to which birds 'Colymbida should refer to, the name was dropped e tirely in 1956 by decision of the Internation Commission on Zoological Nomenclatur and since then the divers (or loons) hav been properly known as Gaviidae. Th English name for birds of this family is als of uncertain definition. The term 'divers' ha been used at various times to refer to any the aquatic birds which habitually dive, i cluding certain ducks, Anatidae; grebe Podicipitidae; and auks, Alcidae. The ter 'loons' for this family is that in common us in North America and, insofar as it onl refers to members of the Gaviidae, must b preferred to 'divers'. However, even th name 'loon' is rather a puzzle. In Nort America it would seem to be derived fro the call of certain species, particularly th Great northern diver *Gavia immer* (the Com mon loon), the call of which sounds like ma hysterical human laughter. This call has be come quite well-known in Britain through th recording of Dr W. W. H. Gunn which wa used to introduce a B.B.C. nature pr gramme. But although 'loon' is now a gener ally understood name for the Gaviidae, eve amongst British ornithologists, one may fin in the older British literature the nam 'loom'. As 'lom' is the Norwegian name for diver, this word probably spread to Britai with the Norsemen and to North Americ with early Scandinavian settlers.

One form of displacement activity is shown here The Wood mouse grooms itself as it is em barrassed by the sight of a camera.

Black-throated diver, also called Arctic loon, nests near the water's edge. It has difficulty in walking on land.

The loons comprise a distinctive group of holarctic birds showing a very high degree of specialization to the aquatic mode of life. They are quite large, from the weight of a large duck to a small goose, with a long body and thick, strong neck. The tail is short, the legs and feet strong, with webs between the three front toes and the bill is stout, long and pointed. These characteristics result in a very streamlined shape. This has come about as a progressive adaptation to under-water swimming, the loons being pre-eminent among birds in this environment. Particularly noteworthy is the structure of the hindlimb. As in the grebes the tibial, or central segment of the leg, like the femoral, or upper segment, is bound by its musculature to the pelvic region of the body. Thus the only externally visible part of the leg is the so-called 'tarsal', or lower segment, and the foot. The leg therefore emerges from the body in a position at the rear which allows great propulsive efficiency in water. But this also means that loons have great difficulty in standing on land and their mode of progression out of the water is by pushing themselves along on the belly.

The loons are also similar to the grebes in having the external portion of the leg laterally compressed for minimal resistance when moving through the water, but they differ in many other respects. Although the general form is similar, as are the adaptations in this form, the ways in which these adaptations have come about are less similar. The loons even have three pairs of muscles in the pelvic region which are entirely absent in the grebes. Thus the two groups are generally regarded as being examples of convergent evolution, and are not at all closely related.

The plumage of loons is of a hard, even harsh texture, except on the neck where it is soft. The young have two successive coats of down—that with which they are hatched, and a second coat which comes between this and the adult-type feathering of the first winter plumage. This replacement of the hatching down may be connected with the fact that loons leave the water only with difficulty and reluctance, and the young therefore are less likely to be brooded on dry land than the young of ducks and geese. And they are not carried on the back as much as the young of grebes.

Adult loons are strikingly marked, with white stripes or spots contrasting with the basic colour of black, grey or brown. The sexes are externally similar. They have a distinctive appearance in flight with head and legs hanging down somewhat and the feet projecting beyond the tail. In the Red-throated diver *G. stellata,* this attitude is seen in its most definite form giving the appearance of a flying banana! Because of their swimming adaptations, particularly the small wings, loons have difficulty in taking flight and need to taxi for a considerable distance to pick up speed before becoming airborne. Once aloft they fly strongly—indeed, they have to, because with their very high wing-loading they must maintain speed in order to stay aloft. Also, as hovering or slow speeds are impossible, they can only 'land' by coming down in a shallow glide onto water, which slows them gradually.

Loons have a wide distribution throughout the Arctic, though the Common loon is almost exclusively a nearctic breeder. During the breeding season all species are essentially freshwater birds, frequenting lakes, ponds, streams and slow-moving rivers. However, enormous tracts of land fulfilling these requirements in the Arctic are found near the sea and loons in such areas may divide their time between fresh and salt water even in the breeding season. Outside that season their habitat is essentially the maritime one, particularly estuaries and inshore waters.

The distribution of these birds is largely determined by their food, which consists almost entirely of fishes, which they pursue and capture beneath the surface of the water. They dive effortlessly from the surface in a smooth forward plunge, swimming with the feet only, except in unusual circumstances, and stay beneath the surface for up to a minute or more, mostly in water of a depth of 6–18 ft (2–6 m). An unusual feature is the ability of loons to submerge only partially. They are thus able to remain with only the head above the surface—a valuable attribute in times of danger.

In winter loons migrate southwards to avoid the more extreme arctic conditions, largely following the coastlines and, particularly the Common loon, travelling in flocks. One population of the Arctic loon or Black-throated diver *G. arctica,* provides an example of loop migration. The Arctic loons of northern Russia winter in southern Europe, migrating south through the Black Sea. In the return migration in spring, however, they first fly northwest to the Baltic, then take a northeast heading, and finally turn east to their breeding areas. The reason for this is connected with the loons' inability to come down on land. The waters of the Baltic thaw out in spring sooner than those inland due to the warming influence of the North Atlantic Drift and the birds take advantage of this. Like many other water birds loons migrate by night and day.

Loons' nests are placed at or near the water's edge, though they vary considerably in construction. Sometimes they are in the form of a simple depression in the vegetation covering the ground; at other times they may be substantial structures of plant material with the nest cup in the centre. Two eggs are normally laid. They are rather more elongated than in most birds and are cryptically coloured olive-brown or green with very dark spots. Both sexes take part in incubation, which lasts about four weeks, and share the care of the young.

The Common loon or Great northern diver breeds throughout arctic North America and in Greenland and Iceland and some smaller islands. It is one of the larger species, up to some 36 in (91 cm) long. In breeding plumage the head and neck are black with a glossy green and mauve sheen, a horizontal line of vertical white stripes on the throat, and a more prominent collar of similar marks on the neck—incomplete at the back. The rest of the upper-parts are black with white spots, the spots being largest in the scapular region. The under-parts are white. Bill, feet and legs are black. In winter the plumage is brown above rather than black, without the spots, and the bill also is paler.

The Yellow-billed loon (White-billed diver) *G. adamsii,* replaces the Common loon in the far north and west of North America and also breeds around the European and Asian

coasts of the Arctic Ocean. Although it is regarded by some authorities as being conspecific with the Common loon it apparently does not interbreed with it in the few areas where they overlap. The Yellow-billed loon is slightly bigger than the Common loon though this is largely accounted for by the slightly larger bill. The bill also is different, being a yellow-horn colour and having an upward sweep to the distal half of the lower mandible. The external appearance of the two species is otherwise rather similar.

The Arctic loon or Black-throated diver has a circumpolar distribution in arctic and sub-arctic habitats. It is a smaller species, some 24 in (60 cm) long, separated by some into Eurasian and American species. Its breeding plumage is somewhat similar to that of the foregoing species, but the head and the back of the neck are grey and the white markings on the back form transverse bands. Also, at the sides of the neck and breast there is a beautiful pattern of fine vertical black and white lines. The bill and legs are as in the Common loon, but slighter.

The Red-throated loon or Red-throated diver is slightly smaller than the Black-throated species, though like all loons it varies considerably in size. It is another circumpolar species and is the most widely

distributed of all the loons. Its breeding plumage is an almost uniform grey-brown above with a chestnut red throat patch, and white beneath. The bill and legs are grey, and the former has a distinctly upturned appearance due to the upward sweep of the distal half of the lower mandible and a depression in the upper mandible in the region of the nostrils. In winter the upper-parts may be seen to be flecked with white. This species is less extremely modified than the other loons and is able to take wing with greater ease.

The feathering of loons, like that of grebes and certain sea-ducks, is so compact that skins of these birds have been used, particularly by Eskimos, for clothing. Even recently the more striking areas of feathering from the necks of loons and the heads of Eider ducks have been used by Eskimos for decorative purposes. FAMILY: Gaviidae, ORDER: Gaviiformes, CLASS: Aves.   P.M.D.

DIVER'S PROPHECY. The Norwegian *lom* which gave the alternative name 'loon' for diver is still remembered in Shetland Island place names, such as Luimisheddon (Old Norse *loma* – diver; *tjorn* – tarn). The Red-throated diver is known as the Rain goose and its movements are said to prophecy

Water shrew *Neomys fodiens* diving, looking like an animated air bubble.

weather. The folk-lore can, however, be broken down to the fact that when the diver goes to sea, fishing at sea is likely to be hazardous. This is not surprising as divers migrate out to sea during the winter when the Shetland Isles are frequently stormbound.

DIVING ANIMALS,
air-breathing vertebrates which are specialized to allow them to continue such essential physiological processes as cellular respiration during lengthy periods under water, in spite of the fact that the breathing movements normally associated with the lungs can not be carried out. Most divers dive in order to obtain food and so there is an advantage in such air-breathing animals being able to stay submerged for longer periods than could be tolerated by their non-diving relatives. But during a dive their cells must be able to continue to respire, in order to release energy for muscle contraction and other energy-requiring cellular processes. Animals which dive to great depths must also be able to meet the hazard of increased pressure, for in the sea pressure increases by one atmosphere for each 33 ft (10 m) of increased depth.

The maximum duration of the dive varies quite widely, as can be seen from the following examples. Among the reptiles the Loggerhead turtle can stay submerged for nearly half an hour, but some water snakes are said to remain under water for up to eight hours. Perhaps they are able to take up dissolved oxygen from the water through the thin membranes of the mouth cavity and the cloaca. Diving birds, such as penguins, puffins and razorbills only stay submerged for a minute or so, but several of the diving mammals have much greater submergence times. Otters, for example, dive for periods up to 30 min, seals and beavers 15 min, and the Blue whale up to about 50 min. But the best diver of all, as far as the duration of the dive is concerned, is probably the Sperm whale, which can stay submerged for about $1\frac{1}{4}$ hours.

These diving animals have evolved a number of specializations which enable them to stay submerged so much longer than could their fully terrestrial relatives. Diving animals do not generally have larger lungs than those of totally terrestrial forms, but they are often able to store more oxygen in the blood and in the muscle.

For example, the blood of a man occupies no more than 7% of the body weight, but in a muskrat the equivalent figure is 10%, in a porpoise 15% and in a seal nearly 16%. Furthermore, their blood can carry more oxygen per unit volume. Whereas in man the oxygen-carrying capacity is about 20 ml oxygen per 100 ml of blood, the equivalent figure for the muskrat is 25 ml and for the seal over 29 ml. This is partly because the oxygen-carrying pigment, haemoglobin, is present in the blood at higher concentrations in divers. The equivalent pigment in the muscle, myoglobin, also affords a large oxygen store; about half the oxygen reserves of seals is located in the muscle tissues.

These large stores of oxygen taken down in a dive last longer than they would normally, because the heart-beat rate is generally slowed down in a dive (a reflex action known as bradycardia). Also the general level of metabolism is reduced, and much of the peripheral circulation becomes shut off. The output of the heart of a turtle in a dive is only about 5% of its normal value. The heart rate of a seal, normally 80 beats per min, falls to 10 during a dive, and the rate at which oxygen is utilized quickly drops to about $\frac{2}{5}$ of its normal level.

Even when the oxygen supply is exhausted, the muscles of the diving animal can continue to function by respiring anaerobically. In *anaerobic respiration oxygen is not required, but lactic acid accumulates as an end-product. On surfacing, the lactic acid is passed into the now fully recirculating blood and oxidized, the oxidation process being apparent as a super-normal rate of oxygen consumption for some minutes immediately following the dive. A seal breathes very deeply for about 15 min after a dive, until the accumulated oxygen debt is repaid.

Carbon dioxide, an end-product of respiration, naturally accumulates during a dive, but diving animals have evolved an increased tolerance of it. Whereas quite low carbon dioxide levels normally stimulate receptors in the brain to initiate increased breathing movements etc., the threshold concentration for this system in diving animals is much higher. Thus the 'respiratory mechanism' is less sensitive to carbon dioxide in most diving animals.

Some animals dive deeply, a walrus, for example, can go down to about 260 ft (80 m), a Blue whale to about 330 ft (100 m) and a Sperm whale to as much as 2,950 ft (900 m). The pressure at a depth of 1,600 ft (500 m) is about 50 atmospheres, and so the changes in pressure experienced by the deep divers is enormous.

A man who dives runs the risk of caisson sickness or 'the bends' if he comes up too quickly. This is caused by nitrogen in the blood coming out of solution and forming small gas bubbles in the blood vessels as a result of the abrupt reduction in pressure. This condition is much less likely to occur in a diver such as a whale, however, for whereas the man is breathing throughout the dive (albeit by artificial means), replenishing the nitrogen in his blood as well as the oxygen, the whale only takes down as much air as the lungs can hold; in fact the lungs may not even be fully inflated. Thus the whale carries only a limited amount of nitrogen when in a dive, insufficient to cause trouble from 'bends' when surfacing.

Warm-blooded animals which dive deeply encounter low temperatures in the depths. Maintenance of body temperature in such circumstances could be an additional burden on already stretched metabolic resources. Good insulation, however, in the form of plentiful subcutaneous fat (blubber), helps to conserve body heat.   A.E.B.

Female Great diving beetle *Dytiscus marginalis*.

DIVING BEETLES,
large water beetles of the genus *Dytiscus*. They are carnivores and are unusual as both adults and larvae live and hunt in water yet their pupae occur on the moist land surrounding the pond. The larvae are astoundingly voracious and can grow up to 2 in (5 cm) long. They will feed on large freshwater animals such as newts, as well as smaller animals, pumping digestive enzymes into the carcase through their large hollow mandibles. The larvae breathe air through two posterior channels whilst hanging suspended from the surface and can then drag themselves below by crawling down the stems of water plants. When fully grown the larvae pupate in the moist soil surrounding the pond but this stage only lasts a few weeks.

The adults are large, up to $1\frac{1}{4}$ in (3 cm), are active fliers and so can colonize new habitats such as water-butts and fish ponds. They are also excellent swimmers using their powerful, flattened hindlegs for this purpose. They have to come to the surface to breathe but dive with an air bubble trapped underneath their wing-cases which is gradually used up during this activity. FAMILY: Dytiscidae, ORDER: Coleoptera, CLASS: Insecta. PHYLUM: Arthropoda.

DIVING MEN. By the standards of seals and whales man is a poor diver, but the records for depth and duration are remarkable when compared to the average ability. Pearl divers sometimes attain depths of 120 ft (36 m) and the record for staying underwater stands at 13 min 42 sec, but the record-holder 'cheated' by breathing oxygen for 30 min before submerging. With his gift of invention, man has embroidered upon these records. In 1867, for instance, a young man calling himself 'Natator' gave nightly performances in an outsize aquarium. Apart from tricks of underwater swimming, he used to eat buns, drink milk and smoke a pipe. History does not, unfortunately, record how he managed these things. The performance took three years to perfect and the nearest Natator came to disaster was the occasion when the front of the aquarium burst flooding the orchestra.

DIVING PETRELS, diminutive black and white seabirds, confined to the southern hemisphere and belonging to the family Pelecanoididae, a peculiar group within the order Procellariiformes. The four species currently recognized are similar in appearance, with compact bodies, short necks and stubby wings and tails. Their short black bills have nasal tubes which open upward and not forward as in other petrels. Most of these features are specializations for diving and swimming underwater. Adaptation for this mode of life has produced a remarkable resemblance in appearance, structure and behaviour between Diving petrels and the small auks, especially the Little auk *Plautus alle,* in the northern hemisphere, although the two groups are quite unrelated.

The largest and most distinctive species, the Peruvian diving petrel *Pelecanoides garnoti* inhabits the cool waters of the Humboldt current. The Magellanic diving petrel *P. magellani* is a little known species found only in southern South America and the Falkland Islands. The Georgian diving petrel *P. georgicus* and the Common diving petrel *P. (exsul) urinatrix* have a much wider circumpolar distribution, breeding on islands and coasts in the subantarctic and subtropical zones and overlapping in several localities. Little is known about many of these island populations.

Diving petrels excavate a burrow in which to lay their single white egg and they visit the breeding grounds at night. Their food consists mainly of small crustaceans and fishes which, unlike other petrels, they obtain close inshore, so enabling both birds to visit the nest nightly. During moult the birds are temporarily flightless while the wing quills are growing. The laboured flight, characterized by rapid whirring wing beats and short

glides, partly explains why these birds do not perform extensive migrations. FAMILY: Pelecanoididae, ORDER: Procellariiformes, CLASS: Aves. J.R.B.

DIVISION OF LABOUR occurs in a number of colonial animals where individuals are differentiated either morphologically or behaviourally (or both) to carry out certain activities to the exclusion of others. Among the colonial Cnidaria specialization of individuals in hydrocorallines such as the millepore corals is morphological. The polyps responsible for food capture, known as dactylozooids, lack mouths, are long and slender and possess scattered capitate (pinheaded) tentacles. They often surround a gastrozooid, a polyp responsible for feeding the colony, and hand prey to it for digestion. Medusae are a third form of polyp which swim freely and carry out the sexual reproduction of the colony.

Differentiation among the polyps forming the body of a siphonophore has developed to such an extent that they are completely dependent upon the rest of the colony and the question arises whether the whole colony should not now be considered as the individual, each polyp having surrendered so much of its individuality. Each siphonophore consists of a pneumatophore or gas-filled float, derived originally from a polyp; gastrozooids each with one tentacle resembling the mouth-bearing manubrium of a jellyfish; dactylozooids, mouthless and with a much longer tentacle, armed with stinging-cells and with strong longitudinal muscles; and gonozooids bearing the reproductive organs.

Division of labour is also pronounced in many social insects, with reproductive and worker castes, the first including the queens and males which, except among certain primitive ants, do not forage but remain in the colony carrying out their reproductive function. The workers are sterile females and their work is to care for the eggs, feed the young larvae, forage for food, and generally protect the colony. Among honeybees, the workers are specialized for foraging by having combs on the middle pair of legs with which to brush pollen from their bodies into pollen baskets on their hind pair of legs, packing it there for transport to the hive. In some species of ants there are major and minor workers, sometimes more specialized workers known as soldiers, with larger heads and more powerful jaws than the other workers. Among termites, two kinds of soldiers may occur, mandibulates with large jaws and nasutes with long beaks. The nasute soldiers have only very small jaws and they defend themselves by squirting an unpleasant liquid from the frontal tube or beak.

The work carried out by the honeybee workers bears some relation to their age. Young workers remain in the hive, feeding the

larvae, building the comb and later guarding the hive entrance. When older they leave the hive daily to forage for nectar and pollen. Nevertheless, though this is the general progression of work with age, it is not rigidly fixed and in a hive deprived of all the young workers, foragers will take over nursing duties and vice versa.

Where division of labour occurs to such an extent that the individuals in a colony become interdependent, there is a temptation to liken this to the surrender of generalized functions shown by cells forming tissues in a metazoan body. This leads to the philosophical concept of the super-organism, i.e. the whole colony has its existence which is more than the sum total of its individual members. J.D.C.

DNA, or deoxyribonucleic acid, a substance of very large molecular weight, sometimes of several million, that is found in cell nuclei. Each molecule is made of two chains that twine spirally around each other. The chains are formed of a sugar, deoxyribose, and phosphate and are linked together by four bases: adenine, cytosine, guanine and thymine. Cytosine links only with guanine, and adenine only with thymine. A similar substance, ribonucleic acid, is found in the cytoplasm. Its sugar is ribose and thymine is replaced by uracil.

DNA has been shown to be the 'blueprint of life', the four bases forming a four-letter code in which all information in the genes is carried. Each molecule can duplicate itself by the two chains unwinding then forming new partners. RNA is formed from DNA and passes into the cytoplasm of the cell where it manufactures proteins on a template basis; each combination of bases attracting an amino acid molecule which links with other amino acids along the RNA template to form the protein. See genetics.

STRUCTURE OF DNA

P	D	A		T	D	P
P	D	C		G	D	P
P	D	A		T	D	P
P	D	G		C	D	P

A = adenine, C = cytosine, D = deoxyribose, G = guanine, P = phosphate, T = thymine.

DOBSON FLY *Corydalis cornutus,* related to the Alder flies, lacewings and Ant lions. One of the remarkable features of this large insect is that it shows very marked sexual dimorphism, the males being distinguished easily from the females by their very long, curved mandibles which lie across each other

A husky, the sledge-dog of the polar regions. The entry on dogs starts on page 577.

A reconstruction of the extinct dodo, using feathers taken from other birds, based on excellent 17th century paintings, without which we should know little more about this bird than what its bones looked like.

and may be almost as long as the rest of the body. Dobson flies rank among the largest neuropterans, with a wing-span that often exceeds 4 in (10 cm). They are found usually near streams and other bodies of fresh water in North America. The adults probably do not feed but the 3 in (8 cm) larvae are carnivorous. FAMILY: Corydalidae, ORDER: Neuroptera, CLASS: Insecta, PHYLUM: Arthropoda.

DODO *Raphus cucullatus,* extinct bird of the family Raphidae which includes the solitaires of Réunion and Rodriguez. The dodo was an inhabitant of Mauritius and the family is therefore peculiar to the Mascarene group of islands to the east of Madagascar. The first Europeans to land on Mauritius were the Portuguese, in 1507, and the name 'dodo' is derived from the Portuguese 'doudo'—a simpleton. Like many other birds which had lived for long without any serious enemies and without human interference the dodo, when first discovered, was quite unafraid of man or his introduced animals. Thus they were easily killed, if not by man, for only the breast meat, apparently, was palatable, then by his introduced animals, particularly pigs. By 1681 the dodo was extinct, and the saying 'as dead as the dodo' has long been used in the sense of completely passé, or extinguished.

The dodo was of considerable size, rather larger than a turkey, at least in bulk, as is known from a considerable amount of fresh and sub-fossil material and from obser-

vations on individual birds which were brought to Europe and, apparently, lived for some years. The body was massive and was supported on short legs and feet. The plumage was grey, paler beneath, the tail was a small tuft of curled feathers and the wings were reduced in size with an accompanying reduction in the size of the keel on the breastbone to which the flight muscles are attached. The head was most unusual, being very large and carrying a heavy, strongly hooked, dark-coloured bill, with nostrils much nearer the tip than is usual in birds. The dodo was, of course, flightless.

There seems to have been only one species of dodo, although there have been claims for a second, similar species, in addition to the solitaires. On the basis of its skeletal characteristics the group has generally been placed in the same order as the pigeons, though there has been a recent claim that the rails, Rallidae, are the nearest relatives.

No authentic dodo skin exists, but heads and feet have been preserved, as well as much skeletal material, and good models of the dodo exist with feathers of appropriate form and colour taken from other birds. Also a number of good skeletons survive in institutions such as the American Museum of Natural History and Cambridge University. It is, however, one of the frustrations of modern zoology that the dodo became extinct before ornithology had become an exact science. We know very little of the life of these very unusual birds. A good field observer could have left a priceless legacy of

information. FAMILY: Raphidae, ORDER Columbiformes, CLASS: Aves.　P.M.D

DODO RELICS. The first mention of th dodo seems to be that in a book, *Voyage t the East Indies* by Jacon van Neck an Wybrand van Warwijk, written in 1598. I describes the *walgh-vögels* (dodo), in th island of Cerne (now Mauritius), as bein 'equal in size to our swans, with large head and a kind of hood theron; no wings but i place of them three or four black little pens and their tails consist of four or five curle plumelets of a grayish colour.' The earlies published pictures are engravings in *Quint Pars Indiae Orientalis* by de Bry, in th frontispiece, where a pair of the birds stand on the cornice on each side surmounting th architectural design of the title page.

The first dodo reached Europe in Jul 1599, the second was acquired later th same year by Rudolf II of Hapsburg for hi menagerie. Both birds are said to have don well in captivity and they soon became favourite subject for German and Dutc animal artists. The bird was painted eigh times by Jan Breughal's famous pupil Roe land Savery. It was included in religiou paintings, coats of arms and etchings. Jaco Hofnagel, the Emperor Rudolf's persona artist, painted it in oils for the Vienna Cour Library.

Many dodos were brought to Europe fron 1599 to 1666. During this period als numerous authors wrote about the dodo either from what they had seen of it i Europe or in its native home, beginning wit Carolus Clusius, in his *Exotica* of 160 through to Baron Edward Herbert, in hi *Travels* (1634) and ending with Bontius i 1658.

Clusius gave a figure of the dodo based o a sketch made from nature by a Dutc traveller. He also described a dodo's leg cu off at the knee which he saw at the house o Pieter Pauw in Leiden. Other known relics o the period include a breastbone preserved i the museum in Paris and a skull, which ha formed part of the collections in the privat museum of the Duke of Gottorp, whicl found its way to the Copenhagen Museum

The most perfect museum specimen wa the skin of a dodo that was on publi exhibition in London in 1638. It was bough on the death of the bird, by John Tradescar who had it stuffed and placed in his privat museum in South Lambeth, in London. Sub sequently it passed to the Ashmolea Museum at Oxford. In January 1775, th trustees of the museum decided that thi wretched, dusty and forlorn looking speci men should be burnt. Fortunately, somebod had the good sense to salvage the solitar remains, a head and a foot.